"A smart, ably argued case for taking the kids out of their rooms and into the world."

—*Kirkus Reviews*

"Rinella's enthusiasm for outdoor activities is contagious, and he offers plenty of fun stories from his own adventures with his family. . . . As useful as it is charming, this should go a long way toward convincing readers to get up, gather the family, and enjoy what nature has in store."

—*Publishers Weekly* (starred review)

"Hunting and fishing stories are Rinella's way of sending out a kind of plea. 'I want my work to inspire people to think about the things that they love, to learn about the things that they love and to find it in them to advocate on behalf of the things that they love,' he told me. For Rinella, that thing is the outdoors; he describes himself as 'an environmentalist with a gun.' "

—*The New York Times*

"Steven Rinella's magnificent *Outdoor Kids in an Inside World* makes the most inspiring argument for outdoor time I've ever read. According to Steven, whatever your access to nature is, it's enough. Let him inspire and teach you and your kids the most important lesson of all: how nature helps you be more human."

—MEL ROBBINS, international bestselling author of *The High 5 Habit*

"I am so sincerely grateful to Mr. Rinella. For many years, I have been laboring to answer the question of how to get our kids off the couch and back outside into nature. Now I can just hand their parents this book—an imperative call to action that contains the secrets to living better through getting outside, and having fun while doing it."

—NICK OFFERMAN, *New York Times* bestselling
author of *Paddle Your Own Canoe*

"A revelation for families struggling to get kids to GO OUTSIDE, or to just stop using the darn smartphone. Steven Rinella uncovers the root cause of the screen-time battle and provides the perfect solution for it. Packed with funny anecdotes, nuggets of wisdom, and actionable advice, *Outdoor Kids* will have everyone excited to leave the house faster than a roly-poly hides under a rock."

—MICHAELEEN DOUCLEFF, PhD, *New York Times* bestselling
author of *Hunt, Gather, Parent*

"Full of empathy and intelligence . . . In some sections of the book, the author's prose is so engrossing, so riveting, that it matches, punch for punch, the best sports writing."

—*The Wall Street Journal*

"Steven Rinella is one of the best nature writers of the last decade. . . . This book was a page-turner."

—TIM FERRISS

"Rinella's writing is unerringly smart, direct, and sharply detailed."
—*The Boston Globe*

"Chances are, Steven Rinella's life is very different from yours or mine. He does not source his food at the local supermarket. *Meat Eater* is a unique and valuable alternate view of where our food comes from—and what can be involved. It's a look both backward, at the way things used to be, and forward, to a time when every diner will truly understand what's on the end of the fork."

—ANTHONY BOURDAIN

"Rinella is an astute observer, with an eye for delightfully telling details."

—*Paste*

"An insider's look at hunting that devotees and nonparticipants alike should find fascinating."

—*Kirkus Reviews*

"Woven into Rinella's thoughtful prose detailing his outdoor adventures (or misadventures, in some cases) are historical, ecological, or technical observations dealing with the landscape, the animals, or the manner in which the game is harvested. . . . Rinella has a passion for hunting and wilderness that comes across in his writing."

—*Publishers Weekly*

BY STEVEN RINELLA

*Outdoor Kids in an Inside World*

*The MeatEater Guide to Wilderness Skills and Survival*

*The MeatEater Fish and Game Cookbook*

*The Complete Guide to Hunting, Butchering, and Cooking Wild Game: Volume 1, Big Game*

*The Complete Guide to Hunting, Butchering, and Cooking Wild Game: Volume 2, Small Game and Fowl*

*Meat Eater: Adventures from the Life of an American Hunter*

*American Buffalo: In Search of a Lost Icon*

*The Scavenger's Guide to Haute Cuisine: How I Spent a Year in the American Wild to Re-create a Feast from the Classic Recipes of French Master Chef Auguste Escoffier*

# OUTDOOR KIDS
# IN AN
# INSIDE WORLD

# OUTDOOR KIDS
## IN AN
# INSIDE WORLD

### GETTING YOUR FAMILY
### OUT OF THE HOUSE AND RADICALLY
### ENGAGED WITH NATURE

## STEVEN RINELLA

RANDOM HOUSE

NEW YORK

2023 Random House Trade Paperback Edition

Copyright © 2022, 2023 by MeatEater, Inc.

All rights reserved.

Published in the United States by Random House,
an imprint and division of Penguin Random House LLC, New York.

RANDOM HOUSE and the HOUSE colophon are registered trademarks of
Penguin Random House LLC.

Originally published in hardcover and in slightly different form in the United States by
Random House, an imprint and division of Penguin Random House LLC, in 2022.

LIBRARY OF CONGRESS CATALOGING-IN-PUBLICATION DATA
Names: Rinella, Steven, author.
Title: Outdoor kids in an inside world: getting your family out of the house and
radically engaged with nature / Steven Rinella.
Description: New York: Random House, [2022] | Includes index.
Identifiers: LCCN 2021048803 (print) | LCCN 2021048804 (ebook) |
ISBN 9780593129685 (trade paperback) | ISBN 9780593129678 (ebook)
Subjects: LCSH: Natural history. | Nature—Effect of human beings on. | Environmentalism.
Classification: LCC QH81 .R48 2022 (print) | LCC QH81 (ebook) |
DDC 508—dc/eng/20211123
LC record available at https://lccn.loc.gov/2021048803
LC ebook record available at https://lccn.loc.gov/2021048804

Illustrations: Kelsey Johnson

Printed in the United States of America on acid-free paper

randomhousebooks.com

2 4 6 8 9 7 5 3 1

Book design by Diane Hobbing

For Katie. Without you there'd be nothing.

We all have this feeling "I came into the world!"
Well that isn't true: You came out of this world, like
a leaf comes out of a tree.

—ALAN WATTS

## AUTHOR'S NOTE

This book is for anyone who feels responsible for the well-being of a child. Not only parents, but also grandparents, aunts, uncles, mentors, friends, and babysitters—caregivers of every stripe. Indeed, raising outdoor kids may well be impossible if attempted by parents alone.

# CONTENTS

# THE FISH SHACK

I found the answer I was seeking under a rock.

The question had been burning in my mind since 2010, when my oldest son, James, was just a few months old—brand-new enough to seem terrifyingly fragile but old enough to have exhausted my and my wife's appetite for sitting on the sofa and staring at him.

*How the hell are we ever going to get everyone out of the house?*

For parents, it's a question that never dies. It doesn't matter which town or city you live in. It doesn't matter if you've got four kids or one. It doesn't matter how old they are. If you're a parent or caregiver who's drawn to the title of this book, you most likely live with the knowledge that nature is important to kids. Just as likely, you feel strained and anxious about how to create impactful experiences for them in the outdoors. Every day, it seems, there's some new obstacle. At first it's the annoyance of changing diapers and feeding a baby while away from the helpful tools of home. Then it's working around nap times and coordinating the needs of children of different ages. The five-year-old is raring to go, but if her baby brother misses another nap, he's going to be a nightmare for the rest of the day. The complications evolve over time, until you eventually land where my wife, Katie, and I find ourselves today as we raise three kids between the ages of seven and eleven: locked in a series of clashes with the kids over our insistence that outdoor time is more important than screen time.

No matter what phase we're in, or how temporarily frustrated I get, I always return to that rock and the lessons it offered. The possibilities it revealed are always nearby, no matter where I am. But that first discovery took place on the coast of a remote island in southeast Alaska.

Years ago, I pitched in with my brothers Matt and Danny for a run-down cabin we'd chanced into on a piece of land a twenty-minute floatplane ride from the town of Ketchikan. We bought it sight unseen, each of us paying about what you'd pay for a decent used car. At the time, the three of us were unmarried. I had no immediate plans to have children, and certainly no long-term strategy about how I'd raise them if I did. All I wanted was a good place for fishing with my brothers that was out in the middle of nowhere, and my brothers felt the same way. We wanted a place that we could call our own, where we could trade our time in exchange for knowledge of the natural world. My life had always been based on the value of that transaction. Ever since I was a kid growing up in rural Michigan, I had taken strength and inspiration from my interactions with nature. The lessons I learned there had guided me toward success as a family member, a student, and a professional. I knew that going deeper toward nature would only bring more rewards.

The fact that the cabin was home to a population of mice and a lone female mink only made it more appealing. At least these animals weren't coated in either mold or rust, which is more than you could say for any man-made objects inside the cabin. My wife, Katie, would later observe that it wasn't really fair to describe the structure as a cabin at all. That was overselling it, she said.

Gradually it became known as the Fish Shack.

The main question we get from friends who visit the Fish Shack is, "How did you guys find out about this place?" My brother Danny has been a professional ecologist in Alaska for about twenty years. He's based out of Anchorage. In a broad sense, as an ecologist, he studies the relationship of organisms to one another and to their physical surroundings. In particular, he focuses on salmon. Salmon are an anadromous fish, meaning that they live in the sea but migrate into rivers to spawn. While many people might regard salmon as a saltwater species, because that's where they spend the bulk of their lives, Danny argues that it's better to think of them as a freshwater fish. Their lives begin in freshwater and, since they die after spawning, their lives end in freshwater. Danny's work with salmon is focused on their freshwater habitats. He studies the gravelly stream bottoms where they lay their eggs. He studies the little streamside brush piles and overhanging vegetation where the juvenile salmon go to find food and avoid predation as they migrate toward the sea. And he studies what happens when all of those dead salmon carcasses rot away on the banks of the rivers (or in the bellies of bears and eagles) and enrich the surrounding environments with the ocean-based nutrients that were transported inland inside of their bodies as fat, bone, muscle, and gut.

It was this type of research that led Danny to the general location of the Fish Shack. He was working on a project gathering baseline biodiversity data about populations of freshwater aquatic invertebrates—insects, molluscs, crustaceans—along randomly selected salmon stream segments in southeast Alaska. In ecology, "gathering baseline data" is an operational term for taking measurements in an environment at a fixed moment. You're asking, "What lives here right now, at this moment in time?" You do this without making assumptions about how things used to look or what they are *supposed* to look like now. In doing that work, Danny became friends with a local man who's a member of the Tsimshian tribe. One day, a couple of years later, that friend called to let him know about an old shack that was up for sale nearby. We bought the place, then chartered a floatplane so that we could fly out and have a look at what we now owned.

At first, we discovered that we now owned a lot of garbage. Of the two-acre parcel, about half was covered in decades' worth of refuse: rusted-out oil drums, rotted lumber, head-high piles of wet fiberglass insulation, jumbles of twisted logging cable, junked-out outboard engines, paint and tar cans, irreparable boats, hundreds of yards of kinked polyethylene pipe, and all manner of other junk. The refuse was so overwhelming that you almost didn't notice the astounding specimens of old-growth hemlock and cedar that towered over the land and shack. The building itself was set on pilings, with half of the shack jutting out to the tideline. The structure was maybe forty feet long and twelve feet deep. Not a straight line or right angle could be found on the place. It looked as wavy as the surrounding ocean. There was no electricity. Water was drawn from the creek and run through PVC pipes that were fastened to the inside walls with brackets and rusty screws. Heat came from a smoky stove powered by a dripline of fuel oil.

In short, it was perfect. I'm talking about love at first sight.

Unbeknownst to me at the time, the Fish Shack wasn't just the best purchasing decision I had ever made. It was the best *parenting* decision I would ever make.

Like many parents, Katie and I have had to move our kids all around the country as we've pursued various work opportunities. At this point, our eleven-year-old, James, has lived in five different homes across three different states. It might sound strange, but that little shack stands in his mind as a point of security. He first visited the shack when he was five months old, and it remains the one physical location that he's known for his entire life. Same for his nine-year-old sister, Rosemary, and his seven-year-old brother, Matthew. Collectively, they've shed a considerable amount of blood on the barnacle-covered rocks that are guaranteed to shred a kid's hands and knees whenever they fall along the beach. In turn, the blood of that place runs through their veins.

The second time we brought James there, he found them: the treasure trove of rocks along the water's edge. He waddled right over to one and flipped it over, and out crawled two crabs. He went wild with glee. Then he started flipping over more rocks in search of more secrets. And that was it. He was hooked.

Of all the activities that our kids participate in at the Fish Shack— stacking firewood, fishing for halibut, checking crab pots, cleaning shrimp—they are most passionate about the task of flipping over rocks along the water's edge as they search for the crabs, snails, pile worms, and sculpins that can be found beneath. The kids seem to prefer human-head-sized rocks, probably because these rocks are small enough to be rolled over but big enough to support a vibrant amount of life underneath. Now and then they need to join forces in order to roll a particularly large boulder. For the really big rocks, they might enlist the help of a nearby grown-up or two, who might be encouraged to come running with a shovel or cedar post in order to pry it free.

With each flipped rock the routine is always the same. They hustle around to examine its former bed, squatting so close to the surface of the shallow water that their butts and sometimes the tips of their noses get wet. A lot of the life-forms that they find are scooped up gently by bare hands; others are caught using a small dip net. Most everything is released unharmed. Now and then, though, a small fish might get gutted, cooked over the fire, and eaten with bare hands. The whole process involves a lot of excited yelling and screaming. There's usually a bit of crying, too, from fingers getting cut up by broken clamshells or smashed under falling rocks. But this form of play, which looks and feels more like work, goes on pretty much all day every day. No matter how hard they try, the kids can never explore all of the rocks near the Fish Shack. That's because the beach doesn't really stay in one place. It's constantly moving with the tides, which are extreme. There's a useful term in ecology, "littoral zone," which describes the shoreline environments of a sea, lake, or river. An area's littoral zone runs from the high-water mark down to areas that are permanently submerged, and at the Fish Shack, it's enormous. A patch of dry ground at low tide could be under twenty feet of water at high tide. On a big high tide, the water has actually floated away boots that were standing next to the front door. At low tide, you might have to walk 150 yards to reach the water's edge.

Watching them flip rocks, with all of the excitement and disappointment and pain, I can't help but relate their work to my brother's. Of course, my brother's professional obligations require scientific rigor and emotional detachment. A scientist isn't supposed to "hope" for a set of results when taking baseline data, as the goal is to avoid bias. My kids, on the other hand, act as cheerleaders and critics for the rocks they roll over. They celebrate the productive ones and curse those that disappoint. By flipping rocks, they are knocking at the door of the natural world to see who's home. They hope, fiercely, to get an answer.

There's a wonderful term for the instinct that drives this ritual: "biophilia." The word was popularized by the American biologist E. O. Wilson. The biophilia hypothesis suggests that humans possess an innate tendency to seek connections with nature and with other forms of life. Kids are especially prone to biophilia. Just take a kid down to a pond, or let her peek into a bird's nest, or help him flip a big rock or a rotting log, and watch what happens. The connection to the life that they discover within or beneath is usually immediate and all-consuming. This is perhaps the most exciting discovery that I've made about my kids, and it's the answer that was lurking beneath those rocks at the Fish Shack. The truth revealed by their abiding focus on rock flipping is their own innate biophilia—a built-in feature that can be harnessed as a way to make nature a normal, everyday part of our family life. No matter the circumstances, no matter the location, some version of rock flipping is available to us. It might be something as simple as looking up from the breakfast table to watch an American robin outside the window and comment on how it tips its head in an effort to hear earthworms beneath the soil's surface before nabbing them. Or observing the way those worms will get flooded out of the ground by fierce rainstorms and driven up onto sidewalks and driveways, where their pale bodies greet us in the early morning as we head off to work and school. Each is a touchpoint with nature, a narrow opening through which we can pass in our search for deeper engagement. And these kinds of openings into the natural world are available to you, too.

I am, of course, aware that almost nobody has a Fish Shack in remote Alaska. Perhaps you live in a place where the closest thing to "nature" is miles away. Maybe everything around you feels man-made, or at least heavily manipulated by humans. Any attempt to discover nature is sure to be thwarted by the presence of people and buildings and the incessant hum and rumble of airplanes and cars. Maybe you don't have access to reliable transportation of your own, or it's prohibitively expensive to explore outside of your immediate surroundings.

Parents and caregivers create other obstacles to nature intentionally, often with good reason. In some households, schoolwork, organized sports, and church activities are given so much priority that there's simply no time left in the day for anything else. You may have safety concerns that lead you to restrict your child's access to your local woodlot or park to times when you or another adult can accompany them. There are strangers around, or you might have concerns about ticks and Lyme disease. There could be ponds or creeks, where drowning is a very real risk.

All of these obstacles are legitimate. There are dozens more that I haven't mentioned, and probably hundreds more that I haven't even thought of. My own family has faced more than a few, which is how I can say with such certainty that catering to our fears creates a sort of inertia that can be hard to overcome. Fear prevents engagement; lack of engagement builds into a habit of avoidance; and pretty soon it's just your family stuck inside four walls, where perhaps the biggest obstacle of all—technology—abounds. Even if you recognize that it might not be good for them to be in their room on an iPad, it's better than not knowing where they are. Technology might be the devil, but at least it's the devil you know.

You wouldn't believe the arguments we've had with our kids over access to Kindles and iPads. I'll just come right out and say it: If my kids had unfettered access to their devices, days might go by before they stepped outside. But even in the face of such a shape-shifting adversary—its hardware and habits so woven into the fabric of our lives we have trouble remembering how we ever did without—it's important not to panic.

This idea that the world is perpetually going to hell seems hard-wired into our psyche. There's a thought, often misattributed to Socrates, that Garson O'Toole (aka the Quote Investigator) traced to the 1907 dissertation of an otherwise unknown Cambridge student named Kenneth John Friedman. It laments the intergenerational discord in ancient Greece, thousands of years ago, where elders saw the young becoming "tyrants," marked by "luxury, bad manners, contempt for authority, disrespect to elders, and a love for chatter in place of exercise."

I'm not sure if the ancient Greeks were lamenting their children's lack of engagement with nature. This particular concern might be more contemporary, though it has certainly become a pervasive thought today. In his 1993 memoir *The Thunder Tree,* ecologist Robert Pyle coined the term "extinction of experience," and since then many researchers have jumped into the fray. There are bodies of work on the demonstrable decline of kids' contact with nature, as well as the negative impacts of this trend—most alarmingly captured in Richard Louv's 2005 *Last Child in the Woods,* which warned of "nature deficit disorder." In recent years, scholars have begun to try to capture this fading picture of human-nature interactions more precisely. In time, we'll probably have concrete data on the physiological and psychological similarities and differences between watching a fishing video on YouTube and standing in the mud with a pole in your hand, but I'm not going to sit around and wait for it. I suggest you don't, either. We already know, both instinctively and empirically, that when kids and adults interact with *real* nature, they get mental and physical health benefits. Two hours a week of time spent in nature, in whatever increments are available, has been shown to radically improve people's outlook, with adult participants in a large-scale study in England self-reporting improvements in both physical health and emotional well-being. Other studies have shown immune-boosting effects, improved cognitive and motor skills development in young kids, and even reductions in crime rates across communities with improved access to green space. But, again, this is probably not news to you. We don't need studies to tell us that we feel better when we step into nature.

Covid-19 complicated everything. Arriving just over a century after the 1918 influenza pandemic, the literal "100-year event" has caused a massive, global withdrawal from public spaces and activities. Every single facet of our own lives, as well as the lives of our kids, has been impacted. Offices were closed and workers sent home. Schools were shut down. Airline travel all but ceased. College campuses were shuttered. Family vacations were canceled. Visits to see Grandma and Grandpa were put on hold, indefinitely. Crosstown trips to the park became impractical or even illegal. Cooped up and constrained, we found our communal appreciation for outdoor time soaring while we simultaneously suffered a troubling increase in indoor time. Previously, we might have been guilty of measuring our own sense of worth by comparing our cars or homes to those of our peers, but suddenly we were measuring ourselves based on whether or not we had easy access to outdoor spaces where we could be alone and therefore safe from infection. Folks from the crowded and urbanized coasts looked longingly inward toward the middle, emptier portions of the nation, where people were able to carry on a somewhat normal existence in their spacious backyards or national forests.

Families without that luxury have seen the impacts on their kids. A friend of mine from New York described to me a "huge uptick in screen time, insanely, dramatically so." The normal, habitual pieces of outdoor time that his kids experienced were suddenly gone. No playground recess. No bike rides with friends. No weekends at the beach. He was left trying to force new outdoor experiences on his kids, but those efforts felt strained and often ultimately unproductive. He'd urge his kids to go outside, but then had to remind them to stay close to each other and avoid their friends. The only alternative was yet another bike ride with Mom and Dad, along the same familiar close-to-home routes. Frustration abounded, both for the parents and for the kids. My friend and his wife felt as though they were failing as parents.

As the pandemic's initial shelter-in-place orders were lifted, people escaped from home en masse and rushed to any place they could find that was outdoors and relatively free of people. In 2020, Americans bought over 13 percent more fishing licenses than they had the year before. Across the nation, enrollment in hunter safety courses skyrocketed. Michigan (my home state) saw a 67 percent increase in new hunting license buyers. Double and triple the normal number of visitors poured into parks, campgrounds, and forests. More than 10 million American households went camping for the first time. With the National Park Service and other land management agencies still reeling from pandemic-related shortages in staff and equipment, the influx of visitors overwhelmed all efforts to accommodate them. Hikers and campers left mounds of trash and improperly disposed-of human waste littering trailheads and campgrounds where garbage service was suspended and outhouses were locked up. Meanwhile, many inexperienced backcountry visitors got into more adventure than they bargained for. Search and rescue teams in the American West experienced the greatest volume of activity in their entire history. While we're probably years away from understanding just how much the pandemic changed us, I think it's safe to say this much so far: The pandemic has reinforced our love of nature, and it has revealed our need for the knowledge, skill set, and equipment necessary to experience it in a safe and sustainable way.

Another thing reinforced by the pandemic is that we place an enormous value on feeling connected. This was hardly a surprise. If humans were to be described in some field guide to mammals, it would say that we are highly social and gregarious. We want connections for ourselves, and we want our kids to feel connected. We generally feel safest when surrounded by loved ones. When times are bad, we tend to go toward others rather than away from them. We want the support and approval of our communities. We want to feel that we belong to something larger and more permanent than ourselves. During the height of the pandemic, many of us maintained our sense of connectedness in a way that truly blurred the lines between digital life and "real" life. We enrolled in online classrooms, dressed up for Zoom cocktail parties, and toasted loved ones during virtual wedding ceremonies. It made it even harder to set aside those glowing screens and get out of the house, but it'd be unfair and shortsighted to label all of the electronics as dangerous or bad for kids. At a time when craziness and unpredictability reigned, they blessed us with something close to familiar.

As Katie and I strived to create an atmosphere of familiarity for our kids, we would often find ourselves lying in bed at night and discussing how everything around us was inherently impermanent. The pandemic rubbed our noses in that reality by taking away so much that we'd taken for granted. Of course, impermanence has always been the norm. Friends move away. Family members die. Social media communities dissolve. We leave our hometowns for school or better jobs. As our communities repeatedly splinter, we're forced to engage in a lifelong rebuilding process. I often find myself mentioning different categories of friends that I have: My friends from back home. My friends from college. My friends from Seattle. Unfortunately, but undeniably, the collections of friends that are left behind tend to fade in relevance as the years go by and we grow apart. Likewise with family. My father was once the most impactful person in my life. He's now been dead for twenty years. I still struggle with how to fill that hole, if it needs to be filled at all.

Part of our job, then, as parents, is to teach our kids to deal with the impermanence of these connections. When Katie and I got our kids their first pet, a brilliantly purple betta fish, we viewed it as being a lesson in death and loss (bettas only live a few years) as much as a lesson in caretaking. We placed its small aquarium on the counter of their bathroom. They were ecstatic about this fish and professed their love for it. In my mind, I was already counting down the days until the fish died and imagining how the kids would respond and what they'd learn from the experience. I know it might sound weird, but in a not-so-roundabout way, we gave the kids the fish in order to begin teaching them about the inevitable loss of friends and family—and even, someday, of their own parents. Bad things will happen in life. That's for sure. What's not certain is how well we'll cope with them.

Considering all this—our desire for connections, the impermanence of those connections, and our impulse to prepare our kids for an unpredictable and unwieldy life—it feels imperative that we foster strong bonds between our kids and nature. As creatures of the earth, we are inherently and intrinsically connected to the natural world. This world is dynamic and defined by change, but it *is* permanent. A relationship with nature fulfills, precisely, our yearning to belong to something bigger than ourselves.

Every time we turn over a rock and look closely at what we find, we get a glimpse of that bigger thing.

I should let you know that I once vowed to never write this book. Back during my early thirties, while Katie and I were flirting with the idea of having kids, I would get annoyed whenever my friends who had already become parents developed what I considered to be an unhealthy obsession with their offspring. Even worse, in my estimation, were writers who gave up on their usual subjects of inquiry and turned their attention to parenthood. That you quit your job in order to be a stay-at-home dad or struggled with your identity after having kids hardly seemed like things worth getting literary about. We're all familiar with that old adage that kids are better seen than heard. I agreed—better seen than heard, better heard than discussed. Whatever happened to me as a parent, I wasn't gonna let it rewire my brain.

I was wrong, obviously, and the depths of my miscalculation are evidenced by the fact that you're sitting here reading this. What caused my change of mind will be obvious to anyone who's ever watched their own child come gasping into the light of the world, slimy and naked and packing along with them a boundless payload of heartbreak and joy that they will give to you in mixed dosages for the rest of your life. Until the moment I became a father, I never felt truly and absolutely responsible for anyone. Becoming a parent is an epiphany: *You're up!* As part of my responsibilities to my children, I knew that I was wholly responsible for teaching them everything I knew about being a human who feels at home in nature.

I'll admit that it's easy to feel the totality of the natural world in a place like the Fish Shack, where nature is omnipresent. It wraps around you and covers you like a sleeping bag. There are very few disturbances from the man-made world to distract your mind and body. But the Fish Shack could be gone from my life tomorrow. Due to matters of health, finance, or family, it's perfectly possible that I might not ever get up there again. Regardless, I know for certain that the gift of nature can be given under pretty much any circumstance, pretty much anyplace. I know because I've seen it happen, everywhere from New York City to Seattle. Nature can teach us—and more importantly, our kids—to go through this existence with a sense of awe and purpose.

This book will show you how to learn.

# OUTDOOR KIDS
## IN AN
## INSIDE WORLD

## CHAPTER 1

# THINKING NATIVE

---

The fat from a whitetail deer is waxier than beef fat and has a higher melting point. If you're eating a particularly fatty cut of venison, such as ribs or neck, taking a sip of cold water can cause the fat to solidify and coat the inside of your mouth. It can be pretty off-putting. People usually compare it to having a sip of candle wax. What's more, it doesn't always have a good flavor, and the flavor only gets worse when it's been in the freezer for a few months. My brother uses venison fat to make hand lotion and lip balm that he gives out as Christmas gifts, but culinary uses are fairly limited.

I was explaining all of this to my kids one day while we were butchering James's first whitetail deer in our kitchen. He had killed the deer after he turned ten and became old enough to hunt alongside a licensed mentor here in Montana. In doing so, he was following in the well-worn footsteps of a family of hunters that included not only his father, but also his uncles, his grandfather, and two great-grandfathers. This particular doe had been living near some irrigated agricultural fields and had built up an impressive layer of fat. As we worked, the pile of trimmed fat grew big enough that it seemed awfully wasteful to just throw it in the trash. This got me thinking about gray jays and magpies, which absolutely love the stuff. I started telling the kids how those birds will actually learn to associate humans with food; they'll sometimes follow you around while you're hunting, as though convinced that it's just a matter of moments until you produce for them a massive windfall of fat and protein. They'll get so excited when you're butchering a carcass in the field that they'll nervously risk coming within arm's reach to snatch away gobs of fat. I appreciate their boldness, but I usually make it easier for them by hanging some bits of fat on nearby tree limbs so that they can enjoy their meal without fear of getting caught by this strange, two-legged predator that seems intent on hogging the bulk of the meat.

When we finished our butchering job, I froze the trimmed fat into a solid gob about the size of a volleyball. The next morning, I tossed it up on a section of our rooftop that we could see from the living room window. The swarm of magpies that descended on the fat within a day's time was remarkable enough that the kids begged to use my phone so that they could send around a video of the feeding frenzy to friends and relatives. That night, we enjoyed a meal of venison that came from the same deer that the magpies outside were eating at that very same moment. I mentioned to them that we should feel as lucky as those birds to have such a fine meal.

The most interesting thing about the experience with the deer fat, at least for me, was a subtle shift in the relationship between my kids and the local magpies. Prior to the fat incident, the kids were aware of magpies at least in the theoretical sense. If you had asked them, they would have described the birds as black-and-white with long tails. We had magpies listed on our tally of the birds that visit our yard. After the fat incident, however, the kids discussed magpies with a far greater level of intimacy and knowledge. Of particular interest to them was the magpies' ability to assess risk. Within days of discovering the fat, the birds developed precise notions about the physical capabilities of our dog. They managed to hop around within feet of her, in a perfectly nonchalant fashion, without ever giving her a chance to sink her teeth into their feathers. These interactions became an endless source of fascination and conversation in our household.

I recognize that butchering deer and feeding fat to magpies might seem a bit extreme, especially for parents who are struggling just to get their kids out of the house for an hour-long trip to the park. But my point is to accentuate the types of interactions that I try to foster between my kids and nature. Beyond the imperative of getting my kids out of the house, my goal is to put them on equal footing with the surrounding landscape and its creatures. I want them to conceptualize themselves as being part of nature, so that they see it on an eye-to-eye level.

It's an approach that sits between two poles, one that I'll call looking down at nature and the other looking up. Our society is well accustomed to the perils of the former. To look down at nature is to regard it as lowly, dirty, savage, or uncouth. It's the mindset that regards worms as gross, dirt as filthy, and wild animals as flea-bitten and dangerous. This view of nature leads inevitably to desecration. It creates room, morally and spiritually, to disregard nature or permanently destroy it in the name of progress or civilization. To demonstrate what I mean on a minor scale, I'll explain what happened along the shores of the small Michigan lake where I grew up. When I was a kid, the lake was bordered by a shoreline of reeds, downed trees, and overhanging weeping willows that provided habitat for muskrats, ducks, frogs, and all manner of fish species. The shoreline buzzed and crawled with life. As magical as it seemed to me, many people didn't like it that way. They didn't like the muck and mud that oozed between their toes. They didn't like the feeling of reeds brushing against their bare ankles or aquatic vegetation grabbing at their toes. They didn't like the creepy crawlies that slithered and swam. Eventually, a resident of the lake solved these problems with an application of herbicide followed by a dump-truck load of sand. This approach caught on, and over the years large stretches of lakeshore habitat were wiped clean to resemble the beaches at all-inclusive ocean resorts. If you asked around, no one would tell you that they destroyed their beach habitat out of a hatred for nature. They'd just say that sand feels good and looks good, end of story. The wildness that was buried beneath the sand and herbicide would be irrelevant to the conversation, because it was never considered in the first place. Such are the perils of looking down at nature, which, in some cases, could be described as not seeing nature at all.

When I say looking up at nature, I'm referring to a more contemporary perspective that regards nature as being more pure or beautiful than ourselves. This perspective holds that nature is somehow diminished through human involvement, even when that involvement is responsible and well-meaning. In environmental circles, this perspective is often described as preservationism. It's easily understandable if you consider the juxtaposition between a preservationist and a conservationist. A conservationist seeks to answer the question "How can we use nature responsibly and sustainably?" A preservationist asks, "How can we protect nature from any use at all?"

While preservationism makes sense from a purely environmental standpoint, I do believe that looking up at nature comes with its own human risks—especially for kids. Think of those millions of tourists who visit Yellowstone National Park every year, just a ninety-minute drive from my house. Many of them never even leave their cars or the parking lots. There they are, visiting some of the most stunning displays of the natural world on earth, and they do so only by looking through the glass of a windshield or standing behind some sign that warns of the dangers posed by wildlife or bubbling geysers. Sure, grown-ups can easily understand the logic behind enforcing passive observation of these natural wonders. If hordes of people were allowed to trample everything in Yellowstone, the magic of the place would be diminished. But kids don't necessarily enjoy that level of insight, and I can't help but wonder about the sense of displacement and alienation that we create in our children by cordoning them off from nature. Imagine for a moment if Disneyland took the same approach. Imagine that the rides are there only to be looked at and never ridden. Imagine if we explained that Mickey and Minnie, or Elsa and Anna, are too pure to be touched by the marauding, corrupting hands of our children. Would Disneyland still enjoy the position that it holds in our children's hearts? Or would they quickly lose interest and move on to other things? If such visits are balanced by journeys to places where our kids are welcome to get muddy and bloody by mixing it up with nature, that's great. But if their only exposure to nature is in places where protective barriers are necessary, how can we expect our kids to feel connected to the natural world? If we want our kids to feel a true and pragmatic sense of stewardship for the environment, we need to let them relate to it as a peer, as something that they're entwined with through symbiotic connections.

The title of this chapter, "Thinking Native," is meant as a prescription for how you and your family can begin to see nature eye-to-eye. The process starts with you, and by extension, you will bring your kids along. Thinking native has nothing to do with trying to mimic the thoughts of Native Americans or any other indigenous peoples. I'm using the term "native" here in the way that a biologist would, to denote a species that normally lives and thrives in a particular ecosystem. When we say that whitetail deer are native to North America or that emperor penguins are native to Antarctica, we mean that they are from that ecosystem naturally: Humans didn't put them there. When we say that the common rat is non-native to North America or that coconuts are non-native to Hawaii, we mean that they were brought there by humans. As a species, *Homo sapiens,* we can think of ourselves as being native to every place we happen to be. We distributed ourselves, and weren't carried around the world by some other creature. Still, many people find it difficult to consider themselves as being a natural part of their own ecosystem. Because we represent "civilization," we conclude that we exist at a remove from nature. We might think of it as being beneath us, or above us, or simply far away. In order to ground ourselves, as well as our kids, we need to discover pathways toward regarding ourselves as legitimate members of whatever natural ecosystem we happen to live in.

Take a moment to consider something called Gaia theory, which might stretch the limits of your imagination, as it does mine. Developed in the 1960s and '70s by a chemist and inventor named James Lovelock, the theory holds that the living and nonliving components of the earth have evolved together as a single self-regulating system. It's a complex and messy concept, but you can get the gist of it by thinking about the composition of the earth's atmosphere. What's notable is that our atmosphere remains constant in its composition, which allows for the existence of life on earth. Many of the gases that can be found in the air we breathe—nitrogen, oxygen, carbon dioxide—are either created or processed by living organisms. If it wasn't for life on earth, all of the oxygen would combine with other gases or minerals in the planet's crust and wouldn't be present in the atmosphere to support life. Thus, we see that life is necessary for life. Similar processes are at play in all kinds of other ways, ranging from interactions between living and nonliving materials that stabilize the salinity levels in oceans to interactions that stabilize global temperatures.

There are many criticisms of Gaia theory. Some say it's a far-out fantasyland concept that suggests the earth is driven by an ingrained sense of purpose rather than random chance. But still, there's something extraordinarily pleasing and reassuring about the broad concept of the earth as a single living organism: the rivers as our circulatory system, the trees as our lungs, and humans as inextricable components living on the surface and (hopefully) lending ourselves toward the betterment of the whole.

A tall order for kids to comprehend, perhaps, but I believe that we can model this philosophy of life and nature in a way that helps them understand how nature impacts their lives—and, in turn, how their lives impact nature. Just as we connect to communities formed by school, work, church, and sports, it's vital that we teach our kids to recognize themselves as belonging to a living ecosystem. In other words, our kids need to understand that they are not above, outside, or apart from their physical environment—they are completely intertwined with it, and it with them.

When you commit to removing the barriers between your family and nature, it means that the whole lot of you, together, stay engaged with what arises around you. You stay engaged with the beauty of nature, the fear that it can inspire, the damage that it can bring, and everything in between. This mindset shift does not need to happen at a global or even national level. It begins small, just by opening yourself—and your kids—up to what's already happening immediately around you. No matter where you are, nature abounds. I promise you. You don't need to be in the wilderness of Alaska or on an Iowa farm. Your yard is perfect. A friend's yard is perfect. A neighbor's woodlot will work. The local park is great. Even the small balcony of a skyscraper will cut it. The point is to remind yourself that nature surrounds you at all times. You are living amid nature. You are *in* it. You are *of* it.

When you're exploring your place in nature, remember that your attitude is more important than your acreage. Believe me, I understand that your attitude can be hard to control at times. As parents, we get lazy and make mistakes. We get careless. We get exhausted. But being mindful about nature can help us with our own problems as parents as much as it can help our kids. Observing nature requires quiet contemplation. The practice of studying nature is calming. It focuses your thinking and gives you a break from the constant buzz of politics, work, social media, and everything else that we wish would just go away now and then. Try this for a minute: Instead of reading this book and judging your own performance as a parent, just think about a dense forest with a grassy floor, sunlight streaming through the treetops. You feel that, right? Something happens to your brain when it goes to nature, and the same will be true for your kids.

When you allow yourself to become enthusiastic about the natural world around you, your enthusiasm will be infectious to your children. It won't all be a picnic. Your kids may roll their eyes at you, or worse. The whining and fighting during that two-hour car ride to the lake may make you want to bag the whole trip. No matter what, though, stick with it. I have faith that you'll eventually find, or reconnect with, the addictive qualities of nature. Which is good, because engaging with nature isn't something you can just do once or twice and then walk away. It needs to become a practice, a discipline. You need to be willing—and, hopefully, excited—to assume the role of a tour guide as you demonstrate engagement with nature to your kids. I'll admit it, I'm more than happy to farm out my kids' arithmetic lessons to our public school teachers. The school closures of the

Covid-19 pandemic made many of us painfully aware of how much we rely on these teachers to give our kids their formal schooling. But nature is an arena that can't be adequately accessed from a classroom. Instead, we need to take on this job ourselves.

The outdoor activities described in this book are tremendously valuable pastimes and disciplines in and of themselves, but the lessons that can be derived from pursuing these activities with your kids will not be fully realized if you approach them absent a mental shift that places you, and them, directly within the context of the natural world. I'm reminded of a conversation that I had on an airplane one time when I was flying solo with my two older kids, in Katie's absence. As I struggled alone with snacks and diapers and keeping everyone buckled up, an elderly man behind me tapped me on the shoulder and said, "Enjoy this. Right now, at their age, it's all physical. Later, parenting becomes mental. That's a lot tougher." I mention that story because I regard thinking native to be the tough, mental portion of this process. The other stuff, the physical acts such as gardening and fishing—that's where the fun is at. And it's my hope that in time you'll begin to sense yet another dimension, a kind of everyday spiritual practice, in the arc of these prescriptions.

For now, though, you just need to make up your mind to do it—to take that first step toward finding your own path to falling in love with the natural world, or rekindling a love that burned out somewhere along the way. It may come more naturally to your kids than it does to you, but since you're the one who's going to facilitate their interactions, you have to accept the challenge of looking nature square in the eye in order to create an environment where your kids' natural biophilia can thrive.

My own parents were able to do this in a way that seemed effortless. When I was growing up, I was completely unaware of their role in this regard. I realize now that they were purposeful and deliberate about raising me on an eye-to-eye level with nature; that I didn't see it happening is testament to just how good they were at their job. Granted, the setting was close to ideal. I was raised amid an unusually vibrant ecosystem in what was then a rural landscape of western Michigan. We had a neighbor's house twenty yards from our front door, but our yard was canopied by mature oaks and pines. The trees had their own resident populations of gray squirrels and fox squirrels. Chipmunks lived in the cracks of the house's foundation and flying squirrels accessed their dens through the holes in the house's siding. At night, when light from the kitchen window illuminated the bird feeder, we would see these flying squirrels come gliding in for a meal. We grew food in our garden and kept raccoons as pets. Downhill from our house was a sixty-acre lake. At night we could hand-grab crayfish and frogs using flashlights; in the daytime, we fished for bluegills and largemouth bass. In the evenings during summer, dark thunderstorms turned the skies inky blue and raindrops roiled the lake's surface as though the water was boiling. In the fall, we trapped muskrats in the lake in order to sell the hides. In the winter, when everything froze over, we fished through the ice. One spring, after the melt, a pregnant doe swam across the lake and got tangled up in the neighbor's fence. The deer broke its hip and had to be put down with a shot to the head; we were all mesmerized by the sight of the fully developed fawns that we found inside when we butchered the deer for meat.

My folks facilitated and encouraged these interactions through their day-to-day parenting. Some of it was probably easy. If my dad caught us watching TV, he'd just kick us outside—if he was in a good mood. If he was in a bad mood, he would send us out to do yard chores. Some of it was probably not so easy. Instead of worrying that my brothers or I might fall off the dock and drown in the lake, my parents would drive us back and forth from swimming lessons during the winter. During the warmer months, my dad would toss us off the dock and into deep water to make sure that we knew how to get back to shore in a hurry. Somehow, he managed to pull this off without it backfiring and making us afraid of the lake. We demonstrated that fearlessness later once we became strong swimmers, by jumping in the lake during those rainstorms on warm summer evenings. I never considered the stress that my mother must have felt as she stood on the porch, watching attentively for approaching lightning storms that would necessitate a hasty retreat from the water. Quietly, without projecting her worries, she weighed the rewards of discovery and exploration for her children against the risks of them getting zapped.

I was taught that questions deserved answers. At times, questions *demanded* answers. If I wondered about a particular bird, I was tasked with finding it in one of the guidebooks that were kept on a shelf above the piano. If my brothers and I brought home a dead bullfrog, we were taught how to clean it and cook the legs. Trees weren't just trees. They had names and attributes. When bluegills showed up in the shallow water in June, it wasn't just by chance. They were driven by factors such as water temperature and photoperiod. Now that I'm a parent myself, I can say that it would have been way, *way* easier for them to just let me watch TV.

Later, raising my own kids in urban environments, I fretted about whether or not I'd do as good a job as my parents did. I feared that the relative lack of nature surrounding us might prove to be an insurmountable obstacle to raising outdoor kids. I feared that their connection to nature wouldn't be as profound as mine simply because there wasn't as much of it to go around. And again and again, I navigated the disapproval of others: I remember sitting on a public beach along Lake Washington in Seattle and watching a woman accost one of my boys, who was only a toddler, for chasing after ducks. I saw the same thing along Lake Michigan, but that time it was seagulls that had been drawn to our lunch. Yet another time, in Florida, my oldest boy got yelled at by an elderly couple for tossing a live shrimp to a heron that was following him along the shore. He was "interfering with nature," she said.

Yet by staying steadfast in my own understanding of the vital interplay between humans and nature, keeping an open heart toward the natural world around me, and working diligently to find it and connect with it wherever we were, I came to understand that my fears about not being able to properly introduce my kids to nature were entirely unwarranted.

Though I'll always advocate for the rawest version of contact with nature you can muster, I do appreciate more than a few tangible, practical benefits of human innovation. One of those benefits, when it comes to our modern cities, is a true reduction in simple physical barriers to getting outside. My own father was born in 1924, in the slums of Chicago's Little Italy. He told me many stories of hopping trains when he was a boy and riding the rails into the agricultural countryside to camp, in secrecy, in the narrow strips of brushy woods that buffered the train tracks from the farm fields. When it was time to go home, he hopped a train and rode back. Back then, there was zero public awareness of the injustice inherent in trapping people in cities with no easy or democratic way out, and no political will to address it. While we still have much work to do on that front, even in the most isolated urban environments there is good work being done to bring people into direct contact with nature, and to raise awareness of the factors that too often deprive them of it.

Said progress does not mean that sometimes, on a systemic as well as a personal level, overcoming these obstacles won't feel like a lot of work, or even downright impossible. I am well aware that not every kid can walk or bike to make contact with nature, nor can every parent just load them in the car. But with the right tools and know-how, bringing any kid into contact with nature is achievable.

By way of a pep talk, I'd like to point out the enormous power that we already wield as our children's gatekeepers, often without even thinking about it. Whenever we shield our kids from unpredictable relatives, or block their access to particular websites, or exclude them from arguments about family financial matters, we are, in essence, limiting which connections they make. We are controlling and customizing their reality. It's hard work, but we often don't perceive it as such.

And of course, we don't just inhibit connections. We also foster them. Intentionally, we build bridges to link our kids with the things that we ourselves regard as socially and culturally valuable. By planning Halloween costumes for neighborhood trick-or-treating, for instance, we are fostering connections to community and cultural tradition. We teach our kids to root for local sports teams as a way to connect with their school or hometown. We introduce kids to Sunday school in order to develop their connections with friends and peers of a similar faith.

As most parents can attest, we also foster connections unintentionally. It's hard to overstate the magnetic quality that social media has; it sucks kids in with the force of a *Star Wars* tractor beam. Right now, none of our three kids has a personal social media account. Yet somehow, they understand the ins and outs of every social media platform out there. They debate the merits of TikTok versus Instagram, and our older two kids somehow knew that Facebook had totally lost its coolness before my wife and I did. It distresses me that this happened, yet how it happened is completely obvious. Our kids see value in social media because they trust our opinions (at least while they're young they do), and they know that *we* see value in it because they see us using it. In the same vein, no matter where we live, if we prioritize engaging with nature for ourselves, and bring them along, they'll absorb that value as well.

James and Rosemary were born in Brooklyn, New York, while we were living in apartments with less than a thousand square feet of space. We observed rats in the subway tunnels, and I gave these rodents the same level of consideration as wild animals that I gave the muskrats of my youth. One time, we trapped a rat on our kitchen counter and discovered in the morning that it had been disemboweled and cannibalized by its brethren. This inspired us—again, with the intent to put our kids on eye level with nature—to explore the cannibalization practices of everything from rabbits to black bears to certain human cultures. We counted bird species and made lists—however brief—of every bird that passed through the diminutive chunks of outdoor space that we regarded as our "yard." I remember one October morning when I flushed a woodcock that was hiding on our patio, and then spent days trying to explain to Katie and the kids just how weird it was for a bird that lives in marshy thickets to get lost and wind up stranded next to our tomato plant. We ate street pigeons that we caught on our patio, much to the bafflement of neighbors. We added to our dinner salads the greens of dandelions and lamb's-quarter that grew from the cracks in the sidewalks. I do understand that most people in cities don't do that. But that doesn't mean they couldn't.

But make no mistake: Pursuing an eye-level relationship with nature can and will lead to experiences that are unexpected, unnerving, and even dangerous. That's part of it, because that's part of the world. I still struggle to make sense out of one particularly dangerous occurrence that happened to James and me. It began in June, when James was three. He and I snuck through Prospect Park in Brooklyn with a small fishing rod in order to catch spawning bluegills out of the man-made ponds. There were no signs that forbade the activity, but I wanted us to be discreet in order to avoid any potential hassles from people who might take offense at someone potentially bringing harm to a fish. It proved to be such an exciting activity for James that I started researching areas that might have even better fishing. A couple of days later, I loaded him into a car and drove forty-five minutes north of the city to look for fish in a reservoir near Bedford, New York, that feeds into the city's water supply. We waded through head-high grass along the shore scouting for spawning bluegills but found nothing. Ten days later, James developed a bull's-eye rash around his navel—a telltale sign that he'd contracted Lyme disease from a tick bite. I got out of the shower and noticed that I had a bull's-eye rash as well. Soon after, James developed Bell's palsy. It was heartbreaking to watch him take a sip of milk and then have it drip out the corner of his mouth. It seemed as though he was suffering from joint pain as well, as he would sometimes cry and hold his knees when we set him down on the ground. In turn, Katie and I cried every night out of fear that he wouldn't get better. Thankfully, he recovered rapidly once he was on antibiotics. I had put off seeking care for my own affliction due to a desire to focus entirely on James. I waited too long, and the infection entered my nervous system and created all kinds of problems for me. It got so bad that I couldn't go up or down stairs without holding on to a handrail. It took a month of daily intravenous antibiotic treatments before I finally got better.

A few summers before that Lyme disease debacle, in 2011, Hurricane Irene rolled through the Northeast. As the eyewall of the storm was passing, I brought James outside in our backyard, fully naked, so that he could feel and absorb the destructive power of nature. We have a photo from that day of James smiling in the yard while he stands in a flooded sandbox. Now he glows with pride when we share the tale of him facing down a storm. And I smile whenever I remember that moment. The story of the hurricane helps capture some of my philosophy about risk. I do not think of myself as careless, though I hate running away from danger. There is great beauty in nature and also some peril; I believe in embracing both. But in all honesty, I do still suffer guilt for not having taken greater precautions to protect my son from Lyme disease. We were lax about insect repellent that day and I hadn't tucked his pants legs into his socks to prevent ticks from crawling out of the grass and up his legs. I didn't check him thoroughly when we got home. That goes for myself, too. In many ways, I let him down that day, because I figured I'd done this a million times without issue, but those are always the situations where you get hit. There's that old saying, Pride cometh before the fall. But there's a limit to how much blame I'm willing to accept. Sure, we got punched by Mother Nature. But we got back up again, with no hard feelings. In my view, the only thing worse than getting into trouble with nature is avoiding it altogether.

Nine years later, when our family was living in the town of Bozeman, Montana, we had yet another opportunity to wrestle with the dangers of the natural world. One Friday afternoon in September, I watched with our three kids as a plume of smoke erupted on the mountainside just two miles from our home. I took the kids up on an extension ladder to access our roof so we could have an unobstructed view. The smoke turned to visible flames, and then high winds whipped the flames into a fury that raced up and over the ridgetop. Within an hour, the flames were being attacked by helicopters and air tankers that shook our house as they passed overhead.

The proximity of the initial smoke plume to a popular hiking trail led us to speculate that the cause had to be some careless hiker who'd flicked a cigarette or done something similarly stupid. Tensions were very high in our neighborhood that afternoon. Katie and I drove over to a friend's house to help her family get ready to evacuate. Smoke jumpers were parachuting down and landing in her driveway as we loaded trucks. We sent and received dozens of calls and text messages as we checked on others and others checked on us. Our kids absorbed the stress of the community members around them. They became visibly concerned about the well-being of our home and neighbors.

That night, after dark, I took them back outside in order to show them the orange flames on the mountaintop as they bounced from tree to tree in a stunning display of raw power. They were worried about the flames traveling toward us, so we paid attention to the feeling of the wind on our skin and decided that the flames would blow the other way for now. I explained to them the passing nature of the man-made world. While I didn't think our house would burn down in this fire, it would not always be here, I told them. We could survive without it. Everything we humans make will go away. That's guaranteed. The mountain, however, is more permanent than anything we could ever create. The timeline of its creation and destruction is something we can't even begin to comprehend. Thousands of small animals will perish in those flames, but the forest will regenerate. The wildlife will return, slowly but surely. I explained to them how a favorite wild mushroom of ours, the morel, will often grow from the ashes of a wildfire the following spring. If we're lucky, I said, we'll pick a bunch of morels up there next year. And no matter what, I will keep you safe. This conversation brought a moment of relief for the kids, however short-lived it was.

In the early morning, I had to leave town for a work trip to Alaska. The fire on the mountain seemed quieter as I drove toward the airport. It didn't seem to have spread at all since I'd gone to bed. By late morning, though, when I landed in Anchorage, it had exploded. The air was hot and the winds roared. We were getting reports of friends and colleagues whose homes were lost. People were opening gates to their pastures and cutting livestock loose in hopes that the animals would figure out a way to avoid the flames. The insurance company called Katie. They wanted to send a crew to our house to clear away the nearby trees. There were predictions that the winds could shift direction. Soon Katie had to begin making her own evacuation plans, just in case, while I listened over the phone from a faraway state. I was not there to protect my family. I was not there to help the kids interpret what they were seeing. I felt helpless. Useless.

In the end, the fire never turned in our direction. It burned more than eight thousand acres and destroyed close to seventy structures before getting doused by rain and wet snow. Despite my early speculation about man-made causes, investigators ultimately determined that the fire was natural. Embers from a lightning strike had smoldered inside a tree, unseen, for weeks. It was nature at work. Being witness to the fire's initial eruption, as well as its devastation, eventually led to many conversations between me and my kids about our complex entanglement with nature—an entanglement that is happening even when we sit inside our own home. Together, we arrived at this collection of thoughts: Like it or not, nature is out there. It cannot be ignored. You can live in fear of it, which is no fun and does little good. Or you can respect and admire it, which opens you up to glimpses of magic.

So I ask you: Where's your closest available magic? Once you've committed to taking a look at nature on eye level, where does your glance fall first? You have to start somewhere, and really, it can be anywhere. It may take a while to reach that true eye-level gaze, and even require daily practice, so make it easy on yourself. Wander over to the nearest waterway with a notebook, and write down what you observe. Commit to trying to identify and learn some facts about the first bird you see after you put down this book. Go outside and dig a hole until you strike a rock or turn over a bug, and go online to see if you can figure out what it is and how it got there. Download an app like iNaturalist and use it to identify that weed in the cracks of the sidewalk—it may well turn out to be edible, or have medicinal properties.

If none of this is lighting you up, perhaps you need to dig deeper. Go back to your own childhood—what did you really love about being outdoors? Or nature, or science, or anything similar? Go back there and grab an idea, then bring it forward into how you live today. What's nearby that you can go see, touch, smell, and even taste that will connect you to that thing you loved as a kid? Or a different route, stepping outside the context of wild nature for a moment: What makes you truly happy? If it's food, perhaps your path to nature is wild edible plants, or a local farmer's market, where you can start asking some questions. If it's art, perhaps you want to try to draw or paint something nearby, and use that time to slow down and reflect on next steps. If it's sports or games, where can you find the closest battle royale to look at from a different angle? Perhaps it's the local songbirds who have to dodge the neighbor's cat that hides beneath their bird feeder. Or maybe it's a hen mallard raising her young in a golf course water hazard, where a secretive snapping turtle slowly takes its toll on the brood.

For a more scientific approach to expanding your knowledge, consider tackling some of the questions below. But please don't be intimidated or feel ashamed if you don't know the answers. They are meant to get you thinking and learning about the natural environment surrounding your particular neck of the woods.

> What is the elevation of your home habitat? Almost three-fourths of the earth is covered by our oceans, which are all connected. The highest point of land on earth, Mount Everest, sits 29,029 feet above sea level. The lowest point of land on earth, the shoreline of the Dead Sea, is actually 1,355 feet below sea level. How far downhill (or uphill, for that matter) from your doorstep is the ocean?

> Imagine yourself as a drop of rainwater that falls on your roof and begins its journey to the ocean. By what network of ditches, creeks, and rivers would you travel? It's helpful to print a map of the waterways in your state and trace the route. What's the name of the bay or estuary where you'd end up before flowing into the ocean?

> How many inches of annual precipitation does your home habitat get? What percent generally falls as rain,

and what percent falls as snow? How does this year's precipitation compare to the long-term average? How does it
compare to the record highs and lows? Set up a rain
gauge and begin measuring precipitation.

Turn on your kitchen faucet and have a sip of water. Try
to actually taste the water. Concentrate on it. Where did
that water come from? A reservoir? An aquifer? How does
that reservoir or aquifer get refilled with new water? Is
your water supply regarded as sustainable? Is it imperiled
by irrigation, industry, or climate change?

What is the dominant wind direction where you live?
Does it change seasonally? What direction do storms generally come from? What wind directions tend to precede
clear weather? How about storms?

What kinds of trees are closest to your home? Are they
native tree species that have always been here? Or were
the trees relocated here from somewhere else?

Identify the nearest large body of water and learn what
fish live there. Are there fish species living there now that
weren't there before the arrival of Europeans? Are there
fish that have vanished from those waters due to man-
made causes?

What birds visit your home habitat? Buy a bird identification book and install a birding app on your phone.
(*The Sibley Guide to Birds* is a phenomenal book; the
region-specific Eastern and Western North America

books are even better. For apps, try eBird, which was created by the Cornell Lab of Ornithology.) Start building a list of the birds that visit your home habitat. Make your own rules about what to include. In my family, we include all birds that are seen or heard from our yard. A high-flying flock of migrating geese is fine, as long as it's seen or heard from home.

What's the earliest known time frame of human habitation around your home habitat? What Native American tribes lived in your home habitat at the time of European contact? What animals did they hunt? What fish did they catch? What crops did they raise, if any? What types of homes did they live in? Were they frequently at war with neighboring tribes? By what processes were they displaced from the landscape?

What were the first European settlers looking for when they arrived in your area? Fur? Gold? Farmland? Who first cut down the trees and cleared the land where you live? What crops or livestock were they trying to grow or raise?

What crops and livestock are raised around your home habitat now? Where do those crops and livestock end up? Are they consumed locally, or shipped far away?

What is the basic geology of your home habitat? What factors, such as glaciers, mountain building, and erosion have shaped your landscape? Are there active mines near you? What minerals do they extract?

What insects share your home habitat? Find and identify four or five bugs around your home. Were you surprised by how quickly you found them? Or did it take longer than you thought? On a warm spring or summer evening, listen carefully at dusk to see if you can hear the buzzing or chirping of insects. What species is making the sound?

When you look out the window in the morning, what direction are you facing? If you have access to an east-facing window, pay attention to the time and location of the rising sun. If you're looking to the west, observe the path of the setting sun and mark the place where it disappears against objects on the horizon. How does the sun's course through the sky, as well as the position where it sets and rises, change over the weeks and months? Acknowledge the winter solstice, which is the shortest day of the year in the Northern Hemisphere. Celebrate the fact that days will now begin growing longer. Do a countdown to the summer solstice, our longest day of the year. Go somewhere with a clear view to the west, so you can watch the sun set on this day.

What can you learn from the stars in the night sky? For eons, humans have used the stars and their constellations to find their way on both land and sea. You can start by finding the North Star, or Polaris, which stays fixed in the northern sky. But what about other constellations, like Orion the Hunter and Taurus the Bull? As the seasons change while the earth orbits the sun, the stars in the night sky shift westward. Likewise, the moon cycles from new to waxing to full to waning and back to a new moon

once every month. Learn why the first full moon of fall is
called the Harvest Moon. Why is it orange?

Again, the preceding questions are meant to kick-start your imagination and get you thinking about your surroundings as a natural
ecosystem in which you survive and thrive. Once you've considered a
few of these questions, you can follow your imagination in any direction that gets you and your kids outdoors on a quest to explore and
understand your surroundings. You will find plenty more inspiration
throughout this book. Feel free to jump around and skip a chapter if
there's something that you're eager to get to. My intention with orga-
nizing this book was to get to the camping chapter right away, as that's
a quick and relatively easy way to get your kids immersed in nature. I
placed hunting toward the end, because although it's second nature to
me, it's an extreme version of engagement that might take a few years
for you to get comfortable with—if you have any interest in getting
comfortable with it at all. No matter how you choose to read, you'll
find lots of information and insight about other activities and disciplines that will keep you making short-term plans and long-term
dreams with your kids.

## CHAPTER 2

# WHY WE SLEEP UNDER THE STARS

---

I'll always remember our first official family camping trip. By that I mean a camping trip involving all five of us: two parents plus three kids ages five, seven, and nine, sleeping in a tent in a place where walking across the yard and into a house was not an option. It happened to fall on a rainy Easter weekend. Ahead of the trip, our kids fretted and fretted about the low likelihood that the Easter Bunny would find them out on a small chunk of state forest surrounded by cattle ranches. I reassured them about the Easter Bunny's prowess at finding campers with a story from my own childhood. When I was their age, I explained, the Easter Bunny found my family at a Jellystone Park Campground in the Smoky Mountains of Tennessee. He or she (my kids and I argue about the gender of the Easter Bunny) saved the day by hiding Easter baskets around our campsite. Unless the Easter Bunny's skills have declined over the years, I assured them, we would be found.

Things started out fine. We pitched our tent, a Nemo Wagontop, off the edge of a muddy road in a flat, grassy canyon bottom in the Yellowstone Basin. We set up our open-air kitchen right next to a livestock watering tank that was maintained by the rancher who leased the cattle grazing rights from the state. The entire area was littered with dried cow pies. On either side of our camp, the canyon walls rose up a couple of hundred feet and then flattened out into the rolling hills of the Great Plains. The upper lip of the canyon was composed of exposed sandstone the color of rust. It was eroded and crumbling and loose; with the push of a hand, you could send head-sized chunks of the rock tumbling down to the canyon floor. Naturally, it took the kids about ten minutes to find their way up there. Within an hour, a few rocks had come rumbling down the hill and rolled onto the road we'd driven in on. I climbed up there to give the kids a stern lecture about the perils of "trundling," which is a sort of technical term for rock rolling. Not only could those rocks strike their own siblings or parents, they could roll down and smack into a vehicle coming up the road and hurt or kill a complete stranger.

Once I was done hollering at them, I turned my attention to our youngest, Matthew, whose face and arms were colored a mysterious bright yellow. Ruling out jaundice, I asked him what had happened. He produced for me a hunk of ochre, a natural earth pigment made of clay and ferric oxide. The piece was about the size of an avocado pit.

The kids showed me how they'd been using it to draw pictures on rocks. I was now feeling a little guilty for yelling at them about rolling the rocks, so I seized on the chance to turn things in a positive direction. I explained to them how ochre has been used by humans for tens of thousands of years for the purposes of making cave art and decorating skin and hair. That they'd stumbled into a chunk of it and were inspired to use it for those exact same purposes was pretty damn cool.

The next morning, a Saturday, the kids were back up in the rim-rocks again. I was reminded of their location every twenty minutes or so when a rock came tumbling down the hillside and skittered out into the grass. Eventually, the three of them came down the hill together with the news that they'd discovered a scorpion and that Rosemary "almost got bit." I told them that this was impossible, as there were no scorpions in Montana—or anywhere near Montana. James tried to solidify his own scorpion-identifying credentials by reminding me of the time when we'd used blacklights to look for scorpions down on the Baja Peninsula. (All scorpions fluoresce under ultraviolet light.) I told him that I remembered that night well, but that didn't change the fact that there were no scorpions around here. The argument escalated. Rosemary was outraged, as she was the one who'd almost gotten zapped by the thing. James implored me to come have a look for myself. I refused, explaining that I had to do pretty much the only thing that grown-ups do while they're camping with kids, which is clean up after kids.

By this point, James was so upset that he was crying. I told him that the only way he would change my mind is by bringing me a scorpion, which seemed like a perfectly safe and reasonable thing to say since we all know that there are no scorpions in Montana. He and Rosemary stormed off and climbed back up into the rimrocks. Within minutes, they came sliding back down the hill with two scorpions on a rock. A quick Google search revealed that we were beholding two specimens of Montana's only scorpion species, the northern scorpion, which is mostly found around rimrock areas in the Yellowstone Basin. It was news to me.

At this point, considering the ochre and the scorpions, I was basking in the thought of how much I loved camping with the kids. They were making discoveries, artistic and biological. They proved that they had the sense to stay away from something potentially dangerous and alert me to what was going on. They were entertaining themselves. They were getting exercise. Here I was fussing around the campsite—but compared with the work it always seemed to take to keep them content at home, what did I have to complain about? It was all so easy! What more could a parent ask?

And then came the rain. Lots of rain. To fully understand the implications of this rain, you have to understand that we were camping in what is pretty much a desert. The area gets, on average, less than fourteen inches of rain a year. So when it does rain, watch out. The soil here is known as gumbo. It's made of very fine clay particles that expand and basically turn into wet cement when saturated. It somehow manages to be both sticky and slippery, and it jumps from surface to surface with tremendous ease. A little boy who walks through gumbo for fifteen minutes will have his shoes so hopelessly encased in the stuff that he cannot find his own shoelaces. If you decide to help him with his shoes, it's all over for you. You will inevitably get coated in gumbo. To put it into perspective, if I had to choose between handling a child who had stepped in gumbo or a child who had stepped in one of those dried-out cow pies that had now rehydrated in the rain, I'd choose the cow-pie child.

Yet no matter how earnestly you warn kids about the perils of gumbo, they will not listen. Instead, they will roll in it. They will throw it at each other. They will throw it at you. They will do things inside the tent that seem to serve no other purpose than to distribute a coat of gumbo over sleeping bags, backpacks, and clothes. Not even your toothbrush will be safe. At night, when you brush, you will feel and hear the fine grit of the gumbo crunching between your teeth.

We made a plan to keep our kids outside of the tent as long as possible, and then have them strip down to their underwear before going inside. But first we had to make dinner in the mud. Our camp kitchen is a pretty simple affair. We have a two-burner Camp Chef propane camp stove that sits next to a small folding table. We keep a water jug on the table, along with everyone's spartan allotment of dining ware: one bowl, one cup, one spoon, one fork. Beneath the table and next to the camp stove are a couple of coolers and a couple of plastic totes. The coolers are for items that need to be kept chilled; the totes are for dry goods. When food is ready, I dish out servings right from the cookware. Everyone sits on the ground or in a folding chair to eat, using their lap as a table. Things get messy, even in good weather. Anyone who has a problem eating food that has touched the ground is likely to go hungry around our camp. In the rain, you need to add in an extra layer of tolerance for soggy burger buns and muddy fingers.

I'm a proponent of packing light when it comes to clothes, too. I'll wear the same pants for days on end when I'm camping, and I expect the kids to do the same. I'm also a proponent of "wearing it dry," which means that when you get wet, you just leave your clothes on until they naturally dry out. This approach yields mixed results with kids. On the one hand, you avoid having giant piles of wet clothes littered around your tent and car. On the other hand, your kids are destined to be soaking wet half of the time and they'll probably complain about it. My packing-light philosophy has sparked a few spirited arguments between Katie and me. (The worst was when I talked her out of packing extra clothes for Matthew on an overnight camping trip when he was three years old. Right off, Matthew waded into the water up to his thighs. I waded in after him and carried him to shore, assuring Katie that he could wear them dry. She then took a more careful look at his pants and asked me, incredulously, if "wearing them dry" was also going to take care of the load of poop that he'd dropped into them.)

At bedtime, Katie and I rehashed this argument once again after we got the kids into their PJs. There, in the doorway of the tent, sat a mound of gumbo-laden clothes that needed to be cleaned, or at least partially dried, before the morning. Katie was, well . . . pissed.

And, she reminded me, there was still the issue of Easter. Considering the rainy mess we were in, I whispered to Katie that maybe the Easter Bunny wouldn't find us after all. She told me that the Easter Bunny most certainly would find us, and that he'd better get outside of the tent with her as soon as the kids fell asleep and start hiding eggs.

Like everything else, the plastic eggs and candy were already a little wet when I pulled them out of the bag and began assembling them. I managed to get a few dozen stashed within a seventy-five-yard radius of our campsite. It continued to rain all night, except for when the rain turned to a wet, slushy snow. The robins started singing loudly before it was even half daylight, and the kids were out of the tent in their rubber boots and PJs in the full frenzy of Easter morning excitement. We watched as they gumboed up their pajamas (so much for our rule about always leaving something dry to wear in the tent) and started opening up dozens of plastic Easter eggs that had been infiltrated by rainwater and snowmelt. The chocolate candies looked like Hershey's Chocolate Syrup and the jelly beans were all stuck together in a gooey mess. Soon, every square inch of skin and clothing that wasn't covered in gumbo was covered in sticky sweet substances. The inside of our truck fell victim as well when it became a favored hiding place in a sugar-fueled game of hide-and-seek.

As the morning wore on, the air temperature dropped and dropped. Around noon, the wet gumbo on the ground started making a slight crunching sound when you walked across it. It was freezing up. Matthew was the first one to come up to me with that helpless look that kids get when they realize, too late, that they are uncomfortably cold. His hands were clenched together against his chest, pale and useless. I asked what happened to his gloves, and he gestured up toward the rimrocks with a look on his face that said, "I don't know, maybe up there?"

I already knew what Katie was thinking when she called me around to the back side of the tent. "I know what you're going to say," she said, "but I don't care. We're out of clothes. Everyone is wet and muddy. It's getting cold out. We're outta here."

I knew that she was right, though that hardly made it any easier to accept defeat. I have always prided myself on being a stalwart camper. I like to tough it out, no matter if it's rain, snow, heat, ice, or grizzly bears. Driving home a day early from this trip had me feeling as though I'd lost my edge and gone soft. The snowcapped mountain range far to the south was visible despite the overcast skies, and the taunting wildness of those distant slopes made going home feel even worse. Deep down, though, I recognized my own failings in getting us ready. I hadn't adequately considered the weather. I hadn't packed the right clothes. I didn't bring a proper shelter to keep us dry while we prepared food. What's more, I hadn't reckoned on how to clean up the gumbo in the event of rain. Now, thanks to those missteps, I had to go home and spend hours drying and cleaning camping gear so that we'd be ready for our next ill-fated outing. I allowed myself to descend into a spiral of negativity.

But then, as it occasionally does when you're a parent—and often when you are near the end of your tether—something magical happened. While wallowing in self-pity about what this meant for me, I happened to hear what the kids were saying in the backseat of the truck. They all agreed that trundling was the coolest thing in the world, however dangerous it might be. And they each had an empty soup can full of bits and pieces of ochre that they were excited to add to their rock collection. There was talk of bringing the ochre to show-and-tell at school, and maybe employing it in some kind of Halloween costume in the fall. On the floor of the truck were other muddy treasures: cow bones, deer antler, a sharpened stick, and a wide assortment of cool-looking rocks.

The best thing about the trip, James and Rosemary agreed, was that they had schooled their dad so bad when they proved me wrong about the scorpions. They were already tinkering with the best way to tell that story; I had a hunch they'd eventually land on a rendition that made me look pretty foolish. The practice of developing this narrative seemed to bring them as much pleasure as finding the scorpions in the first place.

When we got home, I spent some time thinking about how the kids' perspectives on the trip were so wildly different from my own. They were focused on having fun and accumulating adventures, whereas I had fallen into the trap of focusing specifically on grown-up measures of success such as arrival and departure times and how orderly we kept our campsite.

I wondered what kind of mental and emotional framework I was providing for their experiences in nature. Israeli teacher and psychologist Haim Ginott is probably the thinker to credit with introducing, in the 1960s, an approach to interacting with children that asks adults to take a moment to comprehend the enormous power that they have over kids. He described the adult as the "decisive element" whose "daily mood makes the weather" for the child. Although I hate to admit it, I have concrete memories of my own father freaking out during camping trips when I was a kid. My father's outbursts were usually about messy or damaged camping gear. I can still feel, in a visceral way, his anger and frustration as he tried to maintain order on overnight family outings or got angry all over again when it was time to unpack, as he struggled to get all of the gear back in tip-top shape. In fact, his inability to keep his cool while camping is one of the things that I remember most clearly about those experiences. It definitely influenced my later desire to find ways to go camping that didn't involve him. Eventually, I just preferred to go with my brothers or friends because it was less stressful.

Clearly, one of my failures as a parent is that I tend to let my personal demands for order spill over into my children's experiences in nature. I can't entirely avoid making the mistakes of my own father. That's probably true for all of us, to some extent. We carry inside of us the bad and the good of those who raised us—and so will our children. In my defense, I'll say that camping, while often idealized, is in many ways harder for parents than everyday life. The annoyances are far more immediate, and your tools for dealing with them—running water, a dresser full of clothes, the fridge—are far away. There are bound to be tears. Everything's wet. Someone got burned in the fire. The dog got into a fight with another dog in the campground. Somehow your hair has marshmallows in it. The zipper on your sleeping bag is stuck open. The kids left your flashlight on and now the batteries are dead. Your spouse has made a dozen nasty comments about things that you failed to pack.

Yet somehow, no matter what, I think that everyone in my family comes away from camping trips with the sense that we just pulled something off that was well worth doing, and that we ought to do it again soon. In fact, the very things that can make camping so annoying—dirt and discomfort—are what make it so memorable for my kids, and so valuable to me as a parent. I want my kids to learn how to be comfortable with being uncomfortable. What do I mean by that? Consider a scene from the documentary *Happy People*. It's a film by the director Werner Herzog about a community of subsistence trappers and fishermen who live in a remote Siberian village. In it, a man is building a cabin and making his own nails from wire while his back is covered in literally thousands of mosquitos. I squirmed more from just watching the scene than the man squirmed from being *in* the scene. It's enough mosquitos to drive most of us mad, but this man is capable of just ignoring the bugs as he goes about this work.

I do think that being tough enough to withstand some bugs is a great thing, just on its own. But I also view that level of tolerance for bugs as indicative of a higher level of tolerance for annoyances and discomfort in general. I've experienced countless scenarios in my life where tolerating discomfort has saved the day, in areas ranging from travel to work to life-threatening emergencies. If you've ever been stuck in an airport overnight, or lived in a decrepit old house where the furnace fails on the coldest day of the year, or taken a long walk after your car breaks down in the middle of nowhere, you know what I mean. You can be the kind of person who complains and turns moody, or you can be the kind of person who rises to the occasion and meets the challenge with grace and humor.

I've been around a lot of people who have this ability; none of them developed it without practice. Some of my friends were trained very specifically in this mindset by the military. Most, though, just figured it out through a lifestyle of getting themselves—both willfully and unintentionally—into decidedly uncomfortable circumstances, often in pursuit of a life lived close to nature. These are the kinds of folks I want to be surrounded by, and ultimately, the type of adults I hope my children will one day become. When my kids ask why we have to do some uncomfortable thing or another, like ice fishing or taking a long hike in hot weather, I've found myself answering their questions with this glib-sounding but entirely truthful answer: We're doing it so you'll be able to hang out with cool people when you grow up. That's an easier concept for a kid to grasp than a faraway adult notion like their own future resilience. Who doesn't want to hang out with cool people? But ultimately, the core of my motivation is much more profound. I want my kids to build up a tolerance for discomfort that will serve them in innumerable areas of their lives—whether they're stuck in an airport, stalking a deer, struggling through a difficult project, or dealing with the types of painful losses that none of us can escape.

Someone could argue that the uncomfortable aspects of camping are artificial, or at least entirely avoidable, since you could put an end to the discomfort simply by packing up and going home. (Which, if you remember, is what happened on our Easter weekend camping trip.) But kids live close enough to the moment, or so strictly inside their immediate context, that they experience camping trips as a sort of alternate or almost temporarily permanent form of reality.

Matthew has always had a tremendous dislike for wet clothes. Starting when he was tiny, he would freak out if the sleeves on his shirt were damp. He also had an alarmingly rigid sense of what you're supposed to wear to bed at night. After a short lifetime of his parents dressing him in PJs at bedtime, he got to thinking that it was somehow bad or shameful to do otherwise. These are admittedly minor issues. But camping has provided us with a way to introduce a sort of flip-side life, in which everyone has to endure the annoyances of going without. Sometimes we balance our plates on our knees as we sit around a campfire. Sometimes the only way to get dinner is to pick up a dirty hot dog from the ground and wipe it clean on a pant leg. Sometimes we're up way later than normal. Sometimes we sleep in the same underwear that we've worn for two or three days. Sometimes we go to bed without brushing our teeth. Sometimes our clothes are wet all day long.

If your kids are among the fortunate ones for whom deprivation is not a constant, putting them in situations in which they have to improvise or go without demonstrates that there can be an elasticity to the circumstances in which we live our lives. They can learn to be comfortable with the fact that nothing in life is guaranteed, and take in the truth that we can definitely get by with far less than our culture has convinced us we need. Likewise, camping presents us parents with an opportunity to be okay with an occasional dollop of mayhem and the improvisation that inevitably ensues.

My love of camping dates back as far as I can remember. As little kids, my brothers and I would go into a small woodlot across the road from our house and construct all manner of protective shelters. We built tree forts up in the tops of oaks and we built underground forts deep in the sandy Michigan soil. In the summer, we'd paddle our canoes out to an island on a neighboring lake and pretend to live off the land by catching and cooking small bluegills. We were close enough to the beachside houses that we could yell back and forth to the "mainland," but it still felt plenty wild. For years, I carried a scar on my hand from grabbing the fire-heated handle on my mess kit while cooking fish out on the island. I took a lot of pride in that scar.

Eventually, sleeping outside became second nature to me. I could plop down just about anywhere—beneath a truck, on a beach, in the snow—and be totally comfortable for a night of sleep. I have spent countless nights camping everywhere from South American swamps to Arctic mountain ranges. I have no fears about bears or mountain lions or things that rustle in the leaves at night. I recognize that my comfort level is not universal, and that many parents are downright fearful for themselves and their kids when it comes to sleeping outdoors.

Notions of what amounts to an acceptable level of risk in childrearing vary across time and geography. In 2014, the writer and journalist Burkhard Bilger published a wonderful piece in *The New Yorker* titled "The Ride of Their Lives." It's about eight-year-old kids in western Oklahoma who are being trained as bull riders, a "pairs competition in which one partner tries to kill the other, like an ice dance with an axe murderer." The bull riders' parents figure it's the best possible preparation for real life. Bilger contrasts this attitude with the outrage sparked by a playground renovation near his home in Prospect Park, Brooklyn, which featured "a rock-lined stream meandering through it and an old-fashioned pump that children could crank to set the water flowing." This set of parents fretted about slipping and sharp edges and called personal injury lawyers to inquire about forcing the city to remove the rocks. A stonemason was called in to grind them down.

The notions of "rewilding" and raising "free-range kids" (a term coined by the author Lenore Skenazy in response to the public outrage that resulted when she acquired the epithet "America's Worst Mom" for letting her nine-year-old take the New York City subway alone) has gained a lot of traction in recent years. The media generally seems to want to position allowing your kids the free rein to run wild—in nature, or in your neighborhood—as some kind of revolutionary child-raising technique.

At the risk of sounding like a crotchety old man, back when I was growing up, that's just how things were. In the summer or on weekends during the school year, my brothers and I were out the door right after breakfast and usually didn't return until dinnertime. We'd hunt, fish, swim, paddle, or just stomp around all day in the woods and marshes. This all went on with the complete approval of our parents long before any books were written on the subject. Nature felt no more scary or foreign than the contours of our own home—nature *was* home. I bring this up because I think it's important that cutting kids loose in the outdoors not be thought of as an act of defiance against prevailing parenting strategies. It should just be a regular part of their lives.

I know, it's easier said than done. It sometimes requires deliberate action. My own parents made a choice to put down their family roots in a place with easy access to nature. My dad was raised by his Italian immigrant grandparents on the South Side of Chicago. Racial tensions prevented him from straying more than a few blocks from home. Around the clock, night and day, he grew up with the sound of pneumatic presses from a nearby foundry banging in his ears. Eventually, when he moved north to the woods of Michigan, he bought a decrepit house on a lake for thirty thousand dollars and started his life over. With that move, he overcame some enormous obstacles that otherwise could have prevented him from raising nature-obsessed kids.

Not everyone has the luxury to pack up and relocate, and not everyone wants to. Money, family obligations, work, and loyalty to your community are all legitimate reasons it might not be feasible or desirable to move to some wilder locale. That's not a problem, because moving isn't necessary. As I'll explain again and again in this book, I had tremendous success introducing my first two kids to the natural world while we were living on some intensely populated landscapes. We took every opportunity we could find to expand our explorations outside of that home area, and no set of experiences proved to be as rewarding as camping out.

The hardest part about getting your family started with camping is building the necessary level of inspiration to develop a plan and round up the necessary gear. For my family, we rarely camp just to camp; we are out there so we can fish, forage, visit friends, hike up to a remote lake, or explore a part of the state that we've never visited. This sense of purpose lends some urgency and shape to our outings. It enhances the feeling that it's time to go, now. There is no right way or wrong way to find this inspiration. Dig into your own wish list to find an entry point. What's near you that you want to explore? Go back to the list of questions in the first chapter of this book, and remember not to overthink it: What catches your eye? What gets you most excited when you think about extended contact with nature? What about your kids' interests of the moment? Consider the time of year: What will be blooming? How full will the streams and rivers be? What birds might be migrating through? What animals might you encounter?

There are thousands of campgrounds scattered throughout the country, though they vary widely when it comes to how natural the setting will be, what types of amenities you'll have access to, and how many people you'll encounter. Choose the type of campground based on the experience you and your kids want to have, remembering that the more amenities a campground offers, the more people it will attract, especially during the busy summer camping season. For beginning campers, car camping is by far the easiest entry point to a night or two in the wild. Because you'll be basing your camp right next to your vehicle, it's possible to bring along every last thing you need—including luxuries like air mattresses and pillows and the toys, games, and stuffed animals that will make the trip feel more like home.

As you're preparing for the trip, enlist your kids to help you organize gear and pack it up, taking the time to talk about why you're taking each thing before you add it to the bag or box. Start as early as you like. If you're planning a trip with other families, which can be a great way to start out, get everyone involved. Camping trips are special events, and you should savor the anticipation.

Far and away, the best pieces of camping equipment I ever purchased for my kids were a few ten-dollar minnow nets. They have logged literally hundreds of hours playing with them in ponds, rivers, and lakes. As we're packing up, it's a little ritual to get out those nets and use some fishing line to sew up any holes that were torn into the mesh on our last outing. My kids got an almost equal level of excitement from getting their first pocketknives and fishing poles. Even the simple task of visiting a hardware store for a few dollars' worth of steel rod to make homemade marshmallow-roasting sticks is enough to get their imaginations and taste buds intrigued.

You could also work together on some plans to do a few extra-fun, out-of-the-ordinary things during the trip. While you may need the Easter Bunny's help to pull off an egg hunt, scavenger hunts for natural items are always possible and make great activities for small or large groups. Feathers, birds' nests, bugs, animal bones or droppings, and rocks shaped like arrowheads all make for entertaining scavenger hunts. Remember to pack field guides so you can identify flowers, plants, animal tracks, and bird species. On clear nights, you can try finding as many constellations as you can.

You can also play around with building some primitive survival shelters. It's a fun exercise and a worthwhile survival skill to teach children. Emergency shelters like lean-tos and wickiups (teepees) can be fashioned with natural materials like dead branches and leaves. A tarp can be added for even more protection from the elements. But kids get a thrill from just learning how to sharpen a stick with a pocketknife. To use a risky piece of equipment like a knife appeals immensely to their desire for autonomy and danger.

Every kid is different and will tune in to different activities with varying levels of enthusiasm. And sometimes they just need to tune out and do their own thing. In a large group or as a small family unit, a well-planned camping trip (in cooperative weather) gives everyone, adult and child alike, some space to relax and play in whatever way feels most inviting to them. String up a couple of hammocks, set parameters around camp to let kids know how far it's okay to roam, then deputize older ones to watch over younger ones as appropriate. Then you can stretch out and enjoy.

Obviously, camping is easier when the weather is pleasant; you'll save yourself a lot of heartache by paying close attention to pinpoint forecasts for the area where you'll be camping. NOAA, Weatherbug, and Weather Underground are popular apps that supply accurate, up-to-date local weather information. But forecasts can change suddenly and without your knowledge once you've left civilization. Localized storms can pop up unpredictably despite a forecast of sunny skies. So when it comes to weather, it pays to hope for the best and prepare for the worst. It's perfectly acceptable to be flexible by delaying a camping trip if the forecast doesn't cooperate. But once you're out there, you'll need to adopt a "show must go on" mentality unless it is unsafe to be outside. Obviously, you'll need waterproof gear and boots for everyone so that you can all enjoy situations that would otherwise be miserable.

As time passes and you and your kids gain camping experience, dealing with inclement weather can actually become a fun part of the adventure. I've come to believe that hating bad weather is largely a learned characteristic. To test this theory, I'm waiting to see at what point my kids begin to hate gumbo. When that happens, I'll no doubt wonder if my attitude rubbed off on them, or if they naturally arrived at that conclusion through their own experiences. Our kids take their cues from us, and that's how they come to dislike rain and mud. Help reinforce their natural instinct to enjoy nasty weather for what it is. A wet snow is great for packing snowballs or looking for fresh animal tracks. A warm rain brings up worms once it gets dark. Except for the person who has to clean it up, everyone has fun tromping through the mud.

However, there are certainly times when getting "weathered in" at camp can't be avoided. It's one thing to tough it out during a light rain shower, but a combination of heavy rains, high winds, and lightning is a different story. In cases where there's a legitimate safety concern or the weather is bad enough to make being out in the elements downright unpleasant, you'll need a plan for riding out the storm inside your shelter. Times like these are made for napping. Last spring, we got caught in a nasty thunderstorm while we were at turkey hunting camp with two other families. Luckily, it hit right after lunch. After a few days of getting up at 4 A.M. and hiking around all day, we were all happy enough to rest in our tents for a couple of hours until the storm passed. But bad weather doesn't always coincide with a convenient time for a nap—so you'll need a plan for staving off boredom. This is one time when you might consider letting kids use their tablets to play games for a little while. Alternatively, you can try demonstrating that it's okay to have an hour or two of nothingness pass by without filling it with the light of a glowing screen. Board games and puzzles make for a nice distraction for the whole family on car camping trips. A deck of cards or a book can save the day during bad weather on backpacking trips. We've passed a lot of hours engaged in a memory card game called Who Pooped, where you match various animal species with images of their droppings. The kids love it, and it lets me feel better about myself knowing that they're learning some valuable wildlife education skills—though some of the game's technical details are less than perfect.

Here's another radical suggestion: Take advantage of the downtime that seems so hard to come by during our everyday lives by simply talking to one another. Discuss some of the adventures you're looking forward to when the weather improves. Make up your own ghost stories. Have a joke-telling contest. Share a memory from when you were a kid. Talk about the animals who might be huddled in dry places trying to avoid the rain—and what kinds of run-ins you might expect when the sun comes out. In my family's case, we're often out in the woods hoping to make contact with wildlife. But that doesn't mean my kids aren't going to scream if they think they hear a bear outside the tent—and I'm not above worrying about the momentary mayhem and long-term inconvenience of one of the kids getting hosed by a skunk.

Sitting in your tent while the wind blows and the rain pelts down is actually a great time to push into that thing that might have kept you from planning this trip in the first place: fear.

Sensationalized news stories and scaremongering parents aside, the truth is that animal attacks are extremely rare. Out of the millions upon millions of people who go camping and hiking each year, the number of people who get mauled by bears, mountain lions, and alligators is extremely low, with only a handful of fatalities nationwide. On average, black bears kill just one person per year in North America, while brown and grizzly bears account for only a few deaths annually. Deadly mountain lion attacks are even less frequent—over the past century, a little more than one hundred people have been attacked by cougars, but only twenty-seven of the victims died. Rattlesnake, spider, and scorpion bites are more common occurrences—but again, deaths are very rare, even for children. Out of the roughly seven thousand people who are bitten by rattlesnakes each year, only five die. Your child is much more likely to get bitten by someone's pet dog running down a trail off-leash than to be dragged off by a cougar or zapped by a rattler or black widow. For additional perspective, consider that all of my own kids' emergency room visits have been caused by backyard swing sets, scooters, living room couches, staircases, and Legos. A wild animal has yet to make that list. Though I'll mention that the closest my kids have come to being injured by an animal was when a rabid squirrel jumped into a swimming pool with them at a friend's summer home in the Hamptons.

That's not to say you shouldn't take whatever steps are necessary to avoid unpleasant encounters. Research what critters might be roaming the area where you'll be camping. Get your kids involved in this research with you. Local field guides or a call to the regional headquarters of your state's fish and wildlife agency are both great places to start. Once you learn what you might encounter, take a moment to study images of the animal's tracks and droppings in order to gain a greater familiarity. Rather than adding to anxieties, a bit of knowledge about the things that cause fear will usually make those fears easier to manage. Pay attention to your surroundings and follow general safety precautions. Of course it's smart and reasonable to keep a close watch on small children in mountain lion country, carry bear spray and make sure food is stored safely in bear country, and shake out boots left outside the tent at night in places where scorpions are common. This isn't paranoia; it's just plain common sense. Being smart does not mean you're afraid.

My main point, and I can't stress this vehemently enough, is that you shouldn't allow any overblown fears to prevent your family from engaging with nature. It might help to remember that while the big things get all the attention, it's usually the little things that you really need to worry about. A bad sunburn can keep a child up crying all night long, and a twisted ankle can ruin an entire trip—which is why I always work with my kids on spatial awareness, including awareness of the ground beneath their feet. Some kids will scratch mosquito bites until they're covered in scabs. If your child has an allergy to bee or wasp stings, you had better remember to pack the Epi-Pen. A tick hidden under a child's hair that goes unnoticed for too long could transmit debilitating diseases that require antibiotic medication—as my family learned the hard way. (The chance of disease transmission is low if a tick is removed before twenty-four hours have passed, so check your kids regularly and thoroughly.) An application of insect repellent that contains no more than 30 percent DEET will help you avoid a lot of these troubles with biting bugs. Some parents are leery of anything but natural bug repellent, but that stuff really doesn't cut it. If I were you, I'd be more worried about insect-borne pathogens than isolated, short-term exposures to effective insect repellent.

Bugs, bears, or snakes don't worry me nearly as much as water. When my kids are playing in or around fast-moving or deep water, it's with a full measure of caution and supervision on my part. Thousands of people drown each year in the United States and, sadly, a significant portion of these drowning victims are children. My kids are all pretty accomplished swimmers who swim several times a week during the summer, along with lots of time fishing and boating on rivers, on lakes, and in the ocean. Still, they always have a snug-fitting life jacket on when we're in our boat or canoe. Even if you're not boating, it's not unreasonable to put life jackets on very young children or kids who can't swim if they're playing near water. Whenever we're at the beach or fishing from shore on a lake or river, I don't let my kids wander out of my sight, and if the surf is high, they're never more than an arm's length from an adult. Again, there's no need to be so nervous that you refuse to let your kids anywhere near water. Just operate with the watchful eye of a lifeguard and let them have fun.

After a car camping trip or two, you might be ready to graduate into backpacking with your kids. You'll quickly get a sense of your family's readiness for backpacking just by taking a few hikes, whether that's during a car camping weekend or as a separate day trip. When camping with the kids, we take a lot of hikes—some short, some long—as a form of training for when they'll be ready for more ambitious journeys. We generally do our hiking with a goal in mind, such as looking for mushrooms or reaching a swimming destination, but for lots of folks, aimlessly meandering through the woods is one of life's greatest pleasures. Regardless, hiking with kids involves special considerations. You can get more adventurous as you gain experience, but I would not recommend starting out by doing off-trail excursions through brushy or steep country. Instead, choose a route on a well-used hiking trail where your efforts are rewarded with some distance. Remember, however, that a hike that might normally take you an hour on your own will probably take double that time with youngsters. (A quick Google search on a particular hiking trail will usually turn up reviews written by/for parents.) If it's the first time you're visiting a particular system of trails, carry a trail map and load a GPS navigation app onto your phone. They can be a lifesaver if you get lost. Even if you know exactly where you're going, it's a fun and useful field exercise to teach kids the basics of reading a compass or map and using navigation apps.

Before hitting the trail, get prepared. You want to have all the essentials while minimizing weight. Gradually, start training your kids to carry a little weight in their backpacks. Have them tote a water bottle, snacks, and a jacket so that they start to understand the concepts of preparedness and self-sufficiency.

Make sure you aren't skimping on your kids' footwear and apparel.

You can't expect them to enjoy hiking if their feet are blistered or wet and cold. They need a decent pair of trail shoes or hiking boots, durable clothes that dry quickly, and a rain jacket or a poncho. No matter what the weather, always bring an extra layer. Try to time your outing to coincide with a good forecast, but prepare for bad weather anyway. Your kids should understand that a little rain or wind is no reason to bail on the trail.

Not to say that this activity is always, or automatically, fun. Boredom and exertion while hiking can take a toll on some kids, and hiking with most children really can test your patience. Resist the urge to get way ahead and yell at them to keep up if they're dawdling or falling behind. Try to remember that they're the reason you're out there—that their experience comes first. Adjust your pace to hike with them and set goals together for reaching certain landmarks or distances. One neat trick I've grudgingly accepted to keep my kids motivated on the trail is allowing them to track their step count on a fitness watch or smartphone. And I'm not above using the occasional bribe to keep them going. We always confiscate the bulk of our kids' Halloween candy and then use it throughout the year as a well-timed motivator. Look for every opportunity to break up the monotony by pointing out anything that might pique their interest, like cloud formations, wildlife, or lightning-scarred trees.

Spread around the responsibility for motivating the group by occasionally having them take short turns leading the way. Older kids, especially, will fill up with pride at being put in charge of navigation. When they do something impressive—or, better yet, for no reason at all—tell them that you love them, you're proud of them, and that you are so happy to be there together. Over the years, I have stressed the importance of animal tracks so heavily that my kids know to protect them from getting trampled underfoot until I have a chance to inspect them. I'm filled with pride whenever I come around a bend in the trail and find Rosemary standing over an animal track in the mud and imploring me to have a look for myself. I always thank and congratulate her for maintaining spatial awareness and being a good guide.

As you hike, encourage kids to keep an eye out for special totems they can bring home to display in their bedroom—and try not to get frustrated if they pick up every other rock or feather or flower along the trail. Discouraging their curiosity is a big mistake. Plan for plenty of snack and drink breaks, and during those breaks, give them the freedom to climb a tree or a rock formation if that's what they want to do. Resist the urge to stand nearby when they're climbing a tree. Don't intrude on their space when they're building a fort. At first, it might be stressful to let them strike off by themselves, even for a short time. But for their sake, give it a shot. This kind of play is their business. Keep watch from a distance if you must.

At our Fish Shack in Alaska—where, despite the shack's four walls, we're essentially camping, given that we spend 99 percent of our waking time outdoors, no matter the weather—there are three extracurricular activities that the kids do when we're not fishing, eating, or sleeping. Like I mentioned earlier, flipping rocks to look for sea creatures is far and away their favorite. Next to that, they like playing on a rope swing made from an old buoy that hangs from a rope tied fifty feet up in a giant Sitka spruce that leans out over the tideline. We have several launch platforms rigged up on stumps and trees so that they can test their daringness. When the swing gets old, they usually turn their attention to making a campfire. Once the fire's been started, they have a number of games and tasks that they'll engage in. One is to scrounge around for a dry stick with just the right thickness and length. They then squat on their haunches in front of the fire and repeatedly burn the end of their sticks into a smoldering coal that's perfect for making streamers of smoke. Once the stick has been burned down to a length that is no longer deemed acceptable, the whole thing gets tossed into the fire and the search for a new stick begins.

I recognize that young kids running around with smoldering branches might sound chaotic and maybe even a little dangerous. I'll be the first to admit that it can be taken too far. When we were kids, my brothers and I got a visit from the local fire chief after we discovered that cattails dipped in gasoline make one hell of a torch. (It didn't help that the fire chief's kid was playing with us.) But in a managed environment with the light touch of a grown-up, and in the absence of forest fire risk, playing with fire can be an organized and important ritual. What I don't want to do is teach my kids that fire is something to be feared, especially when making and managing a fire is such an important wilderness skill. Even for household safety, I'd rather my kids understood fire well—what makes it, what puts it out, and what it feels like to get burned—than to have an irrational fear of it or ascribe magical powers to it. Nor would I ever discourage the sense of adventure and empowerment I see when they're marching around with their flaming wands, painting the air with smoke. Some parents might still struggle to understand why we'd allow such activities, but I'd ask them to consider a 2015 study led by Mariana Brussoni of the Child and Family Research Institute in Vancouver, British Columbia. Her team systematically reviewed the literature on "risky outdoor play" and found overall positive effects on healthy child development. And that wasn't just in terms of physical exercise: They found "social health" benefits as well, along with a lower incidence of aggression and injuries among children engaging in those activities.

Flaming torches aside, a campfire is often the centerpiece of a night in the outdoors, providing warmth as well as entertainment: getting it started, adding the occasional log, poking the fire with a stick, and simply watching the flames burn until there's nothing left but a bed of glowing coals. Start with the most basic camp chore there is: Send the kids out to collect tinder (newspaper, dry grass, an old bird's nest, etc.), kindling (small, dry twigs), and firewood. If your campsite doesn't have an established fire pit, dig one together and put them to work finding rocks to ring the pit. Once you've got a safe area to build a fire, describe the elements fire needs: fuel, heat, and oxygen. Have the kids build a small, loose nest of tinder, then lay down a tent of kindling on top. Long-reach butane lighters are great for preventing small fingers from getting burned as you light the tinder and get the kindling burning. Once the kindling is burning, allow your kids to slowly add larger pieces of dry, dead firewood until you've got a rip-roaring campfire.

Always keep campfires small and manageable and have a water source, a shovel, and a pile of dirt or sand nearby. That way you'll be prepared to extinguish any flames that threaten to get out of control. And teach children to always make sure all campfires are completely dead before you leave a campsite. Never leave a fire that's still smolder-ing, smoking, or warm, and check fire restrictions beforehand to make sure they're allowed. As conditions get drier during the summer wild-fire season, it's not uncommon for campfires to be legal one day in a specific area and illegal the next.

When I think of campfires, I think of a weekend last summer when we were camping at a U.S. Forest Service campground near a large lake in the northern Rockies. The kids and I went into the surround-ing woods to look for some dried branches on the ground that we could use for firewood. We found that the place had been picked clean by other campers. The campground host was selling little bundles of firewood for five dollars apiece, and the kids thought this was a per-fectly acceptable alternative to finding our own wood. There was no way in the world I'd buy firewood, I told them. I used to cut and sell firewood for money back when I was in high school and college. To spend my own money buying firewood now would be painfully ironic.

We expanded our search and discovered a massive mound of drift-wood that had been piled up by the wind and waves on a south-facing shoreline. The water had since receded, leaving the wood high and dry. All the bark had been rubbed away and the surface of each piece had been sanded smooth as the waves of the lake jostled it against the shoreline gravel. It was an abundant supply of designer firewood, each piece a beautiful work of art. We gathered a few armloads of the best and then turned our attention to some crayfish that we'd found hiding beneath the rocks and logs down along the water's edge.

That night, I taught the kids a trick that I learned from the Kalinga, an indigenous group of the Philippines that lives in the central high-lands of Luzon Island. To cook small crustaceans harvested from local rivers, they simply roll a burning piece of firewood away from the fire and then lay the raw ingredients out on the smoldering surface to cook. We did the same, letting our crayfish turn a beautiful rusted color before popping the sweet, flavorful hunks of tail meat into our mouths. We followed this up with something that the Kalinga would no doubt appreciate—roasted marshmallows.

After our snack, we sat in the glow of the burning firewood that we collected ourselves and explored the mechanics of crayfish claws. There wasn't as much light pollution at the campground as there is at our home. We could appreciate an enhanced view of the night sky. I taught the kids how to find the North Star. Based on that stellar marker, we pointed out the directions toward various friends, uncles, and grandmothers. We speculated on how long it would take to walk to their homes. That night, the five of us crowded into a little shelter no bigger than the bed Katie and I normally sleep in at home. We were bug-bitten and smelled of woodsmoke. Closing my eyes, it was easy to imagine us transported across time, a family clan fending for ourselves and working together to live off the land.

After that trip, and the gumbo-assault Easter trip, and every trip, we arrive home the next day to bathtubs, mattresses, and a refrigerator. We eye these items, so easily taken for granted, with a new appreciation. At the same time, we acknowledge them for what they are: luxuries. Nice to have around, but hardly a necessity. It's an invaluable lesson for everyone, a booster shot for the resilience I know my kids will need to cultivate to make it through life intact, and happy. And it costs little more than a couple of nights spent sleeping on the ground.

## CHAPTER 3

# THE FORAGING HABIT

When we were living in Seattle and Brooklyn, Katie and I had a handful of walking routes that we'd use every day when it was time to get the kids outside for some exercise. Our shorter routes would lead us to the closest park, usually returning along a slightly different path than we took to get there. Our longer routes might connect a couple of different parks and include a place where we could buy an ice-cream cone or stop to skip some rocks across the surface of a pond.

As most parents who live in a city can tell you, such walking routes can start to feel a tad over-familiar, even borderline boring. At times, it can seem that the only thing that changes are the places where your kid crashes her scooter and scrapes her knee. One of the ways that I battled the onset of route fatigue was by making it a habit to point out every wild edible that we encountered along our path. I'm talking about wild nuts, fruits, mushrooms, berries, leafy greens, herbs, onions, and so on. Before I really started focusing on this, I honestly had no idea just how much of that stuff is out there on the urban landscape. But now that I've spent a few years keeping an eye out for it, I'll pretty much guarantee that, no matter where you are right now, you're within a five-minute walk of something that you and your kids could pick and eat. It might not be immediately available due to seasonality, but it's there, ready and waiting to sprout from a limb or burst from the earth.

I should clarify here what I mean by wild, as my definition of the term is rather broad when it comes to the subject of wild edibles. In terms of plants and animals, an official definition of "wild" puts it as something that is not domesticated or cultivated. That does not conform to my personal notion of the word. It would technically exclude the edible acorns falling from an oak tree in Central Park that was hand-planted there as a sapling many decades ago, and I would damn sure regard those park acorns as wild. It should also be understood that wild does not necessarily mean native. Consider Euell Gibbons, by far America's most famous forager, who popularized wild foods among the masses in the 1960s. His groundbreaking title was *Stalking the Wild Asparagus,* a reference to a plant that's native to Europe and Asia and was introduced to North America as a cultivar by European settlers in the 1700s before going rogue and spreading out on its own.

Also consider the noxious Himalayan blackberries that have practically taken over portions of America's Pacific Northwest. Despite their name, the plants were originally from an area between the Black and Caspian Seas of Eurasia. In the United States, they cause millions of dollars' worth of damage annually by forming impenetrable barriers of painfully thorny vines. They overrun parks and other green spaces, they outcompete landscaping and gardens, and they make life hell for road workers, surveyors, landscapers, timber harvesters, farmers, or anyone else cursed to deal with a blackberry thicket in their line of work. But the person who's picking them for homemade jam along a downtown bike path will certainly argue against any suggestion that the berries aren't wild. Despite the fact that most land managers would like to see them eradicated from the continent, the species has so thoroughly rooted itself into the cultural fabric of Seattle and Portland that foraging for them can be competitive in some high-traffic areas. My kids and I used to go blackberry picking in a massive growth of the vines along the shoreline of Lake Washington. The berries accessible from the sidewalks were usually picked over, so we'd climb into water up to the kids' knees in order to pick berries from the side of the patch that no one else was willing to exploit.

I mention this stuff about the subtleties of wildness because I want to encourage as expansive a view of wild edibles as possible. The lessons that your kids can learn from harvesting and eating them are valuable enough that it's worth seeking as many opportunities as nature can provide. One of the priorities of this book is to encourage you, the parents, to assist your children in discovering ways in which they can experience a sense of control over and connection to the tasks that are required to keep them alive. Most of us heat our homes simply by turning a dial on the wall. We cool ourselves by turning the dial in the opposite direction. We don't see our drinking water until it pours from a faucet. Even the challenges and intricacies of our waste management are hidden from view. Just flush the toilet and that's it. Don't get me wrong, I'm not lamenting the gifts of technology and civilization. Being liberated from certain responsibilities can let us focus more time and energy in the places where we feel inspired and impactful. I personally don't envy the task of wastewater treatment, and that's not meant as a disparagement of the labor and expertise that goes into it. It's just that some things are best left to professionals, for all of our sakes. But I do think it's important to recognize how frighteningly simple it could be for our kids to conclude that their earthly existence is managed outside of their view, in a hidden world manipulated only through a network of dials, keys, and levers.

In the first half of the twentieth century, the conservationist Aldo Leopold had already warned of two "spiritual dangers" that come from not owning a farm: "One is the danger of supposing that breakfast comes from the grocery, and the other that heat comes from the furnace." Leopold has been dead for more than seventy years. If he were here, he'd be mightily concerned about the fact that only 1.3 percent of the American workforce is engaged in the agricultural industry. Less than two centuries ago, that number was 70 percent. Go back much further, to the era before European contact, and you'd find that virtually every individual in the New World was directly involved in the production of food, through either gardening, hunting, fishing, foraging, or, in limited cases, animal husbandry.

For many of us, the disconnectedness between us and the sources of our food is cause for serious unease. It's as though we've willfully discarded our physical link to what is arguably our most fundamental human need. So many of our contemporary discussions of responsible eating include some reference or another to the benefits of "knowing where your food comes from." Just look at public enthusiasm for farmer's markets and local food cooperatives. Participants are often motivated, first and foremost, by a desire to close the gap between themselves and their food by meeting those people responsible for its production. Chefs, too, have increasingly embraced a tighter connection to the sources of their food. It's now common practice for professional chefs to visit the farms and ranches where they source their meat and produce, and to proudly proclaim these personal relationships on their websites and menus.

Our desire to get cozy with our food goes beyond nostalgia for some bygone agrarian past when we all spent our days toiling away with a hoe and rake. There's a hierarchy of food quality—whether it's real or perceived is almost beside the point—in which physical proximity is rewarded. A few years ago, Katie and I were eating dinner in Washington and the waiter pointed out that our salad greens had been harvested from a garden within sight of our table. We had a beautiful view, for sure, and I immediately placed a higher value on our meal knowing that it emanated from a place that I could literally see and feel. There was an implied freshness, too, which matters more than a little when it comes to food. Mainly, though, seeing the location made the lettuce on our plates become *believable*. I know that sounds funny, because of course food is inherently tangible. If it weren't, you wouldn't be able to chew it up and swallow it. But eating something so close to the source of its production removes the lingering traces of abstraction that result from our industrialized food supply. Most of our food comes to us through elaborate interplay between corporate farms, global distribution networks, and giant retail conglomerates. Its existence says as much about the magic of technology and capitalism as it does about the magic of nature. Eating something close to the source removes all of the background noise and allows you to focus on the splendor of the thing itself. This is especially true when it's a wild food that exists entirely outside of human effort. (Or, in the case of the Himalayan blackberries of Seattle, that exist in spite of human efforts to eradicate them.) If you imagine food acquisition as an A-to-Z process, buying produce at a farmer's market and bringing it home to cook is at best only half of the story. Completing the process requires that your child be the active agent of procurement. It requires that the hand removing the food from the earth is their own. Only then, when every influence besides nature has been stripped away, can your child experience the surge of self-confidence that comes from truly feeding themselves. In that moment, they glimpse absolute control.

I can imagine some of you reading this throwing up your hands and saying, "This is ridiculous. Our family doesn't have the time and wherewithal to start living off the land like some modern pioneer family." To which I would say, you don't need to. Or at least you don't need to do it all the time. Think of it in terms of visual art. Appreciating art does not require that you live at the museum and indulge yourself with a never-ending barrage of masterpieces. It's possible to live a life that's informed and inspired by art despite getting only occasional glimpses of our most celebrated works. A brief exposure to the pinnacle of beauty doesn't make you lament the ugliness of the ordinary. If anything, it makes the ordinary easier to appreciate because you learn to see it in a different and more thorough way. Grubbing your way into a patch of Himalayan blackberries and getting bloody little scratches all over your arms doesn't cause you to hate store-bought raspberries. But it definitely helps you see them in a more appreciative and nuanced way.

Foraging is one of four food-procurement strategies I'll explore in this book—gardening, hunting, and fishing being the other three—each of which is intended to inspire in our kids a radical engagement with nature centered around sustenance and self-sufficiency. Hunting and fishing require licenses and are governed by sometimes complex regulatory structures. Gardens require the necessary physical space, plus a static living situation where you'll be around long enough to harvest what you've sown. Foraging, though, is largely free of red tape. It's instant gratification, since nature has already done so much of the work for you, a form of guerrilla food acquisition. All you need to do is show up.

Foraging is so easy, in fact, that I do most of it without realizing that it's happening until the very moment that I find something. One day in Seattle, my kids and I were walking our normal route to a local park so that they could race their scooters on a smoothly paved loop from which you could see a beautiful view of Puget Sound. A construction crew was excavating municipal water lines along our route. They had the sidewalk dug up and the road was closed. Rather than going to the next park entrance, we cut through the bushes alongside a chain-link fence surrounding an elementary school playground. Rosemary was wearing shorts and she commented on the "pickers" that were grabbing at her legs. I immediately assumed she was talking about blackberries, but when I stopped to more carefully assess her situation I realized that she had stumbled into a patch of wild rose. I explained that the plant has a special place in my heart, as it's captured in the names of four women who are very important to me. My daughter already knew that she was named after my mother, Rosemary, but I reminded her that Rose is also her maternal grandmother's middle name and the first name of one of her great-grandmothers on my side of the family.

Rosemary's initial instinct was to argue that these weren't "those kind of roses," because there weren't any flowers. I told her that there are more than a hundred rose species in the world, including about twenty that are native to our own continent. They can be found everywhere from Arctic Alaska to south Florida, and from coastal Maine to the deserts of Arizona. The ones with the gigantic flowers you know from grocery stores and floral shops are the result of a mutation that has been exploited and manipulated by humans in cultivated varieties. Most of the wild roses produce only small flowers that you wouldn't immediately recognize as roses at all.

I directed her attention to the rose hips toward the top of the plant—small pear-shaped formations the size and color of a strawberry. The hips, sometimes called haws or heps, begin to form after the flower is pollinated in the spring and then ripen through the summer and fall. We popped off a few of them and I showed Rosemary and her brothers how to nibble away the edible outer portion. The taste brings to mind the relatively flavorless skin of an apple, though it's rich in vitamin C; even the weakest rose hip has a higher concentration of vitamin C than an orange does. Native Americans used the hips for both food and medication. We agreed that trying to make a full meal from rose hips would take a lot of work and that you'd get pretty scratched up in the process. But we also agreed that rose hips are pretty cool, and that it's especially cool knowing that they grow wild within a few minutes' walk of our house. We'd have no excuse for coming down with a case of scurvy with that much vitamin C lying around.

I'm always surprised by how game kids are to try foraged foods, especially in small quantities. My kids will readily take a nibble of a wild onion when they'd never in a million years grab a scallion from the fridge and start munching on it. Same with the spicy greens of dandelions, which they'll happily taste despite the fact that they loathe the similar flavor of arugula. They'll even partake of the occasional acorn, which has an overpowering bitter taste when raw. (There is no store-bought equivalent to acorns; nothing that bitter, which requires such labor-intensive processing in order to become edible, would stand a chance in an American supermarket.) They "like" these things even though they don't really like them, which is all part of the fun. But please don't think that my kids are unlimited in their abilities to stomach weird foods. Just the other day, I was fishing with all three of them along the Missouri River. Our visit happened to coincide with a massive hatch of an aquatic stonefly known as a skwala. The bugs were over an inch long and coming off the water's surface in hordes. They were stuck to our clothes, stuck in our hair, and crawling down our necks and up our sleeves. It was a bit unnerving. I tried to convince the kids that the bugs were harmless and wouldn't bite. Since my verbal assurances weren't working, I decided to get physical. I took one of Matthew's cheese crackers, pressed a stonefly into the cheese, and ate it. I let a couple crawl around on my tongue before eating them. While no amount of begging or coercing would get my kids to try a bug of their own, I did manage to alleviate the tension by putting my money where my mouth is, so to speak. They stopped worrying about the bugs.

Most parents will find that their kids' own natural curiosity will inspire them to try tasting new things, but there's no doubt that the enthusiasm and confidence of the instructor are equally relevant factors. I'm not a good actor, so thankfully my excitement about finding stuff to eat out in the wild is both genuine and infectious. As for my confidence, I earned that through research, firsthand experience, and help from generous people who know more about this stuff than I do.

When I tell my kids that something is safe, or safe to eat, they trust me. Developing the trust of your kids is vital, and with that trust comes major responsibility. I was forced to consider this responsibility after a pair of mushroom incidents that occurred in the Seattle neighborhood of Madison Park. The first involved two king bolete mushrooms growing in the strip of grass between the road and the sidewalk less than a hundred yards from our house. These mushrooms are often referred to as porcinis. They're common in the mountains above the city, but I was pleasantly surprised to find them here. My kids were immediately suspicious when I mentioned how good they are. Despite my fondness for wild mushrooms, they're constantly getting warned by various teachers, playground attendants, and well-meaning babysitters about the perils of messing around with "poisonous mushrooms," as though just looking at a wild mushroom was enough to kill you. But I assured them that all of those warnings were overblown and that this particular species was perfectly great. We took them home with us and ate some of the thinly sliced pieces sauteed in butter with a little salt. The rest we dried on a window screen and saved for later inside a glass Mason jar. I chalked the experience up as a major success. We were making friends with wild mushrooms.

Not long after that, a few blocks farther from home, I was even more surprised to find a species of mushroom called a fly agaric. I had no doubt what I was looking at, as it is perhaps the most widely recognized mushroom in the world. The crimson cap with white spots has been featured everywhere from the Smurfs to the Mario media franchise to the Disney film *Fantasia*. Most visual depictions of the mushroom scene from Lewis Carroll's novel *Alice in Wonderland* feature the fly agaric. The mushroom is often characterized as deadly poisonous, and it might be particularly dangerous to kids, though mycologists have yet to find definitive proof of any fatalities caused by the fly agaric in the past hundred years. However, the mushroom has been responsible for a great many hallucinogenic episodes, both intentional and unintentional, across several continents where it can be found. A number of indigenous Siberian tribes used the mushrooms to induce trance-like states, sometimes through the ingestion of urine from people or animals who have eaten the mushroom. Its mind-altering capabilities are best described as unpredictable. The two major toxins can produce reactions ranging from mild auditory and visual distortions to seizures, amnesia, and abnormally long periods of deep sleep.

My kids were drawn to that insane-looking mushroom as though it were an Easter egg lying out on the ground. They didn't necessarily want to eat it, though they damn sure wanted to mess with it and then take it home to show their mom. I, on the other hand, didn't want them to even go near it, let alone take it home with them. Explaining to Katie that I had decided to let them tote around a hallucinogenic and potentially fatal mushroom seemed like a discussion that I'd rather avoid. The kids got annoyed when I forbade them from even whacking it with a stick. They struggled with my explanation that I didn't want anything bad to happen to the mushroom. I liked it the way it was because it was so cool-looking. They looked at me as though I was some kind of hypocrite. Wasn't I the same guy who was recently extolling the virtues of wild mushrooms and saying that the risks are way overblown? And if it's so dangerous, why not smash it up? The best I could do is explain that it's a complex world out there, which is part of the appeal. Engaging with nature requires that you keep an open mind. It also requires that you keep on your toes.

Despite the dangers of wild mushrooms, they're by far my favorite things to forage with my kids. What's so fun about wild mushrooms is that they're good at hiding. Thanks to their muted tones and the lack of predictability about where, when, and even if they'll pop up, there's always a sense of uncertainty about whether or not you'll find them. In common parlance, we use the term "hunting" for mushrooms. No one would use that term for wild blueberries. You pick berries; you hunt for mushrooms. The hunting, as much as the eating, makes finding mushrooms rewarding.

For kids, the lack of a clear mental search image adds to the challenge of hunting mushrooms. In other words, most kids aren't pre-equipped with a clear notion of what exactly they're trying to find when you take them out mushroom hunting for the first time. Consider morels, for instance, which are one of the most coveted wild mushrooms out there. They have a mild, nutty flavor, and are best served as simply as possible. A little butter, a little salt, and you have a sublime dining experience. Kids generally like them, too, at least compared with other mushrooms. Morels aren't slimy or spongy, and there's no overpowering mushroom taste. But morels are very secretive and mysterious. They defy cultivation, so they are wild by definition. Even on the rare occasion when you do see a morel in a grocery store, you can safely assume it was harvested in the wild, and you'll be paying between thirty and fifty dollars per pound.

The inherent wildness of the morel means that most people don't grow up with constant reminders about what they look like. Pretty much the only people who are familiar with morels are people who hunt for them. A wild blueberry, on the other hand, is a basic facsimile of a domestic blueberry. Most kids have had countless encounters with blueberries. They see blueberries in their breakfast cereal, in their yogurt, in their desserts, et cetera. When you tell them to look for a wild blueberry out in the woods, they have a pretty solid notion of what they're trying to find. It doesn't hurt that wild blueberries grow up off the ground on bushes, either. It's almost like Mother Nature is putting them on display. When it comes to morels, she usually keeps them hidden away in the grassy shadows.

James had been on at least a dozen morel hunts before he had the honor of being the first person in our group to find one. That day, our whole family was out hiking around. I had mentioned the possibility of finding morels only because it happened to be early June and therefore the right time of year for our particular elevation in Montana. (You can find morels as early as March in South Carolina; in Alaska, they can go strong well into July.) The five of us hiked a couple of miles along a trail and poked around half-heartedly in a few aspen groves that looked like decent morel habitat, but we didn't see anything and quickly turned our attention to finding little balls of hardened spruce pitch. Some Native American groups and frontiersmen used the pitch as a chewing gum, as well as an adhesive and caulk. My kids found it to be a far cry from Big League Chew, though, and they spent more time trying to get it all spit out of their mouths than they did trying to chew it. Matthew was only five, and eventually he had a little meltdown about walking so far and we all stopped to take a break. James was sitting on a log and reached down to tighten the strap on his sandal, and he realized that there was a morel growing just a few inches from his heel beneath the log he was sitting on. He didn't notice it until he had almost touched it. He yelled with excitement. A few minutes later, we had found a total of seventeen morels, some as big as three inches tall, growing within an arm's reach of where we'd taken our break. Had James not discovered that first one, we would surely have passed them all by. It was a proud day for him.

Along with chanterelles, giant puffballs, and chicken-of-the-woods mushrooms, morels belong to a collection of mushrooms often referred to as the foolproof four. It's an informal grouping of wild mushrooms that are widely available and easily identified, without deadly or dangerous look-alike species. (Although you'll sometimes hear reference to "false morels," a name given to a handful of mushroom species that are vaguely similar in appearance to morels, it takes only a passing familiarity with mushroom anatomy to tell real morels and their look-alikes apart.) Beyond the foolproof four, there are dozens upon dozens of great-tasting mushrooms that are safe to eat, if you take the time to consult your mushroom field guides, so I'd recommend expanding your repertoire as you go. Nowadays I'm a bit more cautious, and I've built up a knowledge base that keeps me safe. But back when I started getting adventurous with wild mushrooms, in my mid-twenties, I developed an appreciation for what I dubbed "the poison wait." It was that stress-filled hour or two that would follow my consumption of a new or unusual wild mushroom species. Even with that cavalier approach, I've only had one bout of gastrointestinal distress, from an unknown species of bolete that I found in Alaska. Had I done even an ounce of research, I would have realized my mistake before it was too late. So don't let your worries get out of hand. I'll refer you to another quote from the writer Aldo Leopold, this time my personal favorite: "It must be a poor life that achieves freedom from fear."

Aside from any dangers, whether real or imagined, the biggest obstacle to collecting wild mushrooms is their ephemeral nature. They are here today, gone tomorrow. This can lead to some paralysis for parents who might reasonably ask, "What's the point in getting everyone out of the house and into the car when there's a good chance we won't find anything?" I have a couple of answers for that question. First, as frustrating as failure might be, there are many lessons to be learned from it. I'll point out that I have gone looking for morel mushrooms far more times than I've actually found them. Rather than getting irritated, I try to convince myself that learning where and when you don't find morels is somehow integral to learning where and when you do find them. I accept this logic, as I understand the importance of trial and error when it comes to outdoor pursuits. But I also recognize that it's incredibly tough to get kids excited about lessons learned from a failed outing. They want to find things, and they want to find them now.

That might seem like a tall order, but it's not. There are plenty of forageable foods that you can pursue with your kids where success is all but guaranteed. Tapping into these resources requires little more than a willingness to keep your eyes open as you go about daily life. And there's little need to worry about competition. While I have no way of actually backing this statement up, I'd say that 99 percent of most harvestable wild foods simply rot away on the ground. In my mid-twenties, long before having kids, I spent a few months working on a book in San Jose, California. During that time, I could have lived off the oranges and grapefruits that littered the sidewalks there. (I drank plenty of greyhounds and screwdrivers during my stay.) The citrus trees were originally planted as ornamentals, yet it seemed that the bulk of them went unharvested. Routinely, I would see garbage bags filled with the fruit and left out next to trash cans. If I lived there today with my kids, I can tell you that we'd make a hell of a lot of smoothies from fruit we gathered ourselves.

In some cases, we spend millions of dollars annually trying to get rid of wild edibles. The dandelion, which is perhaps the most widely recognized plant species in the world, as well as the most reviled, is entirely edible. You can eat the roots of young plants, or use them to make a coffee substitute. With a little cream and sugar, my kids love it. In the early spring, before the dandelion produces its flowers, you can eat the leaves as salad greens. The crown, when properly cleaned of dirt or sand, can be eaten raw or cooked. Wild foods expert Samuel Thayer, in his book *Nature's Garden*, suggests making "dandelion noodles" with the stalks. As for the flowers, you can dip them in batter and mix them in with a batch of tempura vegetables.

I'll always recall the place where I first showed James and Rosemary how to husk black walnuts, because it's the same location where I got married, and where Katie's mom later arranged to have all of our kids baptized. The property overlooks the shores of Lake Michigan not far from the town of Saugatuck. Part of the experience of visiting this place is stepping over and around black walnuts that have fallen to the earth from a few towering walnut trees. Our friend Kelly, one of Katie's bridesmaids, recalls rolling her ankle on one during our wedding procession. It reminded her of running on the cross-country team back home in Nebraska, when they competed in a park called Walnut Grove. On each subsequent visit to the Lake Michigan property, I found a similar situation: countless calories' worth of black walnuts (193 calories per ¼-cup serving, to be exact) lying on the ground in varying states of decay or gnawed around the edges by gray squirrels. The black walnut is a native species in the eastern United States; long ago, Native Americans cherished the resource. But nowadays, in this location, thousands of wedding attendees stroll past them every fall and summer hoping not to trip.

Then there are those sought-after prizes that no one passes by. In the gardening chapter, you'll see that I argue in favor of concentrating your efforts on growing things your kids actually want to eat—think carrots and raspberries rather than arugula and brussels sprouts. In the foraging realm, that equates to going after wild berries. It's pretty much an objective reality that wild berries taste good. You won't find many kids who will argue against that point. My own children enjoy eating wild strawberries, which are surprisingly small but carry more flavor than any strawberry you will ever buy. They're also keen on wild raspberries and blackberries, where impressive yields help make up for the fact that the thorns will scratch up your arms and hands. And they like eating salmonberries and crowberries at our shack in Alaska, even though the salmonberries are a tad tart and the crowberries have a lot of seeds.

By far, though, huckleberries are their favorite. That's in keeping with Montanans in general, as huckleberries are hugely popular hereabouts. The name of the berry often causes confusion with people from other parts of the country. They'd look at a huckleberry and call it a blueberry, which isn't wrong. In fact, there are dozens of species of shrubs in the *Vaccinium* genus that produce "blueberries" ranging in color from red to blue that folks variously call blueberries or huckleberries or even bilberries, depending on their regional influences. However, the term "huckleberry" does have an indisputably wild connotation that sets them apart from blueberries, at least around here. If you go to a local gift shop and buy huckleberry jam or huckleberry syrup or huckleberry chocolates, you can safely assume you're buying a product made from wild berries that were picked off the side of a mountain by a pair of human hands rather than a harvesting machine driven down a neat row of bushes on a farm.

There are good years and bad years for huckleberries, depending on precipitation and temperature and probably a myriad of other mysterious factors. You don't need to go into the woods to find out what kind of year it is; instead, all you have to do is pay attention around town. On a good year, you might overhear people talking about huckleberries when you pick up your kids from school; or you'll see roadside vendors selling quart- and gallon-sized bags of the fruit near busy intersections; or you'll notice that local restaurants and bakeries are advertising huckleberry this-and-that on sandwich boards set out on the sidewalks. Last summer, which was a stellar year for huckleberries, we picked up on all of these cues plus the additional bit of motivation that came from a neighbor who picked a gallon and a half just six miles from home in the national forest. He pointed out on a map where to park along an old logging road and said you couldn't miss the berries. "Just go uphill," he said. "They're all over." He then showed me photos of the neatly packaged huckleberries that were now loaded into his freezer.

Before leaving, I gathered up all manner of tubs and wide-mouthed water bottles that we could fill with berries. I was thinking about how cool it'd be to have a bunch of the fruit packed away in our freezer. Huckleberries taste good on top of kiddie favorites ranging from pancakes to ice cream, or you can turn them into homemade jam or chutney and use that to top everything from PB&Js to roasted duck. I imagined pulling out the occasional package of huckleberries throughout the winter in order to remind the kids of the splendors of nature. It would also reinforce the value of thrift—that saving good things for later is ultimately more rewarding than using them up right away. The challenge, I recognized, is that huckleberries don't just taste good when added to things. They also taste good right then and there, straight off the plant. In fact, a lot of kids seem to be almost offended by the idea that you'd put a berry into a bucket when you could just as easily put it into your mouth.

Katie and I rounded up our own kids, plus a friend of ours and her two kids. The kids insisted that we bring along our dog, Tracker, a brown-colored mixed breed that we'd gotten a few months earlier from a shelter. We crammed into the truck and drove down a winding dirt road. The deep ruts and bumps made everyone's heads bob and sway in an arrhythmic fashion. The kids complained and fought about who bumped into whom. At one point, I noticed a shoe-sized lump of blackish purple goo that had been deposited ahead of us on the shoulder of the road. I assumed it was a bear dropping; when I rolled down my window to investigate, my assumption was confirmed. The kids all stuck their heads out of the windows to have a look.

"Probably a black bear," I said, "because of the skinny diameter of the turds. But it's hard to really tell for sure. There are grizzly bears around here, too."

When we got to the place my neighbor described, we parked the truck and everyone climbed out. I grabbed my bear spray and placed it into a chest holster that keeps it in a readily accessible position near your sternum—the thinking being that you could still get at the spray even if a bear has you facedown in the dirt. Before all the kids could run off up the hill, I called them around me. I didn't want to scare them off by overemphasizing bears, but I also didn't want to be negligent by not mentioning bears at all. I chose my words carefully and began my short lecture by saying, "Bears love huckleberries as much as people do. Even more than people do. So, if we're lucky enough to see a bear . . ." Then I covered the usual stuff about the need to maintain spatial awareness, how you should never turn your back and run away from a bear, and that it's important to stick close together at all times and make plenty of noise so we don't surprise them.

We moved up the hill and entered a timbered slope shaded by lodgepole pine and Douglas fir. Sunshine came down through the canopy in dappled light, illuminating the vibrant green leaves of huckleberry bushes and shining off the networks of spiderwebs in a way that made them seem ten times thicker and stronger than they actually were. Each huckleberry bush had anywhere from zero to thirty berries. The berries were small, like maybe half the diameter of your typical farm-raised blueberry. Some of the berries were past their prime and dried out like deflated balls. Others were early and still pretty hard. Most, though, were perfect. Firm enough to drop them into a bottle without squishing them, but still soft and packed with intense flavor.

I pointed out a cluster of the berries and told all the kids, "Don't mess with anything but this kind of berry. You don't wanna go around just randomly ingesting stuff. If you see something else that you're curious about, ask me before you eat it."

I mustered a stern voice and continued, "And remember, our primary goal is to collect berries to bring home. Go ahead and eat a few if you need to, but let's mainly see how many we collect in our bottles."

Already the kids were bored with my lecture. "Okay," I said. "Go!"

They moved up the slope at a run. It seemed that their most immediate priority was to put distance between themselves and our starting point. They naturally utilized a faint game trail without me pointing it out to them. I marveled at the native sense of navigation that we humans tend to carry inside of us. Send ten people through a patch of woods, and it's likely that eight of them will choose the same route. Tracker, on the other hand, plowed haphazardly through the thickets. Uphill, the trees were sparse where foresters had thinned the timber stand years ago. Here the berries grew thick.

When you put a bunch of little kids together in a task such as berry picking, you're likely to witness an enormous range of behaviors and attitudes that are often blatantly contradictory. Today was no exception. Over the next couple of hours, while keeping my eyes peeled for bears, I witnessed acts of intense focus, carelessness, greed, generosity, deception, honesty, hubris, selflessness, and even a bit of questionable pet handling. Rosemary accumulated a layer of huckleberries in her bottle that was thick enough to cover the bottom. When she accidentally kicked the bottle over with her foot and spilled the contents, she decided to eat them instead of putting them back. At one point, I heard her yell at her little brother to get away from the bush where she was picking. Then, minutes later, she took pity on him and passed along a handful of berries that he greedily stuffed into his mouth. Later, she asked me to give her the berries from my bottle so that she could have more than James. As for Matthew, I noticed that many of the berries that he picked were being fed to the dog. In short order, Tracker got the hang of things and started picking her own berries. The kids would call her over to particularly good bushes so that she could maximize her consumption. Soon, the inside of her mouth was stained purple. I considered the question of toxicity, remembering how certain benign foods such as grapes and chocolate can prove fatal to dogs. But I didn't have enough of a cell signal to do any research on the subject. Instead, I just hoped that she knew what was best for her. Apparently, she did.

It didn't take long for me to abandon my hopes of accumulating a huge haul of berries for the freezer. There was way too much eating and not enough saving for that to happen. It also didn't take long for me to get more casual about the risk of bears. The sparseness of the trees and the lowness of the bushes meant that we could see a long way in all directions. The dog remained alert at all times and often paused her eating to investigate strange sights or sounds. Plus, we were making a hell of a lot of noise. There was little risk of anything being able to sneak up on us, or wanting to sneak up on us. I began to relax.

I wasn't aware of it at the time, but about two hundred miles to the west and over the Continental Divide from where I was standing, my friend Deirdre McNamer was finishing her work on a novel titled *Aviary*. Early in the book, an elderly woman named Cassie considers the relationship that younger generations have with their phones and computers. McNamer writes:

> Watching her fellow humans' involvement with their communication tools, Cassie had the growing sense that bodies, as bodies, were becoming vestigial on a mass scale. More and more people clearly conducted their social lives, their travels, their shopping, their entertainment, and their learning in a realm that had almost

nothing to do with moving their corporeal selves through space. They existed mostly in the big brain, the forest of pixels.

Here, though, on this afternoon, we weren't letting that happen. We were out of the forest of pixels and into the forest of trees. It was easy to look around and recognize the world as a great flawless system, a place you could easily find happiness. For me, it was one of those crystalline moments when you're forced to recognize that someday your kids will be gone from home, and they'll live far away, and they'll have days when they're too busy to even think about you. When those days inevitably come, you hope, as a parent, that certain indelible experiences are locked away inside of your own brain as well as the brains of your children. Here was one I wanted us to keep, this landscape populated by these young primal human creatures, crawling under and over logs, wiping cobwebs from their skin, staining their hands blue, gorging themselves on the fruit of the earth.

## CHAPTER 4

# TENDING THE SOIL

Over the years, my family has generated a few stories that get told time and again with a lot of laughs. One of those is the salad worm incident, which happened when Matthew was an infant and James and Rosemary were just toddlers. We were living in Seattle at the time, in a beautiful old rental house with creaky floors and a working fireplace. The yard was surrounded on two sides by a head-high brick wall and on the other two sides by impenetrable barriers of vegetation. Inside the walls was a jungle of overgrown landscaping. There was a garage that we couldn't use because it was full of the landlord's junk, and next to that garage was a busted-up apple tree that I tried unsuccessfully to prune back into productivity. Beneath that apple tree was a fallow patch of dirt grown up with weeds and blackberry vines. While the kids played in the yard or "helped" me out by digging randomly placed holes here and there, I defeated the weeds and planted a wide assortment of vegetables and leafy greens in the muddy soil of a Seattle spring. With the mild weather, long days, and fertile soil, the garden went absolutely insane with life. We couldn't eat our way through it all, but we tried. One evening, sitting outside for family dinner, I noticed that James and Rosemary were silently transfixed by something on the table. I looked in the direction of their gaze and there, on the rim of James's plate, was the plumpest, healthiest-looking inchworm I'd ever seen. It was making a break for it, all coated in ranch dressing and headed away from the salad in an easterly direction. My initial instinct was to question my own abilities as a vegetable washer, but I quickly recovered and silently reached over to flick the worm off the plate—and the deck—with my finger. I then looked back to James and Rosemary, expecting them to revolt against eating any more of the pest-infested veggies. But instead they were still just sitting there, completely unfazed as they munched away on their lettuce.

There are a couple of things that I appreciate about that story. First, it makes me nostalgic for those days when our kids would eat their salad without an argument. (Whether by serendipity or some accident of parenting, they mostly ate it without complaint when they were toddlers. Eventually, for whatever reason, they all became suspicious of salad. Matthew's suspicion then developed into full-on hatred that went far beyond the normal, run-of-the-mill hatred that most kids have for the stuff. Recently, he pointed out to me that the primary difference between kids and adults is that adults like salad.) Mostly, though, I appreciate the story as a testament to their acceptance of the earth's fecundity. The worm wasn't icky or frightful to them; instead, they seemed to regard the creature as a wholly expected guest, as natural on our porch as we were.

Most of us make the logical association between gardening and plants, as producing the latter is the objective of the former. But I find that kids are just as likely to associate gardens with creatures of the animal kingdom. Because when you get at eye level with a garden, you see bugs. Lots of bugs. You've got the good ones, like pollinators such as bees, wasps, and butterflies, plus aphids that can help feed those pollinators. And then you've got the annoying ones that cause all kinds of trouble. In my opinion, one of the worst of these is the squash vine borer, which thwarted years' worth of efforts to grow acorn squash and pumpkins in our garden in Brooklyn. It's an orangish moth, native to North America, that actually looks more like a bee or wasp. The female lays her eggs near the base of a plant's leaf stalks. Upon hatching, the larvae eat their way into the plant and migrate to the main stem. There they grow fat on the plant's insides until the host suddenly goes limp and dies. Whatever juvenile squash happen to be developing on the vines are left to rot, their umbilical-like connection to the earth severed.

It took us a year or two to find the culprit that kept crushing our dream of growing gigantic Halloween pumpkins and delicious acorn squash. Eventually, through a series of internet searches, we learned our nemesis's identity. With that, we were able to learn about its vulnerability. If you inspect the vines of your squash plants, you may find cracks and bends in the stems that are oozing what appears to be wet sawdust. Gently open the vine at those spots with a sharp pocketknife, and you can dig the pinky-sized grub out into the light of day. As good as it felt to dislodge the two or three worms we'd find on each inspection of the garden, it was a pyrrhic victory. All of our plants died soon after the surgical procedure. But James, who was just two at the time, expressed untempered elation at seeing the ousted worms. He'd giggle and jump around every time I placed one into his palm. After a few days of hunting them down, it occurred to me that his understanding of the garden was completely different than mine. It wasn't a place where we were losing our battle to grow squash. It was a place where we were winning our battle to grow worms.

We said goodbye to the vine borers when we moved to Seattle, and said hello to legions of garden slugs. They would feed so aggressively on the tender young growth of leafy greens that the plants would end up naked, their pea-colored stalks sticking out of the ground like lonely toothpicks. The slugs were easiest to find during the dark of night, when they'd leave their hiding places to climb up the plants and resume the destruction. James and Rosemary loved looking for them because it meant they got to stay up past bedtime. We'd head into the garden with flashlights and scissors, going from plant to plant as we snipped the slugs in half and let them fall back to earth. In time, we changed our strategy and became slug trappers instead of slug snippers. The kids and I dug into the recycling bin for a bunch of beer cans and cut the bottom third off with a pair of old scissors. We then sank the makeshift cups into the garden so that the tops were flush with the soil. An inch or so of beer in the cup proved to be shockingly attractive to the slugs. The first time we set a dozen cans out, we were greeted in the morning by literally hundreds of drowned slugs lying in the pale flat beer.

I could see how someone might find the whole thing macabre, especially the act of dumping the limp carcasses into a little pile in the bushes, but I never divulged to my kids that such a sentiment would be ordinary. I find that squeamishness is mostly a learned trait. The surest way to make your kids fear worms and other creepy-crawly things is to demonstrate those feelings yourself. Instead I have always chosen to be entirely matter-of-fact about slugs, larvae, moths, and worms, an attitude that I picked up from my own parents. They are natural components of the elegant task of growing food in the dirt.

Beyond the notion that there's nothing gross about a worm, there are countless lessons that our kids can learn from gardening. These include patience, the value of hard work, and the taste of real food. In my mind, though, there are two basic lessons that stand out above all else:

1. Through our actions, we have the power to make things thrive.
2. Neglect is deadly.

My kids are young enough that I haven't yet explored with them all of the areas in life where these principles are applicable. We haven't explicitly discussed gardening as a metaphor for business, marriage, friendship, or their own physical health. Instead, for now, my kids seem to regard gardening as a very matter-of-fact enterprise. We garden in order to make food that our family can eat. I trust that the time we spend growing our own food will only generate more and more wisdom for my kids as they mature. I know that's how it has worked for me. When I was a kid, I viewed gardening as a sort of transaction. Mom and Dad made us pull weeds and till the soil because they wanted to get green salads and sliced tomatoes in return. As I entered my twenties and thirties, though, I began to see gardening as an enterprise that is rich in metaphor. A healthy garden gave me a sense of personal well-being that far surpassed any accounting of how many calories the soil put out. A garden served as verification that it's possible to maintain a healthy, working relationship with the land. It made me feel as though I was walking hand in hand with the earth. When I was older still and started a family, gardens became a valued mechanism by which I could hopefully create these same experiences and revelations for my own children. It came full circle, in a way.

As a parent, one of my shortcomings is that I'm not naturally skilled at letting my kids make their own mistakes. Whether they're trying to fix something with superglue or teach the dog a new trick, I have a hard time holding back advice. At my worst, I'll actually jump in there and do it for them. The more I know about something, the harder it is for me to refrain. My motivation for interfering is that I want them to experience the satisfaction of success and to more quickly develop expertise. I want them to know that process and experience are valuable things, and that you can learn from watching others. Plus, the glued thing stays glued; the dog learns the trick.

But I do understand that it's enormously valuable for kids to learn from their own trial and error. If they don't get to witness and experience failure, how will they learn to respect expertise? A pioneer in the study of child development named Lev Vygotsky had a name for the deliberately hands-off teaching approach with which I tend to struggle. He called it "scaffolding," a teaching technique in which the caregiver, teacher, or mentor gently provides the tools the child needs in order to practice emerging skills. More recent research by the psychologist Carol Dweck suggests that allowing children repeated chances to work through failure promotes what's called a "growth mindset"—a teachable set of assumptions about what it takes to succeed. Children (and adults) with growth mindsets don't give up when they fail or encounter setbacks, because they hold the core belief that they can practice a task and improve. In contrast, children with "fixed" mindsets see their skills—and fates—as immutable, so every failure or bump in the road becomes an indictment of their abilities. People in the latter category are far more likely to give up when faced with challenges.

Although I'm aware of this, I find that I'm especially reluctant to let my kids make mistakes in cases where that might result in them miss-ing those rare, golden opportunities that seldom present themselves. If we wait for hours for a fish to bite, for example, I often end up being overly aggressive in my instructions when it finally happens. After all, I don't want us to miss our one chance of the day. I want desperately for them to experience success, or even just be in proxim-ity to it. Also, I'm thinking ahead to the lessons we could learn by cleaning the fish and cooking it, all of which rely on us catching the thing in the first place. In short, I'm sacrificing the lesson of them learning from their own mistakes in order to experience other, ancil-lary lessons that could come after. Similar things happen in many other arenas outside of fishing. If they don't place the birdhouse in the right spot, they won't get the joy of watching it get used. If they don't pick out the right kind of kindling for starting a campfire, they'll never have a flame upon which they can learn to cook.

With gardening, though, I find it much easier to let the kids make their own mistakes without my getting involved. That's because it's a relatively low-stakes arena, where they can take the lead and experi-ment to their hearts' content. You can get 225 sugar snap pea seeds for about three dollars. Every spring, I carefully plant a row or two in just-right soil conditions so that we can enjoy homegrown steamed peas with a dab of melted butter and some salt. Just as reliably, the kids request a small handful of these seeds so that they can sprinkle them around, willy-nilly, just to see what happens. They bury them in the gravel alongside the driveway. They bury them in the lawn. They bury them just about everywhere you can dig an inch-deep hole. Just as researchers have determined that squirrels probably don't remem-ber where they bury their nuts (they detect the presence of the buried nut by smell rather than memory, and are just about as likely to dig up another squirrel's nuts as their own), my kids seem to forget the details of their own seed-sowing activities. What happens instead is that they periodically discover a pea growing in some improbable location and then celebrate its tenacity as well as the fact that their dad was "wrong" about where you should and shouldn't plant peas.

It's interesting to me that my kids recognize major differences between a seed and a plant. They recognize the potential of life within a seed, but they don't necessarily see it as something that's immediately alive. I witnessed a vivid demonstration of this fact last summer, when Rosemary and James each came home at the end of the school year with a couple of potted vegetables. Rosemary had a tomato plant and James had a butternut squash. Instead of just planting them in some weird and random spot, they sought my feedback on where best to put them. I suggested the garden, which seemed logical to me. The garden is watered regularly, I explained. We keep it weeded, and the fencing protects it from deer and rabbits. It has the proper exposure to sunshine and is shielded from high winds. They rejected this proposal, on the grounds that these were their own personal plants and so they wanted their own personal space for them. They had *plans* for these plants, no doubt envisioning a bright future, and the bragging rights they would get to claim. They didn't want their plants going into a place that they regarded as being communal and, therefore, not their own.

"Then you tell me where you want them," I said.

Rosemary picked a small planter in the hottest, sunniest corner of our patio for her tomato. For the squash, James picked a back corner of our yard beneath some aspen trees where we didn't mow and the grass grew high. Neither plant produced anything. Rosemary's tomato dried up again and again when she forgot to water it. James's squash got choked out by grass and trampled by kids and dogs. I resisted the urge to play the I-told-you-so card. Instead, I just made sure that we occasionally visited the plants and talked about what we were seeing. Honestly, I was impressed by how resistant they were to admitting that they perhaps picked bad locations. In fact, it wasn't until the plants were stone dead that they suggested we move them into the garden with the other vegetables after all.

If your kids are anything like mine, you'll struggle to make gardening relevant to them unless you grow stuff that they want to eat. Not to say that you shouldn't use the garden as a palate expander, because you should—and if you like a variety of vegetables, that will naturally happen in time—but you also need to raise something that inspires them, and for most kids that's strawberries rather than brussels sprouts. My own parents had a large and beautiful vegetable garden when I was a kid. We grew all of the Midwest garden standards: bush beans, tomatoes, cucumbers, acorn squash, lettuce, broccoli, and so on. We ate it fresh, frozen, and canned.

But when I was little, the southwest corner of the garden was the only portion that really, truly mattered to me. That was the rhubarb patch. My mother had dug up some rhubarb from her own mother's garden in northern Illinois, where she grew up, and planted it in our own garden right around the year I was born. The plant can be grown just about anywhere. It's a perennial. Once you get a patch established, it's pretty much on autopilot and will pop up on its own every year.

My mom was generally hostile to snacking. She expected us kids to eat at designated mealtimes and to otherwise stay out of the kitchen. We regarded her as being "mean" about food, because she limited our exposure to things like Coca-Cola and Cap'n Crunch and anything else that she figured would lead to increased dental visits.

The rhubarb patch was the one place where her vigilance about cavity prevention fell apart. We were allowed free rein there. Granted, rhubarb is not particularly sugary on its own. But the way that we enjoyed it was. When rhubarb was in season, our mom would hand us little cups of sugar through the door (remember, stay the hell out of the kitchen!) so that we could rip stalks from the rhubarb plant and dip them into sugar. This recipe, if you could call it that, was damn good. The sugar diminished the tartness of the plant and greatly exaggerated its sweetness. We developed a strategy in which you gnawed the end of the rhubarb in such a way that it would be particularly wet and pulpy and thereby the perfect medium with which to mop up clumps of sugar.

At the time, it struck me that my mom had made some kind of mistake with regard to rhubarb. As though she didn't realize that the sugar we were putting on the rhubarb stalks was the same kind of sugar that was in the dreaded cereals and sodas. Now I realize that she was being much shrewder. My mother loved to garden and had a deep reverence for the land's ability to provide sustenance for people willing to put in the work. By her calculations, the increased likelihood of a cavity was a small price to pay for her kids' initiation into the magical world of growing food.

Her scheme worked. My love for the rhubarb patch created a sort of food-based focal point in our home habitat. It was a fixed location that served as a geographical marker. You might describe a lost baseball as being somewhere in the vicinity of the rhubarb patch, or you would tell someone that the rhubarb patch was the perfect place to "ghost ride" your bicycle down the hill that sloped away from the garden. In the spring, that patch of ground held a lot of promise. The snow would melt and the mud would dry out as the sun marched northward in the sky and the days gradually warmed. Soon the dandelions would start to leaf out. Then a riot of crinkled and deep green rhubarb leaves would emerge from the reddish, warty growths that first broke the ground as the plants woke up and began to grow. Beneath these leaves, stalks the color of blood would rise up and stretch toward the sky. It felt like magic, this thing born of a collaboration between my own mother and Mother Nature. I had friends whose moms were way cooler about junk food, but they never fed me anything nearly as valuable as that.

Rhubarb takes a while to get going. In order to let it become properly established, it's best to wait two or three years before you start harvesting the stalks. My own family's nomadism has prevented me from taking some of the rhubarb from my mother's yard and planting it. I always figure that we won't be around long enough for my kids to enjoy it. But I have had great luck with strawberries. Even though they are a perennial, you can usually begin harvesting the same year that you plant. The second year is often spectacular. We've established two strawberry patches at two of our homes and each became a kiddie magnet—not just for our kids, but for the neighborhood kids. When the plants are fruiting, which can last for months, kids make it a regular part of their day to comb through the leaves looking for ripe berries. When I propose to them some things we could do to enhance our yield—controlling the growth of runners (formally called stolons), fertilizing at the right times—they are supportive and ready to jump in. I came to appreciate the true impact that our first strawberry patch had on my kids once we moved out of that house and another family moved in. A former neighbor of ours reported that this new family hired landscapers to dig up the patch and replace it with gravel. My kids were baffled, as they should have been. They expressed a sentiment that is best summed up by the saying "You can't fix stupid." My wife and I generally try to cultivate in our children positive feelings about others, but in this case I appreciated the condemnation.

Carrots are in close competition with strawberries as the kid-friendliest crop. Last summer, we built a three-by-eight-foot raised bed and plastered that thing in carrot seeds. Even after we thinned the seedlings enough to give each plant the right amount of room to grow, we had hundreds of them. Some were big enough to harvest in June.

I showed the kids how to identify a carrot that was ready to pick by gently exposing the top of the root and comparing its size to their fingertip. We reviewed how to pull it up without damaging its neighbors, and how to dig out the bottom half of the carrot if you pulled it the wrong way and broke it off underground. Sometimes I'd send the kids out to harvest a few for making pickled carrots or to serve at dinnertime, but I told them to just help themselves whenever they wanted one. I left a little trowel stuck in the dirt there so they'd have the right tool for the job and showed them how to use the garden hose to wash the carrots clean. Our carrot bed was so prolific that they were still pulling carrots out of the ground when the snow started to fly in November.

We prioritize generosity with the vegetables we grow. One year, in Seattle, we had an astounding stand of pole beans that grew on an eight-foot-tall teepee-shaped trestle built from saplings that we'd cut off on a friend's property. The vines reached the top, then doubled over and nearly reached back to the ground. We started to freeze some of the beans but then had to admit that frozen beans aren't half as good as fresh beans. We sent the kids around our neighborhood with bags of beans to give away. We also invited four or five neighbors to come over and pick a few meals' worth. When they came, I'd tell the kids to help them pick some beans and whatever else they might like. Perhaps our neighbors were overenthusiastic in their praise of the beans just to make the kids feel good, but either way the impact was noteworthy. Our kids found a tremendous sense of pride in being able to share their food with others, to the point that I had to throttle back their generosity in order to ensure that we'd have some vegetables left over for ourselves.

One of the reasons that I encourage our kids to give away vegetables is that I'm eager to offset the inherent selfishness of gardening.

I'm sensitive to the fact that everything we do to protect our plants—the weed pulling, slug killing, and fence building—could strike a child as intensely territorial. I worry that we might seem to be too aggressive in our manipulations of the earth, as though we play God in terms of which living things get preference and which get persecution. It would seem even worse if the product of those efforts were too selfishly guarded or, worse, allowed to go to waste. Gardens are best regarded as an earthy tool of humanitarianism. The things you grow are a cocktail made from dirt, sun, water, and love, and it's a drink best shared with neighbors and loved ones.

Tending to a garden is a lot of work. Even with just a couple of small raised beds, all the planting and weeding and watering adds up. Getting your kids involved with the work is important for their understanding of the process. In general, though, I see where parents might struggle with questions about how much physical work of any kind their kids should be doing on a routine basis. I'd argue that my own father went overboard on making my brothers and me work so much. He used chores as a form of punishment. If we were doing something that he approved of, such as hunting or fishing, he'd leave us alone. But if we were loitering around with friends in the driveway, or got caught watching TV in the daytime, he'd assign us weeks' worth of work. If he couldn't think up legitimate chores to keep us busy, such as mowing the lawn, raking leaves, or working in the garden, he'd populate his lists with phony activities meant to torture us. He had a meatloaf pan full of bent and rusted nails that he'd make us straighten on an anvil with a ball-peen hammer. I can't think of a single time that he actually used one of these refurbished nails. One time, he salvaged a load of bricks from a building demolition site and made us spend the summer chipping away the old mortar with hammers and cold chisels so the bricks could be reused. In that case, at least, we built an outdoor fireplace with the bricks. Another memorable summer was spent working a dull old crosscut saw he pulled down from a display of antiques he had affixed to the side of our house. We used the saw to remove the rotten ends of discarded railroad ties that we collected from alongside the tracks when crews were replacing them. To lift the eight-foot ties, we used ice tongs pulled from the same antique display as the saw. We were tasked with cleaning up the inner sections of the railroad ties that hadn't yet rotted so they could be stored away for later applications such as building landscaping beds or walkways. If we were lucky, two or three cuts with that crosscut saw might expose a leg's length of solid wood that was worth maybe a couple of dollars. A single cut took us about forty-five minutes. Amid this mindless work came his occasional reminder, and the only useful piece of life advice my dad ever spoke aloud: You're gonna spend one-third of your life working, so you'd better pick a job you love. Apparently, he was keen on demonstrating some of the things we might choose to avoid.

Back then, I assumed my dad was making us do the work because he didn't want to do it himself. Now I see how ridiculous that is. It would have caused him far less hassle to ignore these projects, or just do them himself. If I had to guess, he would have argued that he wasn't "making" us do the work. Instead, he was forcing us to take advantage of a great opportunity to toughen up and learn obedience, and I am grateful. Still, time has revealed that his tactics had complex effects. As an adult, I find it very hard to relax without feeling a vague sort of guilt about being lazy. That can't be good for me—and it certainly impacts the moods of people around me.

Likewise, the thing I remember most about doing those pointless tasks was the sense of rage that they inspired in me. How was producing things of little or no value supposed to impress upon me the rewards of hard work? It was lunacy.

A notable exception was the family garden, which I respected. I got annoyed with the work and resisted it at times, sure, but if there's a kid under the age of twelve who doesn't need to be pestered to do their garden chores, I'd like to meet them. My brothers and I had to plant bulbs, pull weeds, thin seedlings, and mix turkey manure procured from a local poultry operation into the soil with a spade and steel rake. Later, we had to learn how to use an old rototiller that'd take the better part of a day just to get it up and running each spring. The lack of a protective shroud over the exhaust would usually mean that you ended the day with a welt or two burned into your arms or legs.

Looking back on it, I recognize a huge debt of gratitude owed to my mother and father for teaching me how to grow food. I remember that work with great fondness. The difference between gardening and our other "chores" is that garden work produced something of undeniable value. If we didn't grow the things we ate, we would have had to purchase an inferior version elsewhere. My mother participated in the work and cherished the results of our labor. She preserved the fruit and vegetables from our garden through processes of drying, canning, and freezing so that we could enjoy it year-round. She made her own pasta sauce and fruit jams and pickles, all of which I loved to eat. To help the garden was to help the family—to make people happy. What's more, gardening was respected in our community. People walking their dogs or driving by on the road would stop to compliment my mother on her garden, or ask if they could come into our yard to admire it. It was a thing that inspired respect, and that respect was infectious. In the end, it can't be overlooked that my brothers and I all became avid gardeners as adults. The same can't be said for being enthusiastic straighteners of old, rusty nails.

I made a conscious decision to not be as hard on my own kids as my dad was on me. I recently explained this decision to a friend of mine who retired as an educator for the public school system in New Mexico. He was skeptical of my logic. The friend commented to me that most of his problems with kids stemmed from parents who weren't hard enough on them; the parents who were too hard had it just about right. I understand what my friend was getting at. I'm aware of the disservice that is done to kids who aren't trained to jump in and get a job done when it needs doing. It's a volatile and potentially ruthless world out there, and kids need to be equipped with resourcefulness and discipline in order to thrive in a variety of circumstances. Personally, I like to be around competent people who are willing to get dirty and lend a hand when a problem presents itself. I'd hate to raise kids who don't live up to my own standards.

But I also know, firsthand, the frustrations that come from doing inane, pointless tasks. When it comes to working with their hands, I'd rather my kids focus their efforts in the places where they will realize the value of their labor. As it did for me, gardening fits their sensibilities. There's often a bit of resistance to the workload, especially when they're hanging out with a friend or doing some other activity. I expect this, and I let them know that I'm not asking for their help; I'm demanding it. The friend can help out if they choose. Despite the initial coercion, I see again and again how a task in the garden ends up getting more of their attention than they intended to give it. If I ask them to plant ten seeds, they'll plant twenty. If I ask them to water one raised bed, they'll water three beds along with a few extra things that don't need it. If I ask them to cut a salad bowl's worth of lettuce for our dinner, they'll cut a bowl for a neighbor as well. No other set of routine chores inspires this level of enthusiasm. Definitely not picking up dog poop, and definitely not shoveling snow or cleaning bedrooms or clearing the table of dishes.

One of the things that help them get lost in garden chores is what I mentioned before: the riotous amount of life that can be found in and around a garden. They are simply mesmerized by all those slugs, larvae, moths, and worms. Last summer, I took my kids into a cow pasture to gather our own manure for fertilizer. I imagined this being an unpopular task for them, and it was—until they saw the wiggly white grubs living beneath each cow pie. They got to wondering if their pet lizards would like to eat the grubs (I told them I was certain they would), and suddenly we were gathering pet food and plant food all at once. The kids didn't want to stop.

Another thing that delights kids about gardening is the responsiveness of plants and soils. One can assist in the building of life by working in concert with natural systems. You can literally harness and direct nature's power. Through the chore of planting seeds, you place living organisms where nothing grew before. When you do the job of spreading manure and watch as the plants put it to use, you see how energy is transferred from one living organism to the next. By watering, you can save a wilted plant from death. Do the chore of weeding and watch as your plants stretch and grow to occupy those vacated spaces. It's work, yes—but it feels like the work of a magician.

Ultimately, though, confronting one's limits as a gardener is even more important than realizing one's powers. We can influence Mother Nature, and even coerce her at times to get what we want, but in the end she leaves little doubt about who's actually in charge. As it was with my family's experience growing pumpkins in Brooklyn, a lifetime of gardening is marked by more failure than success. A lot of this failure is driven by our own shortcomings as caregivers. Things that would have otherwise bloomed and prospered end up wilting and dying thanks to our negligence and lack of expertise. Greater still, and more instructive, are the losses that come through no real fault of our own—the hurricane-toppled eggplants, the broccoli seedlings plucked up by wild turkeys, ripening tomatoes ruined by early frost. It's normal to get pissed off when this stuff happens. You get mad at the weather, or curse the insects, or bemoan your own bad luck. But I invite my kids (and try to force myself) to see these setbacks as reminders of the fact that nature exists in a way that is ultimately beyond our control. Even as the ultimate apex predator, with all of our technological prowess and access to information, we find that our ambitions can still be thwarted by the planet and our fellow creatures. And we try to hold on to the idea that it's okay for that to be true. By gardening, we are cultivating a close friendship with nature that now and then boils over into a gentle quarrel. Even in a disagreement, you have to fight clean and maintain respect. Looking into the soil of a garden can be like looking into a mirror. You are bound to notice things about yourself that you might otherwise miss. Making the necessary adjustments, so you like what you see, is the ultimate reward.

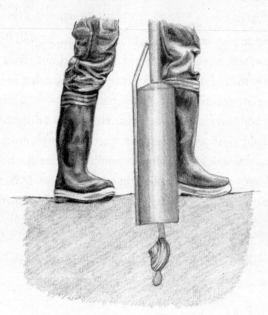

Siliqua patula– Razor Clam

## CHAPTER 5

# THINK LIKE A FISH

---

I like to remind my kids that humans are animals, a simple fact that is surprisingly easy to forget. I don't do it in a way that's meant to either glorify or denigrate our own species. Instead, I think of it as a way to establish a context that can be helpful in understanding our history and biology. However, complications can arise from shattering whatever illusions your children might have about the distinctions between us and the animal world. I was reminded of this one spring day when I was cleaning yellow perch with James shortly after he turned five, when we were living in a neighborhood near the western shore of Lake Washington. Again, it's all about getting eye level with nature.

Our rental house was about eight blocks from a public beach. We had a kayak that could be strapped to a set of wheels and pushed down the sidewalk like a wheelbarrow. I loaded James in the seat, piled on rods, paddles, and life preservers, and wheeled him down to the park. We caught about fifty perch beneath the Highway 520 bridge using little flies made of deer hair tipped with a small chunk of earthworm dug from our garden.

Fried perch fillets were a regular part of our diet when I was growing up in western Michigan. Our family ate hundreds every year. Some years, we probably consumed more than a thousand. They were more popular than pizza. They're still one of my favorite fish, but cleaning large quantities of the little things can be extremely tedious. I was anxious to teach James how to do it on his own, so that I could foist the job off on him the same way that my dad had foisted it off on me when I was a kid.

The first step in cleaning a perch is removing the scales. A lot of folks do this by removing the skin entirely, but this is a sin against God and man. The skin gives the fillet its flavor, so you need to scrape off the scales while leaving the skin intact. This is most easily done with a motorized scaler, which, in that moment, James and I did not have at our disposal. Instead, we were using improvised scalers made by screwing a bottle cap to the end of a stick of wood. Rubbed vigorously against the grain of the scales, the tool flips them off and sends them flying—usually all over your clothes and any surrounding surfaces, where they dry in place like glue. You can contain the mess by scaling the fish in a sink filled with just enough water to cover them. The downside is that the little fish are even slicker when wet—as my father put it, "like snot on a doorknob." You also run the risk of jabbing the needle-like dorsal spines into your fingers and hands. It's painful, especially for kids. But, when you're done, the sides of a scaled perch are beautifully smooth. It's worth the hassle.

The next step in cleaning a perch is to head the fish and gut it. I showed James how to use his non-dominant hand to pinch the fish's gill plates between his thumb and the big knuckle of his index finger. We then placed the fish back side down, with the dorsal fin on the cutting board. I guided his knife-holding hand so that the blade of the fillet knife slipped under the pectoral fins, then we turned the blade about 70 degrees downward toward the cutting board. A push of our hands sent the blade through the body and spine of the fish, at a slight forward angle so that the little pocket of meat that lies just above the gill plate at the back of the fish's head stayed connected to the body. Then we turned the fish on its side, tail facing toward us, and slipped the tip of the knife into the fish's cloaca, or vent. We made our gutting incision by slicing forward to intersect the cut we made when we removed the fish's head. James then dragged the innards free of the fish with the tip of his index finger, and I tossed the fish into a bath of ice water that would be placed in the fridge overnight. The next day, the fish would be way easier to fillet, having firmed up nicely and lost its slipperiness through some magic bit of chemistry that I don't understand.

James was transfixed by the guts that he had pulled from the fish. In particular, he was drawn to a brightly colored orange sac about the size of a grown woman's thumb. The conversation that followed was remarkable enough that I transcribed it on my computer the next day.

"That's her eggs," I said. "There's something like 20,000 of them in there."

"That means a girl?" he asked.

"Yeah, right. A female."

"Those are all her babies?"

"No, that's only half of what it takes to make a baby. You need to combine one of those tiny orange balls with some of this stuff."

From the growing mound of heads and guts I plucked a sperm sac, which looks like a pearly white miniature liver.

"When those are mixed up in the water," I said, "you get baby fish."

I went on to explain how female perch extrude their eggs in long ribbons that hang on aquatic vegetation and underwater structures such as submerged trees or dead branches. The males come along after and expel clouds of sperm, or milt, that fertilize the eggs.

This seemed like an opportune moment to introduce a subject that many parents—including my own, when I was a kid—handle very awkwardly. "It's the same way with humans, basically. The eggs and the sperm, I mean."

"I grew in Mommy's stomach," he said. "She didn't lay her egg out."

"You're right, buddy. That's one difference. Humans don't extrude eggs. And they generally only produce one at a time, too. Not thousands."

I still figured, naïvely, that I'd be able to maintain control of the conversation. But James soon had me cornered.

"Well, if the egg stays in Mommy, how does the sperm get to it?"

With that, we tiptoed unexpectedly into sex education. I found it easier to speak in terms of mammals in general rather than humans specifically, but he got the point. The final words were spoken on the matter several days later, when James was excitedly relaying his newfound knowledge to his babysitter. After some descriptions of the mechanics at play in reproduction, he concluded by saying, "And my mom and dad did that . . . three times!"

Katie and I have had quite a few laughs about that story over the years. When telling friends, I usually explain that my first and only discussion about sex with my father was also initiated by a fishing trip.

We were out fishing for salmon in Lake Michigan when I was ten years old. I saw a boat named *Danny's Wet Dream*. I asked what that meant and almost immediately regretted it. In front of his friends, my dad gave me a few gruff, perfunctory sentences describing what might occur in such a dream. He used the kissing scenes from soap operas as a frame of reference, revealing that such behavior "can lead to a whole lot more." To the day of my dad's death, that's as far as our discussions about sex ever went. I'll always be greatly indebted to the yellow perch of Lake Washington for giving me an easy-ish path into an often fumbled topic.

Fishing—and I'm going to use that term very broadly throughout the rest of this chapter, so that it includes things like clam digging and crayfish trapping—is an incredible relationship-building and mentoring tool. In addition to being a great excuse to get out in nature, it presents nearly endless opportunities not just to talk about hard things (or even sometimes to talk about nothing and just *be* together in companionable silence) but also to practice *doing* hard things, from planning ahead to waiting patiently to managing disappointment to following the rules when you're tempted to cheat. Fishing and related aquatic activities allow you to engage, hands-on and heart-forward, alongside your children in exploring what makes life *alive*. Through the harvesting process, you also get a relatively bloodless glimpse of what happens when life ends.

Even if it seems impossible, or just unlikely, from wherever you are sitting and reading this today, you, too, can go fishing with the children in your life. You can set out to catch a fish, or a crayfish, or a frog. You can learn to gut a fish, and teach your kids how to do the same. It's estimated that as many as sixty million people go fishing in the United States every year—and, just as with camping and other outdoor activities, interest in fishing only grew during the pandemic.

Getting started involves just a small investment in time and gear, and with thousands of public-access fishing sites on lakes and rivers in the United States, I can pretty much guarantee that there's a place to take your kids fishing not more than a few minutes from your home. It might be a small man-made reservoir in a municipal park or a stream that runs through a parcel of city-owned green space, but somewhere close to you there is a body of water that holds fish or other catchable, edible aquatic critters.

Though I was lucky enough to grow up with a lake full of fish literally in my backyard, my own family lives in a much different setting now. My kids have never known anything remotely like what I grew up with, except for our annual summertime trip to Grandma Rosemary's house. Nonetheless, I started fishing with each of my kids when they were three years old, or even younger if you count just having them along to observe the action. Where we live now, there are a few small creeks winding through the suburban neighborhoods. James fishes them regularly, as he's mature enough to ride off on his bike with some friends and their fishing rods. He always remembers to stuff a plastic bag in his back pocket, and usually brings it home with a brown trout or longnose sucker inside. He knows enough to gut the fish and place it in the fridge; we usually cook them up for dinner within a night or two. He relishes the role of being a provider for our family.

I generally admire fishing's ability to inspire meaningful conversations as well as sly observations and literary metaphors. I've always loved the writer John Gierach's line from his essay "The Big Empty River": "Creeps and idiots cannot conceal themselves for long on a fishing trip." And there's a quote often attributed to Karl Marx, though the attribution is dubious: "Sell a man a fish, he eats for a day, teach a man how to fish, you ruin a wonderful business opportunity." And then you've got Shakespeare: "I marvel how the fishes live in the sea. Why, as men do a-land; the great ones eat up the little ones."

For my kids, this is the best part of fishing. They love to explore the world of what eats what. I'm always surprised at the almost universal appeal that this subject has for children. At the time of Matthew's sixth birthday, one of his favorite books was *Who Would Win: Alligator vs. Python*. Inside the book are surprisingly graphic illustrations of a Burmese python swallowing a whole alligator bit by bit. I've got a strong stomach, but there's something about the illustrations that makes me a bit uncomfortable. But Matthew likes to sit on the couch and pore over them, transfixed. Often, James and Rosemary join him there as well, flipping the pages back and forth to behold the process of consumption.

Of all of the things we've encountered in real life, nothing has stomach contents that can rival those of a halibut. Inside their stomachs we've found sea ducks, squid, mud sharks, salmon, shrimp, many species of crabs, and, a few times, these bizarre-looking egg sacs from sharks and rays that are known as mermaid's purses. Northern pike are also great. I remember vividly a pike that I found in shallow water next to our dock when I was a kid. It was gagging on a large crappie, also still alive, as they lay together in a deathlock of almost certain mutual destruction. Whatever slim chance the pike had of getting the crappie down into its stomach was destroyed when my brothers and I netted up both fish and brought them to our dad to be cleaned for the deep fryer.

I remembered this experience one Fourth of July weekend when my kids and I caught a twenty-three-inch-long northern pike while fishing amid a noisy flotilla of holiday revelers. When we filleted the fish for dinner, we found an eleven-inch kokanee (a species of land-locked sockeye salmon) inside its stomach that looked almost fresh enough to get up and swim away. There were a lot of kids from other families hanging around when we cleaned the fish. Sure, there were plenty of exclamations of "ew" and "gross," but those sentiments weren't nearly as abundant as the exclamations of "cool" and "awesome." There was indeed an appreciation for the gluttony of northern pike, but also for the intense proximity of nature in general. Just feet beneath the surface of the water where we'd been hanging out, amid all of the fireworks and sunscreen and coolers of soda and beer, the cycles of life and death had been playing out in vicious harmony.

You don't need big, predatory fish to explore food chains—or, for that matter, sexual reproduction. You might start, for instance, with the ubiquitous bluegill, which is very easy to catch. Place a plastic bobber on your fishing line about two feet above a hook baited with worms and cast it out from the shore in the vicinity of weed beds or lily pads. If there are sunnies around, your bobber should start to wobble and then sink before too much time has elapsed. These small but powerful fish are guaranteed to delight rookie fisherpeople of all ages, who appreciate numbers more than size. Even serious anglers who tend to focus on bigger, more glamorous and challenging species like tarpon or blue marlin will fondly reminisce about cutting their teeth fishing for "panfish" (so called because they are delicious and small enough to fry in a pan) like bluegills, pumpkinseeds, and shellcrackers.

Inside the bluegill's stomach (or the stomach of one of its cousins), you can usually find a well-populated world of miniatures. You'll know you're looking at a prime specimen if the fish's stomach is packed full and firm like a small gray thumb. Help your kid slice open the end of the stomach with a paring knife or pocketknife and squeeze the contents into a small glass bowl full of water. Have them gently agitate the ball of food with their fingertip. It will break apart and blossom into a mosaic of invertebrate life. You'll find larvae, pupae, and adult specimens of various aquatic insects like midges, mosquitos, caddisflies, and mayflies. You'll find dragonfly and damselfly larvae. There might be bloodworms or leeches. Maybe snails or crayfish or clams. It's not unheard of to find vertebrates, too—tadpoles, little frogs, tiny fish decayed beyond classification by the potent acids in a fish's stomach. At other times, there is vivid proof of cannibalism.

I love for my kids to see this stuff. For one thing, I want them to understand the intricate building blocks that are necessary to create life. Mosquito larvae live in the water, where they might eat algae or other microscopic organisms. Bluegills, in turn, will eat the mosquito larvae. A heron or a human might eat the bluegill. You can explain to your kids all day long that life on earth is driven by solar energy that gets transferred from organism to organism all the way to their dinner plate. But there's nothing quite like witnessing and touching evidence of the elaborate array of predator/prey connections that come together to produce the life around us and within us. It's easy to despise mosquitos, but that hatred is harder to maintain when you understand the role that mosquitos have in creating the resources that we rely on. I also like my kids to witness the rawness and brutality of nature. I want them to know that northern pike swallow their prey alive, and that the prey suffocates inside their stomach. I want them to know that the cute little squirrels in the park will, on occasion, consume their own offspring. I want them to know that whitetail deer, of which there are some thirty million or so on our continent, are known to pluck baby birds from nests and eat them. This isn't meant to inspire in them some fear of nature, or worse, revulsion. Instead, my intention is to establish for them a baseline understanding of the lengths that organisms will go to in order to ensure survival. My hope is that my kids will unleash their own instinctual ferocity if they ever find themselves in a tough position.

Now and then, while we're eating family dinner, one of our kids will tell us about some disapproving remark made by a classmate who thinks that their hands-on relationship to nature is "cruel" or "mean." They shouldn't fish, some kid will say. Or it's bad to "kill nature." I don't want to over-prepare them for such interactions, to the point where they're simply reciting counterarguments that their old man pounded into their head. But I do point out to them the most obvious place to probe, which is the moral hypocrisy of someone who eats meat or vegetables raised on industrialized landscapes and then criticizes others for having the bravery and skills to produce their own dinner from the wild. Primarily, though, I hope that their insight into the animal world will cure them of naïve notions that anything, be it bluegill or man, can go through its time on earth without spilling blood.

"But okay," you may ask, "how do I actually catch fish?" That's a great question, because the conversational, philosophical, and nutritional potential of a fishing trip is greatly increased when you actually land a fish. Luck always plays a role in fishing. One of my favorite fishing stories is from a day when my older brother and I were fishing with James and we went all day without catching one of our target species, walleye. James was just four years old and spent most of his time throwing rocks or sticks or digging through his bag of snacks. At one point, though, late in the day, my brother and I were suddenly shocked when we looked down the gravelbar to see that he'd dragged an impressively large walleye out of the water at the end of the twelve-dollar Snoopy fishing pole that I'd bought for him on Amazon. I'll always remember how we tried to interrogate him about where he had cast his bait and what exactly happened—questions that he was simply too young to adequately address.

Typically, though, there are better approaches than simply relying on luck. If you want satisfying fishing experiences, both you and your children will need to become invested in the process. I really can't stress this enough: A major part of the entire premise of this book is getting your kids involved in the process. It's a shift that turns an outing or activity from a chore for you into an adventure for them. Though they may not often admit as much, kids actually *like* being given responsibility, in no small part because they like to feel that they're on the same level as those pesky adults who won't stop bossing them around. Include them in the process. It changes the entire context.

There's plenty of information out there about gear, techniques, and knots, and you can look for information specifically applicable to your local area in field guides and how-to fishing books, YouTube videos, and on your state's fish and game agency websites. But the real first step is for you and your kids to become students of the behavior and preferred food sources of your quarry.

The more knowledge you have about what food sources, water temperatures, depths, and habitat locally gettable fish prefer, the better your chances of success. Many species of fish, for instance, will routinely move into shallow water at night to feed, and then retreat to the darkness of deeper water during the daytime to hide from other predators.

Fish like a good hiding spot, so weed beds, reefs, and underwater rocky structures are great places to look for them. So are downed trees lying in the water. Or look beneath boat docks and swimming floats. Abrupt changes in depth known as dropoffs also hold a lot of fish— they search for food on the shallow side and dart into the deeper water to escape predators. Likewise, current can concentrate fish into easily identifiable areas: inlets and outlets (where a stream enters or exits a body of still water), current breaks behind large rocks or bridge pilings, and eddies where calm water is directly adjacent to moving water. Fish seek out these spots where they can save energy by getting out of the current while capitalizing on food that's getting washed downstream within easy reach. Learning to identify these kinds of places is known as "reading the water." No book is going to tell you everything that you need to know about reading the water at your local creek, lake, or beach, but being observant and curious about these topics will enable you to make discoveries that translate into fish on the end of your kid's line. You should also seek out mentors such as friends, neighbors, or distant relatives who fish. Likewise, you can learn a lot by hiring a fishing guide.

One last tip on finding fish: Just like many other wild creatures (including, sometimes, humans), fish often throw caution to the wind when it's time to reproduce, and this important factor disrupts their general patterns and behaviors. The inherent drive to pass on their genetic line overrides their normal priority of survival, making them more vulnerable to being caught during the spawning season. While regulations sometimes prohibit or limit fishing for particular species at these times, spawning season provides the best (and in some cases the only) opportunity of the year for recreational anglers to catch many kinds of fish.

I grew up during a decades-long stretch of time when we had seemingly unreal numbers of rainbow smelt living in the southern half of Lake Michigan. Every spring, it was an annual tradition for us to drive to the shoreline of "the Big Lake" to go smelt dipping when the fish were spawning. They're often as short as your finger and never much longer than a Sharpie, and they eat tiny plankton. Most of the year, they're targeted only by offshore commercial fishing boats. But when conditions lined up just right with a warm rain right after the spring thaw, the smelt would show up in the shallows at night to spawn en masse. You'd locate the schools of smelt by walking the shoreline with a lantern or waiting at the stream mouths for the fish to appear. Then, you could scoop them up by the dozens with nets before depositing them in five-gallon buckets. Back home, we'd prepare the smelt by gutting them, coating the bodies in cornmeal, and frying them. The cooking process dissolved the fish's tiny bones, so you could just pop them into your mouth and eat them whole. Such meals were the climax of what we called smelt dipping season.

Looking back on those days, the thing I remember most about smelt dipping was the community aspect. On a good night, dozens or hundreds of people would line up together in a party-like atmosphere as they shared equipment, advice, and good cheer. The abundance of the resource meant there was little need to jealously protect your spot or your methods. You could figure out how to do it just by watching the guy next to you. If someone was doing good, it was likely that everyone was doing good.

Rainbow smelt are non-native to the Great Lakes, along with many of the other species that live there. This pretty much guarantees that their populations will be unstable, as there's no natural balance to the ecosystem. For years now, there haven't been enough smelt in that area to warrant looking for them. Who knows if the great hordes of these fish will ever return to the shallows of Lake Michigan?

For much of my life, I viewed the camaraderie of smelt dipping as a one-of-a-kind thing, known only to folks who lived in my home area. But over the years, as I've explored outdoor opportunities across the country, I've discovered many other versions of this activity, where massive spawning runs or migrations of fish or other aquatic creatures create relatively easy opportunities for families to experience some success. If you live in Puget Sound, look into the squid jigging season that runs from around Thanksgiving to Valentine's Day, or the early fall pink salmon runs that occur in odd-numbered years (a fishing opportunity that also makes for a great research assignment for you and your kids; look that factoid up together and explore why that's true). If you're on the East Coast, check into the American shad and hickory shad runs in the spring. Up and down the West Coast, check out herring, candlefish, or grunion run schedules. Look into dip-netting salmon in south-central Alaska in the late summer. And pretty much everywhere, ask around at your local fishing tackle shops about sucker and catfish runs through the spring and summer.

Wherever you're fishing, one harsh reality remains a constant: Sometimes, no matter how engaged your inner fish-brain, or how good a certain spot is "supposed" to be, the fish just aren't biting. Even when they are, there are apt to be lots of long dry spells. You'll occasionally hear fishing described as hours of boredom punctuated by occasional minutes of excitement.

There's no denying that when the fishing is slow, children can lose their focus in a hurry or get bored. It's pretty much inevitable, so try to be understanding and coach them through the frustration. Just as with failure, delayed gratification has its merits. I can't think of any kind of paying work that doesn't involve some degree of boredom, and teaching kids how to work through their own frustration during these times can only benefit you when you're stuck inside on a rainy day.

And remember, always, that success shouldn't be measured solely by the number of fish caught. Instead, keep in mind the real goal of making your children's time in the outdoors as enjoyable and engaging as possible. Try to manage your own expectations by understanding the role you'll be playing once you're on the water. Rather than doing much serious fishing yourself, you'll be spending a lot of time untangling lines, retying knots, and baiting hooks. Some days, it seems all I do is bounce from one kid to the next, dealing with one mishap after another. I recall one such incident when James and Rosemary simultaneously snagged each other's life jackets and then proceeded to spin and turn until they were pretty much hog-tied by fishing line. I had to use scissors to get them freed up. Over time, though, our situation has improved as I've taught my kids to become more self-sufficient. It might be faster to make a cast, tie a knot, hook a fish, or undo a tangle yourself, but you'll know your kids are truly engaging in the process of fishing when they start trying to figure it out on their own. By the time she was eight years old, Rosemary was downright opposed to having me cast her rod for her. She'd rather catch nothing on a cast of her own than catch a fish on a cast that I made for her. I respect that immensely. And it's paid off for her, because she's learning how to catch fish and that makes her happy. It might sound hokey, but these days, I get way more pleasure out of seeing her catch a fish than I do catching fish myself.

There are lots of catching and eating opportunities beyond rod-and-reel fishing, and many of them are very kid-friendly. Take crabbing. Saltwater crabs such as blue crabs and rock crabs, widely available in most coastal waters, can be easily trapped with devices known as pots or rings baited with chicken scraps or the heads and entrails of fish. A boat is helpful, but crabs can also be caught near shore in shallow water, using traps anchored to the bottom with a rock or secured with a rope to a bridge piling or tree. You can even catch them by standing on shore or in shallow water and flinging out a string with a chicken bone tied to the end. Wait twenty minutes or so and slowly pull the rope in to see if any crabs are latched on.

Gathering shellfish occupies an interesting middle ground between fishing and foraging. Unlike the former, it tends to involve very little gear or preparation. Mussels can simply be plucked off the rocks they cling to. Clams spend most of their time underwater, buried in the substrate, so you'll usually have to dig them up with a shovel or a "clam gun." (Freshwater clams make for poor table fare and can build up toxic pollutants in their flesh, but most widely available saltwater clams make for excellent eating.)

The world's best-kept secret when it comes to shellfish isn't technically shellfish at all. Sea cucumbers are actually echinoderms, the same group of animals that includes starfish and sea urchins. They look like poisonous worms from an alien planet, and their sweet meat is very similar to clam strips when deep-fried. Snorkeling gear makes them easier to find, but in places with extreme tidal shifts, they're easily gathered from shallow tidal pools and exposed rocks at low tide. Picking sea cucumbers might seem pretty casual, considering their lack of defenses and inability to run away or hide when danger approaches. But one of the scariest moments of my life—and of my kids' lives—happened when my brother and I were gathering sea cucumbers while James and Rosemary watched from the boat with a friend of ours. All of a sudden I could hear the kids screaming bloody murder. I lifted my head to see two dorsal fins as tall as a man closing in on my brother from behind. The killer whales got within about fifteen feet before satisfying their curiosity and turning away. My brother never even knew they were there. It took a while to calm the kids down; they were very scared and crying. Throughout the day, though, we taught them by example to relive the story as an adventure rather than a moment of terror. Gradually, they were able to get over their fears and see the event for what it really was: a once-in-a-lifetime experience.

When I was growing up in Michigan, far away from any saltwater, we developed a love for catching crayfish. I've passed this love along to my kids, who'll spend hours wading around shallow water and flipping over rocks trying to catch their prey. Crayfish escape their predators by swimming backward in short, fast bursts, so the trick to catching them is using one hand to scare them into the other. It's a great opportunity for sibling cooperation, as one kid can flip rocks while others stand at the ready to snatch up whatever crayfish come squirting out. The hardest part is holding on to a crayfish without getting zapped by their claws. To avoid this, you either have to engulf them tightly in the palm of your hand or else pinch their carapace from the top, placing two fingers just behind the base of their claws. Inevitably, there will be pinches and lost crayfish. Aquarium nets can help circumvent these issues, but even large crayfish aren't capable of doing any serious damage beyond a blood blister or two. If anything, a few crayfish pinches make for good stories.

Bullfrogs are another critter many kids are happy to catch with their hands, or by dangling a hooked worm in front of the frogs' faces. We eschew traditional French preparations for the legs. Instead, we deep-fry them and then drag them through cocktail sauce or ketchup. The meat, commonly described as chicken-like in flavor, is light, sweet, and only mildly fishy.

Admittedly, bullfrog dinners won't be for everyone. But if your family is into it and you want to up the ante, you might consider "gigging" for bullfrogs, using a spear with three to five barbed prongs and an extra-long shaft. It's considered a legal fishing activity in most states, and I've found that kids can manage a frog gig with adequate dexterity when they're just five or six years old. The best action happens at night, when the mostly nocturnal bullfrogs are breeding and hunting for insects and other prey. It takes a keen eye to spot a motionless green frog hiding in floating mats of green vegetation. The deep focus required by this activity will have younger kids forgetting all about their nighttime scaries in no time.

Ice fishing is another worthwhile activity to explore after dark. You can go ice fishing during the day, of course, but there's something otherworldly about being out on the ice on a moonlit night, especially with kids. Often, as the air temperature falls at dusk, you can literally hear the ice expanding beneath you—it emits these gloomy-sounding groans that reverberate across the frozen surface. On many frozen lakes in the Upper Midwest, people gather by the hundreds on weekends to socialize and catch dinner. You'll need to invest in some additional equipment like an ice auger for drilling fishing holes, short rods specifically designed for ice fishing, and perhaps a pop-up tent that provides shelter from the elements. But that's not crucial. What *is* necessary, though, is ice thick enough to support people. Four inches of hard, clear ice is considered safe to walk on, but it's not un-reasonable to wait until it's six inches thick for peace of mind.

In northern-tier states where it's legal, spearfishing through the ice is a popular winter pastime, and it's got a special sort of magic. Whereas spearfishing in the ocean involves diving or snorkeling, when spearfishing through the ice, you stay on the surface. You don't throw the spear so much as hold it over the fish and drop it on them.

An augur is required, for cutting a hole about the size of a large flat-screen TV into the ice. So is a pop-up tent or a sturdier shelter called a "dark house," to cover the hole and block glare from outside light. It's nearly impossible to avoid an expression of astonishment when you first peer into such a hole. The water is lit up from ambient light passing through the ice, making any fish swimming under the spearing hole visible, and it's like having your own private glass-bottomed boat. You feel as though you're peering into some other dimension that was previously hidden from view.

In our family, we do very little intentional catch-and-release fishing. Usually, if we let a fish go, it's because we inadvertently caught a species that we do not care to eat (common carp, for instance) or we're prohibited by law from keeping it. Because I've raised my kids to view fishing as primarily a food acquisition tool, they usually express disappointment about letting fish go. We celebrate those instances when we're able to catch our own dinner, and letting a fish go makes as much sense to them as dropping your fishing rods into the water.

Rather than playing into their annoyance, I try to steer my kids toward an appreciation for the legal mechanisms and ethical considerations that compel us to return perfectly tasty fish to the water. Virtually every type of edible aquatic creature that you encounter is managed through some sort of regulatory structure. Many species are completely off-limits to harvest, while others have specific license requirements, open and closed seasons, size limits, and bag limits in order to prevent the resource from being overharvested. And even in situations when you could legally keep a fish, there are times when it's better not to. Let's say you and your child are having a banner day of fishing for yellow perch, like the day that I described at the beginning of this chapter, when James and I caught the perch that landed us in our discussion about procreation. In that particular lake, there is technically no legal limit on how many perch you can keep. It's tempting to just keep pulling in fish until your cooler is completely topped off. But then you need to ask yourself if you're really prepared to properly clean and eat that much fish in a timely fashion in order to prevent spoilage. Yes, it's a good plan to save some fish for later by freezing what you can't eat right away. But rather than stockpiling so much excess that it will end up forgotten or freezer-burned, a better plan is to take just enough for a few meals and leave the rest for seed.

These situations where we have to release fish are incredibly important teachable moments. They give kids a chance to practice restraint and develop the skill of dealing with disappointment. Ultimately, a child's awareness of their own status as an animal is only half of the equation. Accepting oneself as an animal that lives amid the natural world cannot be taken as a license to live without responsibility. As humans, we have some rapacious tendencies that need to be held in check. We hold the unparalleled power to destroy the resources that sustain us. Just ask the buffalo, the passenger pigeon, and the oysters of the New York Harbor. Restraint and conservation are a must if we're going to live on this planet in a sustainable fashion.

In fact, ethical principles are codified into the rules that govern fishing, and these rules have sharp teeth. Bringing kids into the conversation about these rules, and teaching them what happens when you don't play by the rules, is a perfect primer in stewardship. One day, our family was driving down the highway listening to recordings of the comedian Jerry Clower, who used to get up and tell hunting and fishing stories at the Grand Ole Opry back in the 1970s. In one of Clower's stories, a man responds to a summer of poor fishing by tossing dynamite into the river and harvesting boatloads of catfish. Rosemary asked me what would happen if we did that. I told her we'd land our butts in jail.

Fishing rules go way beyond prohibitions against explosives. There are all those regulations that I mentioned earlier—seasons, bag limits, and so forth—but there are many more that are less well known and more impressive in their complexity. There are rules governing the size and quantity of fishing hooks that you use. There are rules governing where and how you gather your bait, and where you can use it. One stretch of a river might have totally different fishing rules than the next stretch downstream. There are rules against fishing within certain proximities of specified dams, fish ladders, and spawning habitats. There are even regulations that govern what you do with your catch once you're home. Thankfully, in most states, it's actually illegal to waste the edible portions of a game fish. (Don't let the profusion of ordinances worry you; your state's fish and game agency will be happy to help you understand the fine print.)

There are plenty of people who blatantly disregard these regulations as being onerous or nitpicky. Extreme cases of these individuals are known as poachers or violators. Others are better described as just lazy or ignorant, as in lazy about compliance or ignorant about the importance of the rules. I would put my own father in the latter category. He was on board with the general gist of wildlife regulations, but fudged a lot of details out of convenience. It took me many years to unlearn his example. Today, I try my hardest to understand and comply with all of the rules that govern fishing. There's a selfish justification for this, in that I don't want to get in trouble. More important, though, I want my kids to understand that we, as a society, guard our resources jealously to prevent overexploitation. I invite them to celebrate the rules, and to honor them so that these resources can continue to be allocated in a democratic fashion to responsible users.

What could be dismissed as a bunch of fine print on a website is actually often a marvel of adaptive history, biology, and sociology: a finely wrought contract among people that also holds nature in mind. When I consider this contract, I think of one of the most beautiful, memorable days that I ever spent with my kids. It was midwinter out on the western edge of Washington's Olympic Peninsula, a few hours' drive from Seattle. The beaches there face the open Pacific Ocean. They are hard, sandy expanses, colored like clay and windswept and violently washed by waves—perfect habitat for razor clams, one of the most sought-after shellfish on America's West Coast.

I think of fishing and clamming as cousins; both involve water and work. What's more, both fish and clams taste equally good when fried, baked, or placed in a stew involving butter and white wine. I'd been waiting anxiously for an opportunity to introduce my kids to the discipline. In many states, your regular old fishing license allows you to harvest clams, but not so in Washington. Prior to 1929, you could have just gone out there whenever you wanted and dug up as many as you could. But that year, the Washington Department of Fish and Wildlife, which itself was established in 1890, put in place a daily bag limit of thirty-six razor clams. Fourteen years later, in 1943, they began to establish "seasons," or times of year when the resource is legally open for harvest and times when it's not. In the following decades, in response to overexploitation, resource managers continually adjusted bag limits and seasons in order to ensure a stable population of clams. They made a rule that razor clams have to be at least three inches in order to keep them. The seasons were shut down entirely in 1984 and 1985, when some beaches lost up to 95 percent of their razor clam populations due to a naturally occurring bacteria that attacked the shellfish.

Now, the state has a highly adaptive method for regulating the razor clam harvest. The resource is managed on a beach-by-beach basis across five different stretches of shoreline. Each summer, biologists do detailed population assessments on each beach, using models that demonstrate approximate numbers of clams both over and under three inches. For each beach, they establish a TAC, or total allowable catch. Based on the strength of the clam numbers, the TAC can run between 30 percent and 40 percent of the population. Half of the TAC is allocated to members from the Quinault, Hoh, and Quileute tribes, who are the traditional owners of the resource. The other half of the TAC goes to the state, which then opens up a number of harvest opportunities for the general public.

These harvest opportunities are known locally as "clam tides," because razor clams are vulnerable to human harvest only when they are exposed by a low tide. The rotation of the earth and its spatial relationship to the moon and sun dictate that there are two low tides every twenty-four hours. The state tries to open the harvest for at least one clam tide each month between October and May, with priority given to tides that favor participation from the public—typically weekend afternoons. Since weather conditions have a huge impact on the harvest—bad weather and high surf make for tough clam digging—the state will continually update its website with new announcements of additional clam tides so long as the TAC has not been reached.

There's one final wrinkle in the setting of clam tides. It's called paralytic shellfish poisoning, or PSP. It's a naturally occurring biotoxin produced by some microscopic algae. When ingested by humans, the biotoxin can affect the nervous system and lead to muscular paralysis. Worst case, it can kill you. The state monitors all the beaches for PSP, and if levels reach a certain threshold, they will cancel the clam tide altogether.

All things considered, planning a trip for razor clams on the Olympic Peninsula has a sort of tentative feel to it, like you're trying to hit a moving target. But when everything lines up, it feels pretty damn good. And here we were, a few hours early for the perfect clam tide! The low tide would occur before sunset, so there was no need for flashlights and lanterns. Nighttime clamming is fine for grown-ups, so long as you maintain good situational awareness: Every so often, a big wave will come out of nowhere to swamp your boots or knock you over. You might even pull it off with a single kid, if you can keep them within arm's reach at all times. But to go out there in the dark with three kids, two of whom are toddlers, is a good way to get in bad trouble.

So our timing was perfect, as was the weather. It had rained all morning, but now the clouds were breaking up and the sun was coming through. There was just a light breeze and the surf was low. The beach felt endless, with grayish sand stretching north and south for what seemed like eternity. These beaches are admittedly beautiful in their rawest, unpeopled form. They feel desolate, wild, and forgotten. But now the beach was beautiful in the opposite way. The Washington Department of Fish and Game estimates that a favorable clam tide can attract more than a thousand clam diggers per mile. Today was such a day.

The fishing writer John Gierach has another quote I like: "There are only two kinds of anglers: those in your party and the assholes." There's some truth to that, but the sentiment was not on display today. Moods were jovial, cordial, supportive, enthusiastic. People with extra gear were helping to equip those who were lacking. All of us on the beach shared in a collective excitement that seemed to spread like some friendly contagion through the air.

With Matthew in a backpack and the other two kids darting around my and Katie's legs, the five of us followed the receding waters westward as more and more of the beach was exposed. I tried to explain to the kids what exactly we were looking for. I told them it's called a "show," a term for the subtle marking on the sand's surface that reveals the presence of a razor clam hidden beneath. The show is caused by the clam suddenly retracting its neck, which creates a dimpled little hole the size of a dime. A razor clam's show is the essence of ephemeral. It's gone so fast you barely get to behold it. Rather, you have to trap the image in your mind, instantaneously, and then try to view it as a memory. Explaining this to the kids was next to impossible. They kept pointing out potential shows, and I kept dashing their hopes.

"There!"

"No, that's just a bit of seashell."

"That's it!"

"No, that's a little mark from a ghost shrimp under the mud."

"What was that?"

"I don't know, but not a clam."

"There's a sand dollar!"

"You're right. That *is* a sand dollar."

Eventually, an hour or so before low tide, James hollered and his face lit up. Mine did, too. We both stepped over to the same little patch of nondescript mud and pointed at the same little spot of nothingness. We were 100 percent sure of what we had seen, but now it was gone and there was nothing. We marked the spot with a bit of broken shell. I got Matthew out of the pack and set him on his feet. I called Rosemary over as well. I wanted to show them how to use the clam gun. It's a suction device, basically a T-handle welded to the top of a five-inch-diameter metal tube that's about two feet long. You place the opening of the tube directly over the clam's show and then shove it down into the mud about twelve inches or so. As the tube descends into the mud, displaced air escapes out of a pinhole in the handle. Once the tube is down far enough, and hopefully over the clam's body, you plug the pinhole with your finger in order to create suction as you pull the tube back out. It withdraws the entrapped cylinder of mud, and usually the clam, up into the light of day.

Razor clams have an oval shape, like a flattened sweet potato. The shell is pearly and fragile and breaks as easily and sharply as glass. They are gorgeous. I expected the kids to behold the clam and marvel at it, but instead they seemed to marvel more at the mud around them. It was like some pregnant creature, ready to birth treasures straight into their hands.

At that moment, the hunt was on. Predatory instincts were at full bore. By law, each licensed clam digger is allowed fifteen razor clams per day. Each digger must keep their personal limit of clams in a separate container. Since Rosemary and Matthew were too young to dig clams on their own, we had agreed on a family limit of forty-five clams, fifteen each for Katie, James, and me. We caught the last of them just as the water began to turn and come back up to swallow the beach. We were loaded down with heavy clam bags, but we helped some other folks who weren't so lucky by teaching them how to identify a razor clam's show. By now, Rosemary and James were experts and they were eager to demonstrate the skill. Soon, though, the waves were rolling over the clam beds and everyone was back up by the cars.

The kids were a total mess. Literally coated in mud. They'd all gone in the water over the tops of their rubber boots and so they made squishing sounds when they walked. But they glowed with pride for having caught our dinner. In fact, they had caught a lot of dinners: steamed clams, pasta with clams, and—their absolute favorite—fried clams. I knew they'd start getting cold at any moment, but for now they were running back and forth along the water's edge. To the west was one of the most gorgeous sunsets I have ever seen. Rays of orange sun blasted down through cracks in the gray clouds, casting long shadows off the kids' legs as they ran. The shadows made the kids seem even faster and more powerful than usual, like shadows of wild animals chasing down their prey.

## CHAPTER 6

# HUNTING: THE DEEP END OF THE POOL

There were at least two grizzly bears nearby. James had seen the first one without me, through the windows of a two-seat Piper Super Cub when he was being flown into our caribou hunting spot south of the Yukon River in eastern Alaska. He and his pilot described how they inadvertently buzzed right over the top of the bear while circling to approach the makeshift landing strip where we were going to set up camp. I had landed just ahead of James, and neither I nor my own pilot had seen the bear. But James described in great detail how the blond-colored bear spun and ran as the plane passed overhead. It was chubby enough that its fat rippled beneath its fur, and it ran downhill and disappeared into a thicket of brush. He said it was the coolest thing ever.

A few hours later, after our pilots had shuttled in my buddy Martin and his two teenage sons, we caught a glimpse of movement on the mountainside about eight hundred yards away from where we were setting up our camp. It was another grizzly, feeding on blueberries with such vigorous intensity that the bear seemed like it was mad at the fruit. I put our spotting scope on a tripod and helped James focus in on the bear to have a good look.

"You sure that's not the bear you saw from the plane?" I asked.

"No," he said. "No way. That other bear was blond-colored. This bear is *way* darker. And bigger." James slowly moved the spotting scope in order to track the bear's progress. "This is the neatest place in the world," he said.

James, Matthew, and Rosemary had already accompanied me on many hunting trips, both around our home in Montana and also near their grandma's house in Michigan. We'd chase after squirrels, rabbits, and pigeons, and they'd sat in the woods with me while hunting turkeys. We'd made a lot of great memories, and some not-so-great ones. There was the time we were stalking an antelope out on the Great Plains and the kids found a badger skull lying right next to a prairie dog skull. But there was also the time we were hunting squirrels and Rosemary mistook a piece of deer poop for a chocolate chip. And the time we were out chasing wild turkeys and had to all pack ourselves inside a little one-person hunting blind that was only big enough for a single folding chair. The kids giggled about the tight accommodations until the laughing stopped and they all started crying about being hungry and cold.

Those early trips had tremendous value in their own right, though it has taken me some time and distance to see that clearly. Early on, I sometimes brought them along for the selfish reason that I wanted to be in the woods but the only way to do that was to bring everyone along with me. Gradually, though, I came to see it as an investment of sorts. I was training the kids to be good hunting partners for me and for each other. I had always planned to take them out individually as well, in order to give them my undivided attention as they embarked on what I hoped would become a lifelong pursuit. James, being the oldest, was first at bat. I wanted to create an adventure for him that he'd never forget, so we made a plan to spend a few days hunting caribou in September during the herd's annual migration as they moved from their summer calving grounds to lower elevation winter range.

We were almost certain to encounter grizzly bears, so for months we'd been talking about how to deal with them. We discussed the importance of maintaining a strong sense of situational awareness at all times. We discussed the importance of staying close together when we were out walking around, with me out in front and him close behind. And we talked about last-ditch emergency precautions, such as when to use bear spray and how to curl up in a ball and use your hands to protect the back of your head and neck if a bear gets you on the ground.

I had worried that I was overemphasizing the risk of grizzlies; I didn't want to create in my son a sense of what my brothers and I call "bearanoia," a condition where one's fear of bears becomes so great that you can't enjoy yourself in their presence. I've known a lot of people who've succumbed to this fear, but seeing James's excitement about the two grizzlies alleviated any fears I had about it happening to him.

As for me, I was feeling quite at ease now that we were out of the airplanes. That I felt better being on the ground with grizzlies than I did being inside a machine that's flying through the air says a lot about my personal biases. The bush pilots I hired were highly skilled, sure, but I can never shake the feeling of vulnerability when I'm coursing through mountain passes inside a fabric fuselage that you could easily punch your fist through. Being separated from James made it all the worse, as the thought of him encountering trouble without me being there to protect him made me question my own judgment as a parent. Yet it was utterly unsurprising to me that a hunting trip would so quickly bring feelings of fear and responsibility to the fore. Hunting creates around itself an arena of tremendous consequence. There's little room for a casual or passive relationship to a pursuit that ends, so long as everything goes right, with a wild creature dead on the ground.

There are many recommendations within this book that I make wholeheartedly, with zero reservations. I see not even a glimpse of downside to getting your kids involved with gardening or foraging or exploring the traditions of the indigenous cultures that occupied their home habitat ahead of them. Those things will enrich their lives, period. But hunting forces an extreme, hands-on level of engagement with nature that requires high levels of education and a lot of ethical considerations. If we are taking it seriously, and we must, it forces us to reflect on our past, present, and future. It is a matter of life and death, literally. Within that richness lies its beauty, and also its dilemma.

Despite the fact that around 80 percent of Americans support hunting for food, less than 10 percent of our country's population are actually hunters. If the mere idea of you or your kids killing an animal—and eating what you've killed—makes you truly uncomfortable, hunting isn't for you. There's nothing wrong with that. I would never suggest to someone who is outright opposed or even indifferent to the practice of hunting to just go out and try it. However, if you're truly curious, it's a different story. I've introduced many people to hunting, both children and adults. Most of them had developed an interest in eating wild game and expressed a desire to try getting their own. Not all of them became lifelong hunters, but none of them regretted the experience.

To actually become a hunter is to surmount substantial barriers to entry, and stay engaged in a demanding, intricate ongoing ritual. Put simply, becoming a safe, ethical hunter is tough. There is no room for shortcuts. Not only will you need to follow strict licensing requirements, complicated regulations, and infrangible firearms safety protocols, you'll have to become a dedicated student of nature with a keen understanding of the landscape and how animals use their environment. And, especially early on, you'll need to overcome one of the biggest challenges new hunters face: finding a place to go hunting. All of this adds up to a long and difficult learning process that never really ends—which, of course, makes it an ideal lifelong adventure for an outdoor family.

When I first started having kids, I worried about the best way to introduce them to the concept of animal death. I find that such anxieties are pretty common among parents, including those that don't hunt or fish as a way of life. On the one hand, most of us want our kids to acknowledge the resources upon which we rely and appreciate the full material costs of our existence. On the other hand, we want to protect their innocence by stalling their awareness of certain cold realities. I'm sure that even the parents of vegetarian children are reluctant to explain the thousands upon thousands of insects and small mammals that die when an acre of land is tilled, planted, and harvested. We all take different approaches to this. I have watched people cringe when I mention to my kids that hot dogs are made from animal muscle and that the gelatin inside marshmallows comes from the ligaments and tendons of cattle and sheep. They behave as though I'm sharing dirty secrets, which is a perspective that has annoyed me. At the same time, though, I have gone out of my way to shield my kids from certain experiences. When James and Rosemary were around five and three, I prevented them from witnessing the slaughter of lambs in my brother's barn for fear that it would cause some sort of emotional trauma—even though our family would be enjoying the lamb meat around the dinner table the next night.

Not long ago, I remembered these early trepidations of mine thanks to an unexpected encounter with a dead cat just down the road from my brother's place. We were driving away after a family visit, and there was the cat crushed on the side of the road. My brother happens to have a pet cat that was remarkably similar to this one in size and color, so James became distressed; he was convinced that his uncle's cat was lying there dead, and that his uncle would be devastated. The cat was flattened, with its intestines frozen to the roadbed. It had been there awhile. I assured him that his uncle would have mentioned if his cat was missing, but it was no use. James insisted that we turn around and investigate. He wanted to check the cat's eye color, because his uncle's cat has "bright yellow eyes." But the cat's head was frozen and contorted in such a way that its eyes were obscured from view. James worked the cat free from the road and then he managed to twist the stiffened head and neck around until he could see what he needed to see.

"It's not him," he said.

He took the cat down the snowy berm and laid it as gently as possible on the ground where it was safe from the wheels of traffic. There was no disgust whatsoever about the admittedly grotesque condition of the animal. Instead, I noticed in him a sense of relief for his uncle's sake, tempered by a sadness for the cat. It was a simple and honest display of empathy and acceptance. I was proud of him.

From the perspective of a parent, one of the many things I appreciate about hunting is that it has given my kids this kind of pragmatic yet ethically sophisticated perspective on the animals that we live alongside and, by extension, the animals that we eat. In our home, we're fairly strict about eating meat only from animals that we caught or killed ourselves. The first meat that James ever ate, when he was nine months old, was a little piece of pre-chewed deer meat. Same for Rosemary and Matthew. To this day, one of their favorite meals is thinly sliced deer heart dusted in flour and fried in butter.

Over the years, through a discussion of our diet, I have impressed upon them a somewhat complex concept. While we do kill individual deer, we maintain a love for the idea of deer in general. That is, we have a population-based perspective. It allows exploitation of the resource while at the same time demanding reverence for it. We don't just eat deer; we love deer. We study their behavior and celebrate occasions when we see them in the wild. We advocate for the protection of their habitats. This deep connection to both animals and food enriches a human life, and it's an idea that can be applied to the relationship between people and all wild things. In her book *Braiding Sweetgrass,* Robin Wall Kimmerer invokes the idea of a "gift economy" to describe this sacred human/nature exchange; however you define it, you're certainly never going to get that level of impact by serving your kids grocery-store chicken strips.

Looking at the world through the eyes of a hunter might be the ultimate immersive natural experience. It's the purest, if not the fastest, way to fully embody our animal selves. Some anthropologists believe modern human genes still carry the predatory instincts of our ancestors, and we certainly have the physiology. A diet rich in protein and fat is believed to have led to the development of larger brains in early humans, which in turn allowed them to develop tools and more advanced weapons as well as complex languages, which made their offspring still more effective hunters, and, eventually facilitated the modern human brain capacity that creates things like freeze-dried food, carbon fiber, and cryptocurrencies. Hunting, in other words, is in our blood, and it's what made humans who we are as a species today.

There's an undeniable logic in that line of thought, but another contingent of academics and researchers believe the inclination to hunt is a learned trait, not hardwired. The truth is, it's surely a combination of nature and nurture, like everything else, but kids do seem instinctually inclined to mess around with primitive hunting tools. If you've ever watched a child pick up a stick and throw it like a spear, you'll know what I'm talking about. In fact, kids seem to universally enjoy playing with things like spears, slingshots, and stick bows even if they've never been exposed to actual hunting. You might be inclined to think of this as some passing (or enduring) human fascination with weapons of war, but in the animal world, when young brown bears play with their littermates, they're building up the muscles and coordination needed to chase down and capture moose calves and salmon. Other predators are known to bring live prey to their young so they can practice their hunting skills. Likewise, playing with slingshots and spears could be considered a valuable, less-risky prelude to the real thing.

Being that the real thing involves lethal weapons, hunting is one of the few outdoor activities (and perhaps the only one that doesn't involve operating motorized equipment) where we have legal guidelines that restrict the participation of children according to their age. If you want to take your kid down an avalanche chute on a set of skis, that's your decision. If you want to take them deer hunting on a friend's farm, you'll need to adhere to your state's legal age requirements. These age restrictions are based around the fact that the weapons used for hunting are not just dangerous to the user. They can kill other people, both up close and far away.

When I was growing up in Michigan, state law mandated that kids had to be at least twelve years old to hunt small game with a firearm or to hunt deer with archery equipment. In order to hunt deer with the powerful firearms required of that job, kids had to be fourteen. In addition, all hunters had to pass the state's hunter safety course before they were eligible to buy a hunting license at all.

Among our local hunting community, there was widespread criticism of the state's age requirements for firearm deer hunting. My father felt that it should be treated as a private issue for each family to resolve on their own. A child's mentor or guardian, he argued, was better suited than the state to know when that kid had achieved the proper level of responsibility to be trusted in the woods with a gun. As long as a kid had passed the hunter safety course, he saw no reason why they shouldn't enjoy the full set of privileges afforded to older hunters.

It turns out that my dad was ahead of his time, at least on the issue of hunting age requirements. Gradually, around the country, states have been lowering or altogether dropping their age requirements. In Michigan, a kid can now hunt at any age as long as they're accompanied by a licensed hunter in good standing who's at least twenty-one years old. Pretty much those same rules apply in states ranging from New Hampshire to Texas to Alaska. In Montana the legal age requirement is considerably lower than what I experienced growing up. Here, kids can start hunting deer with a firearm at the age of ten if they're accompanied by a licensed mentor. I support these liberalized restrictions, as I think it should be a family decision as much as possible rather than a government one. It had always been my intention to let my kids start hunting as soon as they passed the local regulatory threshold of wherever we were living at the time—as long as they demonstrated the necessary discipline. Hunting requires patience and determination, but, in my mind, discipline, which begins and ends with proper firearm handling, is the key ingredient.

Discipline, of course, can be demonstrated in a lot of different arenas. Whether and how a child applies themself to homework is a good indicator of discipline, as is their general inclination, or not, to keep a bedroom tidy. But so is seeing how your kid approaches the recipe on the back of a box of brownie mix, or surreptitiously watching them take off alone on their bike for the first time to see if they wear their helmet when they think no one is looking. A stellar performance on these lower-stakes tasks may indicate a readiness for bigger challenges and adventures, whether that's hunting or tackling that rock scramble they've been begging you to try.

Growing up among responsible hunters is one way to begin to develop the kind of maturity, focus, and toughness a person needs to have a rewarding life in the outdoors—and, by extension, anywhere at all. Because of the stakes involved in this particular pursuit, however, parents must take the utmost care to make sure that as kids are learning, they're really grasping what's going on.

James had aspired to be a hunter since he was three or four years old, and the same is now true of Rosemary. But long before I ever let them handle guns, I took great care to explain to them how firearms work. I showed them how to tell when a gun is loaded. I taught them how the safety mechanisms function. And, just in case, I taught them that it's possible for safety mechanisms to fail, and therefore you'd damn sure better treat every gun as if it were loaded—that is, pointed in a safe direction, finger away from the trigger, and zealously guarded against any untrained individuals who might want to meddle with it.

In our family, the journey to Alaska to give ten-year-old James a chance to take a shot at his first caribou had begun five years earlier, when we began practicing marksmanship and safe firearm handling with a spring-loaded Red Ryder BB gun similar to the weapon that Ralphie begs for in *A Christmas Story*. And long before he graduated to firearms, we began to talk about the responsibilities that using one in a real hunting scenario would entail.

A primary responsibility of the hunter, I have always explained to James, is to minimize the suffering of your quarry. You need to put the bullet right where you want it, and to do that you need to understand anatomy and ballistics. Together James and I covered these subjects for five or six years, a few minutes here and a few minutes there. Driving down the highway through farm and ranch country was the perfect classroom.

Me: "How about that cow? What if it was a caribou?"

James: "Aim tight behind the shoulder, half the way up the body."

Me: "How about that one?"

James: "It's facing away at a little angle, so you could aim farther back from the shoulder and the bullet would still enter the heart and lungs."

Me: "Okay, try this one."

James: "It's facing toward us, so there's no good shot."

Me: "Good job, buddy."

To drive those lessons home, I often set James up with a paper silhouette featuring squirrels or deer that he could practice on. Although BB guns and the pneumatic rifles to which he would eventually graduate lacked the power of real firearms, I encouraged James not to think of them as toys. They were fully capable of killing small animals or putting an eye out at close range and should be treated accordingly. To avoid confusion, we would handle his BB gun according to the same rules that would apply to shooting more serious weapons: treating every gun as if it were loaded; always pointing the gun in a safe direction; never pointing the gun at anything we didn't intend to destroy; keeping our finger off the trigger until we were ready to shoot; and being sure of our target and what lay beyond it.

It was only once he had proven that he could handle that BB gun with caution and respect that he'd be ready to move on to supervised target shooting, and eventually hunting, with a "real" firearm. Selecting James's first rifle required some thought. Many of the "magnum" big-game cartridges are so overpowered that their recoil, or "kick," makes them extremely unpleasant or even downright painful to shoot for novice hunters, especially children. What's more, beginners exposed to rifles that produce an excessive amount of noise and recoil will often develop an involuntary flinch that makes shooting accurately nearly impossible. Parents who are familiar with baseball can find an equivalency in a child who's struck by a ball while at bat and might need years to regain confidence and reestablish proper form and follow-through. Certain "kid-friendly" centerfire cartridges are indeed light on recoil, but they're also light on energy. They shoot underpowered, lightweight bullets that lack the oomph to cleanly kill big game animals when shot placement turns out to be less than perfect. In the end, James wound up with a Weatherby rifle chambered in 6.5 Creedmore with a stock intended for female shooters. It was sized perfectly for him.

Soon, James and I were "wingshooting," shooting at moving targets with a shotgun. Even with a shell that fires dozens of pellets, consistently hitting moving targets with a shotgun would require hand-eye coordination, muscle memory, and quick thinking. We started by using clay pigeons, discs about four inches in diameter that break apart on impact, letting the shooter know they've hit their target.

Valuable as that practice on paper targets and clay pigeons had been, shooting at an actual animal would be a very different experience for James, as it would for any novice hunter. Even if a hunter-in-training is calmly punching bull's-eyes all day long at the shooting range, a lot of nerves can build up in the moments before pulling the trigger on a live critter. A little nervous excitement is completely normal and to be expected from anyone, but some people, when in close proximity to game animals or as they're about to shoot one, suffer from an overwhelming bout of nerves and stress that can cause shaky hands, rapid breathing, and unclear thinking.

In hunting parlance, this is known as "buck fever." It mostly afflicts novices, but it can strike veteran hunters, too. Hunters experiencing extreme cases of buck fever have been known to shoot wildly at animals without even stopping to aim. Other hunters are reduced to complete inaction, forgetting to shoot at all. This is actually a much better outcome than rushing a shot without taking the time to aim. It's much better to not pull the trigger at all than it is to regret taking a shot that only wounded an animal. Usually, a novice who suffers from buck fever will get over it after a number of close encounters. But even if you're able to maintain total calm, you still need to wait for the perfect shot opportunity. The right time to pull the trigger varies greatly depending on the particular animal being hunted, the weapon being used, and the shooting abilities of the hunter. But a good rule of thumb to follow is never take a shot unless you're sure that the result will be a dead animal. If kids are pulling the trigger just hoping to hit an animal, that's not good enough. They need to be confident of a quick death. If there's any doubt, they shouldn't shoot at all.

A couple of years ago, I bought James a handful of pigeon decoys that he can set out in fields or openings near places frequented by pigeons, and we're constantly amazed by how well they work. Virtually any pigeon passing overhead will drop down to investigate the fake plastic birds, usually presenting James with a shot from his .410 shotgun. In the United States, pigeons are classified as deleterious non-native birds rather than game birds, so you don't need a hunting license to go after them and you can hunt them all year long. Because of this, pigeon hunting allows James plenty of opportunities to develop his skills with ever-increasing autonomy. He'd had some success, but also plenty of failure. Sometimes watching for pigeons is just as boring as waiting to be seen at the dentist's office. Over the past few years, I've watched him develop the skill of patience as well as a capacity to deal with disappointment.

When he is successful and comes home with a pigeon or two, it's time for him to process his kill. Despite their reputation here for being nothing more than loathsome pests that feed on garbage littering city streets, pigeons that live in rural areas are extremely good table fare. Street pigeons are actually a species of rock dove native to Europe and Asia, and in Europe, young farm-raised pigeons called squab are considered a delicacy. We've tried a handful of different preparations for these birds, but James and his siblings prefer pigeon breasts marinated in Italian dressing and then cooked over a hot grill.

Obviously, giving my preteen children access to firearms and then allowing them to consume a bird that many folks regard as little better than a flying rat puts me among a tiny minority of contemporary American parents. I don't consider this to be something that warrants an apology from me. In rural America, hunting and firearm ownership remain a strong part of the culture. In most large cities, however, things are generally much different. Urban areas tend to have a much lower concentration of hunters as well as a much lower concentration of gun owners. When we were living in Seattle, many of the neighboring parents knew that I was a hunter and assumed that we kept guns in our house. Others did not know. Rather than trying to figure out who might or might not have a problem with guns, Katie was very proactive about addressing any concerns that might later lead to conflict or discomfort. Whenever new kids came over to our house to play with our kids, she let the parents know that, yes, there were guns in the house, and yes, they were kept under lock and key.

When you have young kids living in your home or visiting, you can't go overboard on gun safety. Regardless of where you live, you need to keep guns locked away where kids have no possible chance of getting to them. Even within a gun safe or locked case, do not leave weapons loaded. You can create redundancy in your home safety system by adding childproof trigger locks to firearms and storing ammunition in a separate lockable container inside the case or safe.

As it was with my own generation, our kids are being raised in an era of criminal gun violence and senseless mass shootings. I understand that many people demonize firearms as a root cause of these catastrophes, but I discourage my kids from thinking that firearms are magical things with a will of their own. Rather, the guns that our family keeps locked in our gun safe are powerful tools that can be put to use by individuals for purposes both good and bad. We do not use them to hurt people or threaten people, though I would use them to defend my loved ones if I were forced to do so by circumstances outside of my control. Mainly, though, my kids and I discuss guns within the context of hunting, as that's the world in which they experience them. That context requires adherence to strict safety rules. Unintentional firearm fatalities in the United States have fallen by more than 47 percent in the last twenty years, thanks largely to education about safety protocols. In 2018, there were over 90 percent more choking fatalities than accidental firearm fatalities in the United States. In terms of injuries, hunting with a firearm is safer than just about every other physical activity besides billiards and pool—and even that activity is only one tenth of 1 percent safer than hunting with a firearm. You're 27 times more likely to be injured playing softball than hunting with a gun, and 149 times more likely to be injured playing tackle football. Still, every year there are widely circulated reports of tragic hunting accidents. These incidents should not be ignored. If handled improperly, guns are deadly. I do not sugarcoat this for my kids. A mistake could lead to the death of their mother, father, brother, or sister.

In the weeks leading up to our Alaska caribou hunt, we reviewed gun safety measures umpteen times, and talked a great deal about caribou anatomy and behavior. We covered the key points once more when we reached our campsite atop a geological formation known as a glacial moraine. The long flat-topped strip of gravel had been deposited thousands of years ago by a river that once flowed beneath a now extinct glacier. The surface of the moraine was as smooth as a gravel driveway and sat well above the boreal tundra that surrounded us. It was late August. The mosquitos and biting flies were still active, and would be for another week or two, but they weren't so bad up on top of the moraine because there was a consistent breeze aided by the presence of the steep mountain to the south. The slopes were covered in black shale and scattered clumps of dwarf birch and blueberry. The top of the mountain was usually obscured by clouds. In the four days that we were there, we saw the peak only two or three times, and for mere seconds. If you turned your back to the mountain and looked north, there was a streambed cutting through a broad valley as it flowed away toward a larger tributary of the Yukon River. The edges of the stream were dotted with clusters of black spruce that trickled out thinner and thinner farther away from the stream.

From almost the moment we arrived, we could see caribou crossing the stream as they traveled eastward. There were some single animals traveling alone, but mostly it was small groups ranging from a half dozen to twenty. The cows and calves were typically out in the lead, with a few bulls trailing the larger groups. Sometimes fifteen or twenty minutes might pass without any new groups coming into view. At other times you could see as many as fifty or sixty strung out in a line. We watched a black wolf that was headed westward against the flow of caribou traffic, and it reminded me of a car driving in the wrong lane.

The breeding season would be approaching soon, but so far there was no indication of it. The bulls weren't fighting among themselves or behaving aggressively to the cows. Like other members of the deer family, caribou bulls grow a new set of antlers every year. Through the spring and summer, the antlers grow beneath a fur-like coating of what we call velvet. The velvet peels away in the fall, revealing blood-red antler beneath. In a matter of weeks, the reddish color is gone and the antlers turn a lightish brown color like the crust on homemade bread. They shed their antlers in the winter, which then become valuable mineral supplements for porcupines, ground squirrels, and other mammals equipped to gnaw the bone-like structures. In bygone times, the antlers were used as weapons and tools by indigenous people. Unlike other species in the deer family, female caribou grow antlers as well—though the timing of their growth and shedding cycle is different. As it happens, we were catching the herd right when the bulls were shedding their velvet. That bright, blood-red color of the antlers stood out against the muted palette of the vegetation in an almost startling way. As the cows and calves traveled across the landscape, they disappeared and reappeared in a subtle fashion. But not the bulls. You could easily track those towering red antlers with your eyes as they bobbed westward.

I pointed all this out to James. To be a good hunter is to be a good student of nature. And to be a good hunting mentor, you need to play the role of an interpreter who can help the student understand the lessons that nature can teach.

I didn't appreciate the extent of my own father's efforts when I was James's age, but I now recognize how much work he did toward helping me become a knowledgeable and proficient hunter. It's worth noting that many people, including some of my personal friends, have become highly capable hunters all on their own, without the same multigenerational guidance that I benefited from. To that end, there are countless books, websites, and YouTube channels that can help you build up your knowledge base; my own *The Complete Guide to Hunting, Butchering, and Cooking Wild Game* is a comprehensive two-volume set.

When I was just nine or ten, I remember enduring an incredibly awkward situation when my dad challenged the father of one of my own best friends over the fact that he killed well over his limit of wood ducks and then dumped the carcasses in the woods without taking any of the meat from half of the birds. I was embarrassed at the time, but that incident made a lasting and positive impression on me about the importance of utilizing game meat to the fullest extent. Just as there are golfers who can't stop themselves from cheating and reckless drivers who can't help but break the rules of the road, there are plenty of bad hunters out there who will sacrifice safety and ethics in order to get what they think they deserve.

The laws that govern hunting put a lot of emphasis on maintaining the sustainability of our resources, and they were initially drafted in response to the terrible abuse of wildlife resources committed by past generations. For the most part, hunting regulations are similar in design and purpose to fishing regulations. But the former are even more byzantine. For instance, the area where James and I chose to hunt caribou was on federally managed public land in Alaska's Game Management Unit 20. In total, the state is divided into twenty-six GMUs, each with its own unique sets of regulations. To be more specific, we were in one of the five subunits within GMU 20 and each of those subunits has unique regulations.

A peculiar rule that governs caribou hunting in most of Alaska's GMUs is that you can't hunt on the same day that you fly in an airplane. The rule is meant to eliminate the advantage of spotting a particular animal from the air and then landing a bush plane nearby to kill it. So on our first evening at camp, James and Martin's boys were legally prohibited from pursuing a caribou with the intent to kill it. I was happy about this, because I wanted my son to continue to experience the flow of migrating caribou without being distracted by the thought that he should run down there and try to get one. I had hunted in this particular region before, and along the migration paths of other caribou herds, so I knew that we might encounter an embarrassment of riches. This had troubled me, actually. As much as I wanted to show James the spectacular abundance of the resource, I was afraid of spoiling him with an adventure that not even most grown-ups will be lucky enough to experience in their lifetimes.

One of the beauties of hunting and fishing is that they force kids to reckon with failure and to struggle against their own impatience. I look for ways to accentuate those facets of their experience. On a recent snowy day, I tried to explain to my kids why ice fishing was better than sledding—an argument that they felt was absurd. In defense of my position, I pointed out that we already know that gravity works, so there's no suspense in sledding. But we don't know if this fish will bite, and that unknowingness is what makes it so fun. If you want to experience success at hunting or fishing, there's often little recourse other than to shut up and keep waiting. No amount of nagging or fidgeting is going to make the turkeys walk out in front of you.

I have put my kids through all kinds of torture sitting in a boat or on a frozen lake or out in the woods when absolutely nothing is happening. No bites. No sightings. Just cold hands, cold feet, and tears. They'll all register some complaints and demand to know what we packed for snacks, but beyond that they have wildly different ways of battling the boredom and discomfort. Rosemary will usually stay true to the notion that we're out there with a goal of collecting something. So when she gets bored with trying to collect what we're after, she'll switch over to interesting rocks or wildflowers or whatever else. On a recent ice fishing trip, she set herself to wandering through the frozen cattails surrounding the lake in order to count the abandoned nests of red-winged blackbirds. A rainy day spent stuck in a tent will find us digging out books and sometimes iPads, but a case of boredom that strikes in the outdoors is often remedied, ultimately, by the kids' own natural curiosity about their surroundings.

James has a tendency to stay committed to what we're doing for a surprisingly long time; he'll just want to do it differently. If we're walking to the north, he'll want to go south. If we're hunting ducks along a creek, he'll want to hunt by the pond instead. As the youngest, Matthew is far more likely to follow the lead of his siblings than his father. Whether he sticks to the task at hand or wanders off on another pursuit depends entirely on whether he happens to be shadowing his brother or his sister at that particular moment.

I try not to get too upset by their lack of focus, because I know that they're building up valuable mental muscles as they learn how to manage boredom without giving up or turning to external distractions like devices. What's more, these long stretches of time without the glory of immediate success reinforce the concept that cool things happen to people who stick with a pursuit even when it's uncomfortable or deadly boring.

Ultimately, I know that all I can reasonably ask of my kids is that we defeat their impulses to pack up and go home until there's a clear, legitimate reason to do so. Not always, but often enough to matter, our perseverance is rewarded by a surprise of success that is born of a three-way collision between patience, skill, and luck. To be clear, it's not that success itself catches us by surprise; rather, it's the timing that surprises us. Think of it like a rainbow. We've all seen them, we know they exist, and we know that they will continue to exist in the future. But still, we're damn happy and surprised by every one that we witness.

Even with the caribou streaming through the countryside in front of us, I tried to impress upon James that there were still plenty of things that could go wrong. For instance, I said, we could wake up in the morning to find that the herd had changed course. I'd seen it happen before, I told him. One minute you're overrun with caribou, and the next minute you go days without seeing one.

I wasn't fibbing, and it had the desired effect. In fact, it might have worked a bit too well. He suffered an anxious night lying next to me in the tent, made all the worse by the fact that it never really gets dark at that latitude in late August. He asked again and again if he could go out and peer through the half darkness to make sure the animals were still coming. I told him to get some sleep because we had a long day ahead of us. At those latitudes, it gets light outside absurdly early in the morning. At dawn, I gently laid a shirt over James's eyes in hopes that he'd keep snoozing. I didn't wake him up until I figured that he'd logged a good eight hours of uninterrupted sleep. When he did wake up, he hurriedly pulled on his rubber knee boots over his sockless feet and ran across the moraine to where he could see out across the tundra. When he came running back to the tent, he was excited and smiling. "They're still coming," he said. There would be plenty of other days when a child's breathless excitement would give way to crushing disappointment. But that morning wasn't one of them.

The five of us ate a quick breakfast in our cooking tent and slugged back some coffee and hot chocolate. We then went over and sat down on the edge of the moraine, where we had a good view of the surrounding landscape. We sat quietly for a half hour as we studied the movements of the herd. The animals were appearing in sporadic pulses from over the horizon and traveling along two general paths. One line of travel was more than a mile away along the edge of some distant ponds. The other was maybe half that distance. Martin volunteered to take his boys out near the far-off ponds so that we'd have a safe distance between us in the event that one of us fired a shot. James and I would try to intercept the closer line of caribou. We picked out a recognizable clump of spruce trees that would put us right in the action.

We slung on our packs, grabbed the rifle, and dropped off the moraine. The world seemed to shrink dramatically after we lost our van-tage point and started trudging across the low-lying ground. We could no longer see over the scattered spruce trees but instead had to look through them. The ground was wet and boggy and carpeted in clumps of vegetation called tussocks. I was able to step over or around the tussocks, but in places they rose up to James's knees and he had to basically crawl through them. I felt that he was exaggerating the ex-tent to which the tussocks were slowing him down, and I told him to hustle. He told me that my legs are longer and I didn't understand what it was like. The breeze was greatly diminished down here, too. The mosquitos and biting flies crowded to our faces and started to bite our ears and eyelids. I cursed the bugs to James, but deep down I was secretly glad about it. I wanted my kid to have this chance at being annoyed and challenged.

In the weeks leading up to our trip, I had told James that under no circumstances would he be taking a shot farther than one hundred yards. With his limited experience, there's just too much risk of an improperly placed shot that could result in a wounded animal run-ning off over the ridgeline. James had willingly accepted, but now that we were so close to the caribou, he rankled at the limitation. Behind us, a band of bulls crossed our path, just a little beyond our agreed-upon shooting distance. James was eager to attempt a shot and he whispered that he could make it, no problem. I whispered back a firm no. I told him we should keep going and get properly set up by the spruce trees we had picked out after breakfast. We swatted the bugs away as best as we could and pushed on.

Soon we hit a series of caribou trails. The annual passage of the animals had worn deep grooves into the land, down through the moss and lichens and into the dirt and the rock. Some of the trails were so faint and narrow that you'd have to place your feet in an unnaturally straight line in order to walk along them. Others were as wide as a car seat. All of them ran in the same general direction, though crossing and joining and splitting apart again in seemingly random fashion. There were piles of caribou droppings along the trails. They were greasy and smooth and still looked wet. I gave James a thumbs-up and patted his back. The clump of trees that we had been aiming for was right there. The caribou trails split around the clump like water flowing around a rock in a river. We dropped our packs and got the rifle ready. I knew we wouldn't have to wait long before we'd have a shot at a caribou.

I positioned James so that he was sitting right between my legs, his rifle resting on a V-shaped shooting support mounted on top of the same tripod that we use with our spotting scope. We fidgeted around too much as we tried to get in a comfortable position where he'd be ready to shoot when the moment presented itself. The first band of caribou picked up on our movement and spotted us before we spotted them. We were waiting for a bull, but these were all cows and calves. The caribou in this area—as in most areas where they're found—have very limited exposure to humans. It's probable that we were the first people these caribou had ever seen. Yet they still regarded us with suspicion. In this area, caribou are preyed upon by a host of things, including black bears, grizzlies, wolves, and wolverines. They know to keep their distance from anything unusual. And they know to cluster up when confronted by a predator. There is strength in numbers; it's the stragglers who get picked off. The group passed quickly, balled up and leering at us from the corners of their eyes.

"You can't get a clean shot when they're grouped up like that," I told James. "You risk hitting two of them. It's better when they aren't spooked so they stay strung out."

James and I repositioned slightly, and I showed him how I try to melt myself into the ground in order to hide from animals. "Imagine you're a rotting log," I told him. "Move your eyes but not your head. Relax your arms. Your legs and feet shouldn't move."

"What if I fall asleep?" he said.

"I don't think you need to worry about that," I replied.

The next group was also only cows and calves. They passed by just forty yards on our upwind side and never smelled or saw us. "Excellent," I told James. "That's how we'll do this."

Two or three more groups passed us by with a few bulls among them. One of the bulls was moving too quickly and never paused long enough for a shot. Another bull had several cows traveling alongside it and I told James to hold off. Again, I told him, "You'll hit two of them."

We heard a distant shot from the direction that Martin and his boys were hunting. "Sounds like they're seeing some too," James said.

"Let's just hope they keep coming," I replied.

Indeed, the caribou kept trickling through. The bull that James ended up shooting was traveling with a pair of smaller bulls. They were coming directly at us, and got to within fifty yards before they sensed our presence. When they did, the two smaller bulls veered to their right and stopped. The larger bull swung around and ran twenty yards away from us before turning broadside. I whispered to James, "Right behind the shoulder." The bull jumped at the crack of the rifle and made a few steps in the opposite direction before it stopped, staggered, and tipped over. Its legs kicked three or four times and then it lay dead still.

As we approached James's downed bull, I told him to keep his rifle ready in case the caribou got up and tried to take off. Its body had settled down in between the tussocks, so the only things sticking up were the velvet-coated antlers. Once we got close enough, we could see that it was hit through both lungs. Its muzzle was red with blood. I had pounded the concept of "meat loss" into James's head a thousand times, so he was eager to hear that his bullet hadn't damaged too much of the meat. "Perfect shot," I told him. "No damage to the loins, no damage to the shoulders. Really, I don't think anything's messed up except a little of the rib meat. And there's not too much there, anyway."

By now the day had warmed up. There was little wind and the humidity was high. The biting flies and mosquitos were heinous. The warmth of the caribou's carcass seemed to especially draw them in. Shortly after I started field dressing and butchering the bull, my knuckles were so swelled up from bites that it was hard to make a fist. I told James to keep his gloves on, but he refused. If I was getting stung, he said, he should, too. We compromised by having him apply some DEET to the back of his hands. I felt that familiar ping of guilt about putting such a potent chemical on his perfect skin, but it wasn't as bad as having him suffer swollen and itchy hands and then spend the next few nights scratching the bites until they were bloody and infected. Once we started removing the legs from the carcass we were also joined by scores of yellowjackets, or "meat bees," drawn to the smell of blood and flesh. They wouldn't mess with us if we didn't mess with them, but a misplaced hand that came into contact with a bee would lead to a painful zap and an itchy welt.

A mature caribou bull like the one James had shot weighs about four hundred pounds. The yield in boneless meat is probably around 40 percent of the animal's live weight. We were salvaging the head as well, plus the heart, a portion of the liver, some stock bones, and a few pounds of the fat that we could render into oil in order to fry some of the meat for our next couple of meals in camp. All told, the caribou yielded a much bigger pile of usable materials than we'd be able to haul back to camp in a single trip. James was carrying his own small backpack, so we loaded it up with a caribou loin that was wrapped in a protective covering known as a game bag. On top of this loin we piled all of the gear and clothes from my backpack so I could refill it with meat. I put about a hundred pounds' worth in my pack, including a sack of fat that we could render into lard for cooking. We'd have to come back for the rest. If a grizzly was drawn to the carcass, it would focus its immediate attention on the soft tissue of the gut pile. To play it safe, I carried the remaining meat and the head about a hundred yards away from the guts and laid it out in the open, where I could see it from a long way off. When hunting in grizzly country, approaching an animal carcass is probably the riskiest thing you can do. When I returned for the meat, I'd want it in a place where I could easily determine whether or not a bear was nearby, so that I didn't stumble into trouble.

We hoisted our backpacks and started trudging back. The excitement of the day had pretty much wiped James out. His sense of accomplishment and triumph began to fade as he struggled mightily to get over and through the tussocks with his heavy backpack. At one point, he sat down and said he couldn't walk anymore. I told him to get up and keep moving. He did, but slowly. We didn't have even a mile to go and we were making very poor time, and the bugs were traveling right along with us. I got impatient with him for not being tough enough about the hiking. I told him that if he wants to hunt, he'd better be as willing to walk as he is to shoot. He started to cry and I felt like a horrible dad. I sat next to him and apologized. We took our packs off and he leaned on me and had a short rest while I fanned the bugs away from his head. I hugged him close. We made a pledge to keep walking at a nice, slow pace. We picked a few handfuls of blueberries and ate those. He then put his backpack on and started toward camp. He fell a few times while we were crossing some boggy ground, and his boots filled up with water and his pants were soaked. But he held to his pledge and kept moving along.

About halfway back our paths crossed an old caribou trail that was more or less headed in the direction we were going. We followed it because it was easy walking. In some mud I noticed a fresh grizzly track that couldn't have been more than a day or two old. We eventually climbed the wall of the moraine and got back up into the breeze of the higher ground. The bugs weren't nearly as bad. We approached the tents slowly and carefully so we didn't surprise any bears that might have been drawn in by the odor of our food. Everything was just as we left it, but now it started to rain. We hauled the meat over to a point on the moraine that was about 150 yards from our camp but still visible from the tents. I showed James how to string a tarp shelter using a length of paracord tied to a spruce tree for support. We pulled out two tenderloins for the night's dinner, plus the sack of caribou fat so that we could fry the meat in lard over our camp stove. We cached the remainder of the meat beneath the tarp to keep it dry. Then we went to our tent and got James into some dry clothes and his other pair of boots.

Martin and his boys were still out somewhere, probably butchering a caribou of their own. I was anxious to go back and fetch the other half of James's caribou before a bear found it, but I couldn't decide what to do about James. I didn't want to leave him behind all alone, but I didn't want him to get wet all over again, either. He'd already had a pretty long day. The only logical fear of mine was that an aggressive grizzly would come into camp and I wouldn't be there to help him. From atop the moraine, I could see out to where we'd left the rest of the caribou. With my binoculars, I could actually see the meat lying there. To the left, I could see the butchered carcass and the gut pile. The chances were way better that a bear would show up down there than it would up here.

I turned to James and explained a couple of things to him. "It's the fall season," I said. "The bears are in what's called a hyperphagic state, roaming all over and eating everything they can to get fattened up for hibernation." I explained to him that if a grizzly caught wind of the caribou meat we'd carried up to the moraine, it'd probably come in to have a look. I told him that losing the meat was not my main concern. "We worked hard for it," I said, "and it's very valuable to us, but it's not anywhere near as important to me as your safety." So if a bear came toward him and he couldn't scare it away by yelling at it and waving his arms, then he should be prepared to shoot it. I pointed out a couple of trees and told him that if he saw a bear that close to camp, he would need to be concerned. I told him that I was going to jog down as fast as I could, get the meat, and walk back. As I prepared to leave camp, I could see that James was totally cool with the plan. He had zero concerns or worries. If anything, he seemed pleased with the scenario. He was in charge, and he seemed perfectly at home. In that moment, it was easy to imagine him doing okay in this world. For a parent, that's a good feeling to have.

CHAPTER 7

# HOME

In case you're thinking that a caribou hunt in Alaska seems about as likely to happen as a trip to the moon, let's bring things a little closer to home for a moment and talk about pets. Currently in our house we have five of them: two frogs, one dog, and two leopard geckos. The leopard geckos are the senior members of our pet lineup; besides a couple of short-lived pet store fish, they were the first "real" pets that our kids got. When we bought the first one, the guy at the pet store explained that it's hard to sex geckos when they're young, meaning that it's hard to tell males from females. However, something about the gecko's coloration and demeanor struck the kids as decidedly male, so they named him Buddy. We didn't have Buddy more than a month or two before the kids became worried about him being lonely inside his aquarium. So they began to save up money and purchased him a companion. This gecko's slender head and more graceful coloration led the kids to think it must be a female, so they named her Sapphire. It was about a year later when they actually figured out how to sex their geckos, using an online video. Currently, the dominant opinion is that we originally had it all wrong. Buddy is, in fact, a girl. Sapphire is a boy. I asked them if we ought to change their names around, and they acted as though that was the dumbest idea they ever heard. Now, when the kids are showing their geckos to visitors, I'll often hear them explain that "he's actually a girl," and "she's actually a boy."

In the warm months of summer and fall, when our yard and the surrounding areas are rich with invertebrate life, the kids typically keep the geckos supplied with a diet of earthworms, grasshoppers, and various moths that they collect from our vegetable garden or catch inside the house when they come in through open windows. Two summers ago, they fed the geckos dozens of those beetle larvae that they'd found beneath cow pies in a pasture that happened to be located next door to a place where we arranged to have our family portrait taken. In the winter, when all of the wild gecko food is sheltered beneath the frozen ground and a blanket of snow, the kids buy various mealworms and waxworms to feed them. Coincidentally, these are the same worms (insect larvae, actually) that I use for ice fishing bait. Larvae that I purchase from the bait store will often become gecko food, and gecko food purchased from the pet store will often become fishing bait. Whatever its intended use, we store the larvae in our kitchen refrigerator, inside clear plastic bottles. The low temperature of the fridge keeps the larvae from pupating, which, when it happens, pretty much ruins their utility as both food and bait. The clearness of the bottle lets you check to see how they're doing.

The only type of wintertime gecko food that we don't store in the fridge is the crickets that the kids occasionally buy from the pet store. The crickets are typically sold in bulk inside plastic bags, the same bags used by pet stores when they send a goldfish home inside a sack of water. Dozens of the insects will be packed inside a bag. They need to be kept warm, so the kids keep them right next to the aquarium where they can bask in the glow of the warming lamp that keeps the aquarium nice and balmy. The heat of the lamp seems to supercharge the crickets. At feeding time, when the kids are attempting to transfer crickets from the open bag to the aquarium, there are often escape events. Some of these escape events have involved several dozen crickets getting away all at once and dispersing around the house. It's not atypical in our home to hear crickets chirping away from beneath the furniture or inside the walls. One time, an escaped cricket got inside our shower and chirped incessantly for days. It made enough noise to wake us up at night, but the insect had a finely tuned survival instinct and foiled our efforts at remedying the issue. As soon as you opened the shower door to try to find it, the cricket would shut up. It would then stay silent for an hour or so, until it could sense that the danger had passed. Then, once again, it would fire up the chirping and go nonstop for hours at a time. Eventually, through a process of elimination, I was able to deduce that the cricket was actually living down inside the shower drain. This seemed nearly impossible. How could it withstand a shower's worth of water draining through its new home without becoming dislodged and washing away?

As annoying as that cricket was, I had come to enjoy its presence by the time it fell silent a week or so later. What I appreciated about the insect, I realized, is that it embodied the natural world inside our home in a way that could not be ignored. This notion, bringing nature inside, had always been a priority for me as a parent—though admittedly things have gone a bit overboard now and then. (I'm thinking of the Brooklyn apartment where we awoke to find the cannibalized rat on our kitchen counter.) Even for the most dedicated outdoor families, home is where our kids will ultimately spend the bulk of their time. There will always be homework, rainy days, professional obligations, and the simple need to relax and unwind in the comfort of home. In deference to this reality, I have long strived to incorporate a collection of objects and activities into our home life that would serve as reminders of our relationship to the natural world.

Take mealtimes. Hectic work and school schedules mean that dinnertime is often the first opportunity of the day for me to have any sort of real conversation with my kids. Naturally, these conversations usually start out with how everyone's day went and what's going on tomorrow. But the food we're cooking and eating is a reliable way to eventually turn our attention to the outdoors. Other than the occasional pizza night or birthday party, dinners at our home always showcase ingredients that we've sourced for ourselves through hunting, fishing, gardening, or foraging. Acknowledging these ingredients by bringing them into the conversation is a routine that we can all participate in. The conversation will often drift from there in unexpected but welcome directions. We might end up discussing the ants that are raiding our strawberry patch or the minnows that we used for fishing bait at Grandma's house.

You don't need to belong to a family of hard-core hunters or anglers in order for this to happen. Even if you source only a small portion of what you eat from the surrounding landscape, you can cultivate a more intimate connection to the places where that food was raised. Last Thanksgiving, we secured a turkey from a friend who had raised twelve of them on a small farm near our home. We were able to visit the farm and feed the birds, and eventually even dispatch one ourselves with a .22 rifle. We then brought the thing home, feathers and all, and heated a tub of water in order to dunk the bird (scalding hot water loosens the follicles) before plucking it in our yard. My kids will never think of a Thanksgiving holiday meal the same way again.

When children see an ingredient's journey from the field or farm all the way to the table, they enjoy a sense of ownership over their food that is otherwise hard to achieve. James has learned to fry the squirrels and rabbits that he gets with his air rifle. He proudly declares that his own homemade squirrel dishes are his favorite food. Rather than taking this as a condemnation of my own cooking, I'm excited to see this blossoming of self-reliance and pride. You can get a similar impact on a smaller scale just by helping your kids cook with some herbs that they grew on your porch. Even some food that is purchased from a local farmer's market or vegetable stand can get your kids talking about life outside the immediate confines of your home. Go out and buy some locally produced potatoes. Get the spuds when they're as dirty as possible. Help your kids with the job of scrubbing, peeling, shredding, and frying them up as homemade hash browns. Follow that up next week with a bag of the mass-produced frozen variety from the grocery store. Use the contrast between these two experiences as a way of discussing our industrialized agricultural systems in a way that goes deeper than simply condemning corporate agriculture. Our children will inherit a global responsibility to feed more than seven billion human beings, many of whom live far away from productive lands. Ignoring the subjects of industrial agriculture and prepackaged foods in our conversations with our kids is both naïve and shortsighted.

The biggest argument against getting kids involved in the kitchen is that things are faster, easier, and cleaner when they're not around. That's just the honest truth, at least until they reach the age of ten or so and can handle certain tasks safely without direct supervision. Oftentimes, you just need to get into the kitchen in a hurry and put food on the table with the least amount of hassle possible. I get that. I'm as guilty as anyone of letting my kids watch a show on TV while Katie and I struggle to prepare dinner so that we can get everyone to bed at a reasonable hour.

When weeknight schedules are tight, we tend to plan out some food preservation projects that can happen over holidays or weekends. The techniques used to put up food can impart beautiful lessons from the natural world. In northern regions, beavers will stockpile willow branches in deep water, where they can still be accessed beneath the winter ice. In the mountains, the rabbit-like pika will dry and cure grasses to be stored through the winter. You can mimic these behaviors in your own way and produce foods that can be enjoyed again and again over the coming months. Dried meat, or jerky, is probably the oldest "recipe" on the planet. Kids generally love it, especially sweeter varieties flavored with honey, brown sugar, or teriyaki sauce. You can make it using wild game or domestic meat from the grocery store, and there's no requirement for sophisticated equipment. When we lived in New York, I made batches of jerky using nothing more than the oven in our apartment with a crushed beer can holding the door open a crack so that the moist air could escape. We do some vegetarian food preservation projects as well. A jar of jam made from summer berries or some homemade canned spaghetti sauce from garden tomatoes will give you two chances to explore the wonders of nature. The first time is when you make it. The second time comes months later, when you eat it.

When people come into my home for the first time, it usually takes less than a minute for them to comment on the array of antlers and bones that we have displayed on a shelving system that occupies an entire wall of our living room. Some of the stuff is quite old, including a fossilized hunk of deer antler, a mammoth molar, and several bones and partial skulls from the bison that roamed our local ecosystem a couple of hundred years ago. We also have a lot of newer things, including turtle shells that the kids found, a coyote-gnawed skull of a young antelope fawn, and an elk vertebrae that I found in the mountains of Idaho bearing a stainless steel arrowhead that the bone had healed around—a vivid reminder of the astonishing tenacity of the species. My kids can do an impressive job of walking visitors through the collection and handling some of the questions that inevitably arise.

Mostly, though, our wall collection contains the horns and antlers of animals that we've hunted over the years. Many folks would refer to these specimens as "trophies," a term that isn't entirely incorrect even though it has a seriously negative connotation in certain circles. When people hear the word "trophy" they often imagine animal parts belonging to a creature that was killed for no other purpose than to display it on a wall in a boastful fashion. I see the practice of displaying these trophies in a completely different light. The specimens are informative from a biological perspective, beautiful by artistic standards, and of deep significance to me on a spiritual level. Beginning as far back as fifty thousand years ago, humans honored the animals that they hunted by painting them on cave walls, carving their images into weapons, jewelry, and tools, and decorating their homes with bits of hide, bone, and horn. I continue this tradition in my own way, by giving the animals a prominent place of display at the center of my home. By doing so, I not only remember and acknowledge the animals' lives, I also demonstrate to my kids the importance of maintaining this honorific attitude toward the living products of the earth that we utilize for our own benefit. You might think of this practice as a celebration of both our food and our past experiences. These totems are physical reminders of the places where those animals lived, the friends and family members we were with when we hunted, and little details about the hunt that might otherwise be forgotten: the iridescence of a turkey's feathers glinting in the sun, or the taste and smell of a piece of mule deer meat charred over juniper coals during a snowstorm.

I recognize that many people who read this book will never go hunting, and even fewer are going to go so far as to decorate their living room with animal parts. But for me, the practice exemplifies an approach to indoor life that I do wholeheartedly recommend: using your home as a way to showcase and celebrate the elements of nature that are inspiring to you on a personal level. Some of the very items that I mention in this book—the hunk of ochre that tinted Matthew's skin yellow during our first overnight camping trip as a family, clamshells and crab claws found while flipping rocks at the Fish Shack— have all enjoyed periods of prominent display in our house. My kids love to bring these things home, and I fully encourage it, even when it gets a little weird. I'm thinking of a yellow warbler that my kids found on a New York City sidewalk that lived on our counter for a couple of days. They later wanted to give a similar treatment to a Norway rat in Seattle, but Katie and I nixed that idea.

Such behaviors from my kids are testament to the fact that my lessons might be rubbing off on them. They seem to accept the idea that the boundary between nature and home is porous and perhaps irrelevant, and that experiences in the home can be flavored and enriched by experiences in nature. My kids' artwork has proven to be another, pleasantly surprising way in which I've been able to follow along as their relationships with the natural world evolve. A lot of their creations are brought home from school, arriving on our kitchen countertop as a messy jumble of glued-together papers and cardboard that the kids are more than happy to interpret for us. The kids also produce a lot of art here at home. In our coat closet, we have two small "art carts." These moveable art stations are loaded down with a hodgepodge of markers, watercolor paints, colored pencils, fabric scraps, craft glue, recycled bits of packaging paper, beads, popsicle sticks, and other items. The carts saw a lot of action during the height of the pandemic, when the kids were cooped up inside for weeks on end. But even during normal times it's not uncommon for them to get out the carts without any kind of prodding from grown-ups.

They produce the usual streams of kiddie drawings, such as unicorns, monster trucks, aliens, crazed cats, and chaotic battle scenes featuring futuristic weaponry. Mixed in with the stuff, though, is a surprising amount of material that ties in directly to recent experiences in the outdoors. Rosemary has produced drawings about planting pole beans. Matthew has made drawings about setting up camp. James does a lot of drawings about our fishing adventures. When looking at these sketches and collages that are born of their experiences in nature, there are two things that stand out to me. First is the attention to procedure. They are eager to capture the steps involved in doing something, or at least account for the constituent parts. Rosemary's garden drawings are likely to include everything from planting to harvesting. Matthew's camp drawings will usually show the placement of the tents and the campfire relative to some body of water. The second notable thing is how much emphasis they place on capturing the people who were present during an experience. A garden image from Rosemary might show her, me, and Matthew, all performing some role or standing together alongside a collection of plants. One of James's fishing drawings might show him and his uncle, along with his uncle's dog, all smiling.

The kids' allegiance to process and partners in their nature drawings helps me understand what components of an experience stand out in their memory. In the actual moment, a particular experience might be marked by cold fingers and squabbling over who ate all of the Cheez-Its. Later, though, when they reproduce those experiences as artworks, they seem eager to convey their understanding of how the tasks were accomplished as well as an appreciation for the people who were there. As a parent, I find a lot of inspiration in these pieces of artwork. Not only do they encourage me to continue facilitating experiences that will inspire them, but they help guide how I plan those experiences. Understanding what, exactly, stands out to them helps me ensure that I'll deliver more of that in the future. To me, it's clear that they value the presence of loved ones and they have an innate desire to learn.

If you imagine your children's artwork as a way for your kids to speak to the world, you can think of books as a way for the world to speak back to them. We keep a fairly well-rounded collection of children's books in our home, on subjects ranging from manners to puberty to geography. But I have always placed a strong emphasis on books about nature, and these have generally been very well accepted by my kids. In my estimation, the most important book that we own is *Bird Songs Bible,* which Katie purchased for me as a birthday present the year that James was born. It's a large-format coffee-table book with detailed paintings of birds and information on habits and range. It has a built-in speaker and audio library containing hundreds of bird songs that can be called up by number. Over the years, the kids have spent countless hours playing these bird songs, and the book has helped spark in them an honest interest in learning to identify birds by their vocalizations.

We keep a handful of other bird books around the house and make a point of trying to identify every bird species that we either see or hear from our home and yard. I can't overstate how effective this has been in training our kids to take notice of the other life-forms around them. Kids naturally love to quantify and count, and they take a lot of pride in those moments when we're able to open up our list and add a new species. We keep a small bird feeder outside of our window, hung in such a way that it minimizes the chances for stray house cats and avian predators to munch on the birds that are drawn to this admittedly unnatural food source. The feeder allows us many opportunities to study, up close, the coloration and other physical characteristics of the birds that come to visit. The bird books help us to contextualize what we're seeing by placing the particular birds outside of the window within the broader framework of their species' migratory range and family tree. It's my hope that devoting this level of attention to distinguishing bird species will foster in my kids an appreciation for the biodiversity of their home habitat. Rather than just seeing "birds," they are learning to see a community of species that interact with one another and compete for the shared resources that surround us.

When we moved into our current home, my kids' love for the neighborhood birds resulted in a bit of family drama that exemplifies the sort of behaviors that come from a close relationship with nature. The home has an outside patio that is roofed over. The east and west ends of the patio are formed by a fireplace and the house, respectively. The north side of the patio is a large glass wall; the south side is open to the elements. We didn't live in the house for long before discovering that this three-sided structure was a death trap for birds. They'd enter the space through the open-air side and then crash into the glass wall. The carnage was especially horrific during the spring and fall migrations, when we logged as many as seven bird deaths in a single week. Amid everything else going on, I was slow to address this issue and instead wasted my time blaming the architect of the home as well as past owners for not figuring out a solution. The kids, though, were completely disinterested in assigning blame to other people. They demanded that we take action, and that we do it right now.

Together, we researched and attempted various bird deterrents, such as strands of Christmas tinsel and blank CDs hung from monofilament fishing line, but nothing was entirely effective at protecting the birds. The most promising solution that we learned about was a specialized window film developed by ornithologists. Buying and installing the film struck me as absurdly expensive. Katie and I might still be procrastinating about the purchase had it not been for our kids acting as our conscience (a very annoying and persistent conscience, I might add). They succeeded in getting us to do what was right, despite the financial hit, and I have to give them credit. Not only did the bird strikes end immediately, but the moment that we solved the problem was the first moment that I was able to truly feel good about that house. For that, I owe my kids a debt of gratitude.

Clearly, my kids cared about those birds. In nurturing their innate empathy for their fellow creatures, I try to balance fanciful stories of human-like, talking animals with books and shows that provide more realistic and educational material about wildlife. An all-time favorite book of ours is an out-of-print children's book from 1963 called *Possum* by Robert M. McClung. It tells the story of a litter of nine opossums from birth to sexual maturity. The book includes a lot of predation. On the first page, the mother opossum eats a moth while her litter of offspring is still riding inside her marsupial pouch. She then goes on to eat snails, beetle grubs, a snake, and the four green eggs of a catbird that she spooks out of its nest. Once the young opossums are weaned, they feed on turtle eggs, black snake eggs, and a family of newborn mice. In turn, various littermates are killed off. A fox kills one; a great horned owl carries away another. A third is killed by a rattlesnake, a fourth by a car, and a fifth by a snapping turtle. Eventually, a nameless female opossum grows to sexual maturity and breeds with a male during a single courtship encounter that lasts only one night. She gives birth to fifteen babies. The thirteen babies that are able to crawl to their mother's pouch have to compete for placement on her eleven nipples. The two losing babies starve to death. The book sounds brutal, and in some ways it is, but I don't see any reasonable argument against sharing these materials with my kids. I might shield them from a book about road-killed baby opossums, but as long as they're able to look out the window of a car there's no way to shield them from seeing the real thing.

There's an immediate value in teaching your kids about local bird species and widely distributed animals such as opossums, because it

gives them an avenue into understanding their immediate surroundings. It informs the encounters that they're likely to have as they look
out the window, walk in the park, or go on a weekend camping trip.
But books can also inspire kids to consider aspects of nature that are
far removed in terms of space and time. Gradually, they can begin to
open kids to the magic and unfathomable beauty that awaits them out
there. From the school library, we have checked out dozens of titles
relating to the natural world. Books about weather, dinosaurs, ice
age mammals, oceans, volcanoes, whales, jellyfish, and animal poop
(a family favorite). Together, we marvel at what we find. I've spent
many nights lying in bed with my kids as I try to read books to them
from start to finish, only to have them insist that we flip ahead to
some image or another that had caught their eye when they first
opened the book. An all-time favorite of theirs, particularly for Matthew, has been a painting in one of our many books about dinosaurs
that features a forty-five-foot-long marine reptile from the dinosaur
era called a pliosaurus. The creature is fixing to chomp down on an
aquatic reptile called an ichthyosaur that resembles a modern dolphin
and, like dolphins, breathed air. Looking at this picture, Matthew
likes to ponder what would have happened during an encounter between an ichthyosaur and a megalodon, a relic shark species that was
perhaps five times as long as a modern great white shark and twenty-
five times heavier. It's a great question.

The illustration forces you to ponder the deep past of our planet,
the hundreds of millions of years' worth of dream-like creatures that
haunted the landscape and waters that would one day become our
home. When we look at such images, I notice how my kids sometimes
fall into a moment of melancholy as they consider the gargantuan
wonders of the world that they missed by being born today and not in
the distant, pre-human past. I counter this nostalgia by showing them
an illustration that compares a modern blue whale with a human. The
whale is as long as seventeen people laid out head to toe. A mature

specimen can weigh more than three hundred thousand pounds, or the equivalent of maybe five big megalodons. A blue whale's arteries are large enough that you could swim through them.

Looking at the pictures of the blue whale, there's a singular point that I like to emphasize. "Those are alive *right now*," I always say. "The biggest animal to ever exist on earth is still with us, out there now. Someday, if you play your cards right, you'll be able to see one." That golden piece of information usually snaps them back into the joy of the present day.

A thing that I appreciate about kids is that their imaginations are so much more quick and nimble than those of us grown-ups. They are capable of a sort of time travel. Exposed to the right stimuli in the home, they can bounce instantly back and forth between the past and the future without any perceived confusion about where they actually sit at the moment. They can also move from the real to the fantastic without any sort of mental whiplash. Time frames that feel impossibly distant to us might strike our kids as being barely out of reach. It's dinosaurs one moment, intergalactic space travel the next. I think that we parents should use any and all resources at our disposal—books, movies, YouTube, cartoons, the list of prompts at the beginning of this book—in order to continue inspiring and educating these adept voyagers that we're lucky to share our homes with. I believe that the surest path to an appreciation for whatever the world will become is an appreciation for what the world is, and has been.

If there's a limit to the time-traveling capabilities of young kids, it's that they have such a hard time imagining a future in which their parents are gone. Flying cars are regarded as being well within reach to my kids, but they're unable to imagine that Katie and I will someday die. Recently, Matthew estimated that I'd live for at least another two hundred years. I felt a lump in my throat as I gave him a more accurate estimate. From the parents' perspective, the reality of our passing is painfully real and close. So much so that we can't help but brood over ideas about their future, a future in which we won't necessarily be present to hold their hands.

Recently, a colleague of mine emailed me about a lecture she'd attended by an academic and educator named Chris Emdin. He talked about an evolutionary theory called punctuated equilibrium. The theory counters the popular notion that the evolution of species occurs gradually and smoothly—a concept known as phyletic gradualism. Instead, the theory of punctuated equilibrium argues that evolution occurs when long periods of stasis, with little or no change, are punctuated by rare bursts of rapid change brought on by cataclysmic events.

Metaphorically speaking, Emdin pointed out that youngsters are living through—even embodying—such a moment of rapid change right now. Culturally, socially, and sexually, many of our norms are being upended and discarded. From your own experiences as a parent or citizen, I'm sure you can think of examples to support what Emdin was getting at. In the last decade or so, we've experienced profound shifts in societal attitudes toward same-sex marriage, gender fluidity, marijuana, bipartisanship, national identity, and patriotism. You might feel frightened or exhilarated by these changes, depending on your particular generation and worldview, but our kids have no context in which to compare the "now" and the "then." For them, there is no baseline data. Rapid change isn't new. It's normal. And the changes around us are not just societal. With our seemingly infinite power and capability, we humans have ushered in an entirely new geologic epoch. The termination of the last ice age marked the end of the Pleistocene and the beginning of the Holocene. As it turns out, the Holocene was remarkably short-lived. We have now entered the Anthropocene, a term derived from the Greek word for "man." Today, our species stands as the dominant influence on the earth's climate and environment.

The survival of the planet, at least as we know it, depends on how we behave from here going forward. Personally, I don't view it as a foregone conclusion that we'll end up doing the right things at the necessary times. Our kids will be left to experience, or perhaps endure, whatever it is that they inherit from us. Their adaptability will be put to the test. They will be forced to continue to evolve. The greatest gift that we parents can get from our kids, really, is an assurance that they'll rise to the occasion of the future. That they'll find the strength to tackle their problems head-on. Their readiness to pull that off will not be something that they can articulate directly to us. Instead, we'll have to be satisfied with whatever assurances we can garner from their behavior and actions. One of the greatest disservices that we can do to them is to spoil their native enthusiasm for the natural world in which they live. The planet's salvation will not be delivered by a generation that is disheartened and apathetic. It will come from folks who step outside of their home in the morning with an eagerness to be embraced by the sun and the wind and the rain.

# ACKNOWLEDGMENTS

My friends Kelly Bare and Brody Henderson collaborated with me on every single aspect of this project, from brainstorming to writing to editing. This book is as much theirs as it is mine. Thanks also to Savannah Ashour for helping us cross the finish line. The beautiful illustrations are from my friend Kelsey Johnson (@k_raeartworks on Instagram).

I consulted with many admirable parents throughout the process of writing this book, but a few were of particular importance. Thanks to Joe Cermele, Pat Durkin, Mark Kenyon, Ben Long, Clay Newcomb, and Janis Putelis for sharing their parenting experiences.

At Random House, thanks to my editor, Ben Greenberg, for steering this project in the proper direction at all of the important intersections, and to Kaeli Subberwal and Nancy Delia for their invaluable contributions. Also at Random House: Tom Perry, Andy Ward, Greg Kubie, Erin Richards, and Ayelet Durantt—thanks for continuing to bet on the entire MeatEater team.

Thanks to my trusty agent, Marc Gerald, who's been by my side for damn near twenty years. Also to MeatEater's Katie Finch, who keeps all of our publishing projects on task. And big thanks to Kylee Archer at MeatEater for making the world go round.

Finally, I'd like to acknowledge my own mother and father. I miss you, Dad, and I always tell my kids how much you would have loved them. And, Mom, thanks for letting us get scraped up and hurt while we wandered through the woods, and always being there to patch us up when we got home.

## RESOURCES

I find that I'm always more confident and relaxed when I feel adequately prepared. Given the healthy dose of chaos that is sometimes a factor in family adventures, having the right gear and information at the outset can make the difference between an outing that's a success and one that involves a stress-inducing series of setbacks. For those looking for some extra information of a pragmatic sort (for example, on how exactly to cross the threshold from day hike to overnighter), I offer this additional set of resources. Organized by chapter, the sections provide practical suggestions for things like gear, getting your family out the door, foods to forage, kid-friendly fish for beginning anglers, hunter safety courses, and more.

## I.

### CAMPING

## STARTING CLOSE TO HOME

For kids with minimal outdoor experience, a backyard overnighter can be a valuable lesson that helps make future camping trips more enjoyable. Knowing how to use your gear makes everything go more smoothly, and backyard camping is a great opportunity for kids to practice things like setting up their tent, blowing up sleeping pads, and lighting camp stoves. If you are city dwellers without access to a backyard of your own, consider whether you have friends who do and who might be open to sharing the adventure with your family. Or check with your city parks department, as many urban parks offer periodic camping opportunities.

Let the kids lead on your first outdoor mini-adventure. Encourage them to read the assembly directions (with your help if necessary) or watch a video tutorial, then set up the tent and organize their "campsite" themselves. It's okay if they're having some difficulties and they screw up a time or two—step in to help out only when absolutely necessary. Learning to set up a tent builds skills and self-reliance, and it's knowledge that'll come in handy when you are actually out in the woods together and need help getting your campsite prepared before night falls or a rainstorm rolls in.

Make these initial backyard camping experiences as fun as you can. Choose a warm night with clear skies. Cook dinner outside on the grill or over a fire pit. Do some stargazing and storytelling. When it's time for bed, encourage kids with an independent streak to sleep outside without you. Otherwise, it's perfectly acceptable to join them or arrange for them to have an outdoor sleepover with a friend.

For some children, minor scares will be inevitable once the sun sets. Teddy bears, special blankies, and the like are all fair game. Flashlights and headlamps also go a long way toward staving off any fear of the dark, as does letting the family dog sleep with them in the tent. But for one reason or another, sometimes a kid just can't bounce back. You shouldn't give up if your first backyard campout ends with someone, or everyone, back inside in their beds. It's a good learning experience, and an opportunity to fine-tune your approach. What went wrong? Were they really scared? Of what? Or were they just cold? Don't underestimate the getting-cold thing—temperature swings can be wild in a tent. I've found that just getting into a sleeping bag and getting it properly zipped up is challenging for a kid.

The goal, however long it takes to reach it, is to pull a successful all-nighter. When they want to sleep out again, you've won. And chances are good that after a few fun nights of sleeping in the yard, they'll be begging to go on a real camping trip.

## FINDING A CAMPGROUND

With thousands of campgrounds scattered throughout the country, it's likely you won't need to travel too far in order to spend a weekend outdoors. Choose campgrounds based on the experience you and your kids want to have, keeping in mind that the more amenities a campground offers, the more people it will attract, especially during the busy summer camping season.

A good place to start researching is the website www.recreation.gov, which lists thousands of campgrounds managed by federal agencies in national parks, forests, historical areas, and seashores. At rec.gov you can make campsite reservations, buy permits and passes for entry into parks, and rent RVs, cabins, and camping gear. If you're planning on doing a lot of camping, fishing, or hiking, it's more economical to buy an annual pass that is valid in all national parks throughout the country than to pay daily entrance fees. There are also programs like Every Kid in a Park, which offers fourth and fifth graders free entry to national parks and historic sites, as well as senior discounts for grandparents. (Bring them along and save some money on your car pass!) Most states have similar campsite reservation websites managed by their individual wildlife and parks agencies; these also sell daily and annual state parks passes. These passes provide access to features like visitor centers, boat launches, and various kid-friendly educational tours and activities led by park rangers.

## DEVELOPED CAMPGROUNDS

At developed campgrounds, all you have to do is back your vehicle into your assigned spot and pitch your tent, and you'll be ready to let the kids roast some hot dogs over the campfire and dig in at your allotted picnic table. Many developed campgrounds have electrical hookups and bathroom facilities complete with showers, and some even have small convenience stores. Keep in mind that developed campgrounds in national and state parks are often booked up throughout the summer. If you're interested in camping at busy, well-known places like Yellowstone or the Grand Canyon over the Fourth of July weekend, you may need to reserve a campsite months in advance. Otherwise, you'll be forced to find a campground that sets aside a small number of sites for walk-up customers on a first-come-first-serve basis—and you'll certainly have to arrive early and wait in line to score one.

Private campgrounds are also an option, though many lack truly natural settings. They might not be the most serene or idyllic places, but they do offer a gateway to trails, rivers, forests, and lakes nearby, and your kids will still be building up valuable skills like sleeping away from home and tolerating discomfort. Sites are often conveniently located along major travel routes or in small, touristy satellite towns just outside national parks and mountain or beach resort areas. From small mom-and-pop operations to national franchises like KOA, they vary widely in their offerings—some don't have much more than a parking space and a flat spot to pitch your tent, while others feature electric hookups, fishing ponds, playgrounds, pools, vending machines, laundry machines, and showers. A quick internet search will lead you to listings of campgrounds around specific destinations, towns, and travel routes. Most have a website or at least a phone number where you can make reservations. Fees for developed campsites range from a few dollars to the price of a night in a nice hotel depending on demand, the available amenities, and maintenance and operating costs.

When you stay at a developed campground, whether it's privately owned or in a national park, you'll almost always be sharing space with other campers—often a lot of them. Campgrounds are usually full of friendly folks who don't mind children playing nearby, but you'll still need to follow the rules and be respectful of people's privacy and space, which means your kids can't play in occupied campsites during the day or roam around screaming at night.

## PRIMITIVE AND DISPERSED
## CAMPING ON PUBLIC LANDS

If you're looking to get away from the crowds, consider primitive campgrounds or dispersed camping in public lands. Primitive campgrounds are just that—you and your kids will need to be a little more self-sufficient. At best, each site will have a tent site, a fire ring with a rusted metal pit and cooking grate, and maybe a picnic table. Usually, but not always, there is a communal water pump and outhouse-style pit toilets that may only be operational at certain times of the year. You and your kids may need to get comfortable digging a cat hole.

Available in most national and state forests, these types of sites often offer a more pristine and less crowded setting than you'll experience at developed campgrounds, and fees tend to be low. Some sites operate under a reservation system (try rec.gov, state park and wildlife websites, or apps like The Dyrt), while others are available on a first-come-first-serve walk-up basis; for walk-up sites, have cash on hand, as you may be depositing your campsite fee in a drop box.

You're likely to have even more breathing room in areas on public lands where dispersed camping (camping that falls outside of designated campsites) is legal—that includes hundreds of millions of acres of federally managed national forest and Bureau of Land Management lands, as well as some state lands. You can find these public lands on trail maps published by the U.S. Forest Service and National Geographic and through smartphone apps like FreeRoam. Once you're in the area where you'd like to camp, you can simply pull your car off on the side of a road and set up wherever you like. This often allows you to get close to an area with breathtaking views, hiking trailheads, or large tracts of wilderness with good fishing or hunting opportunities. It's important to remember that areas where dispersed camping is legal often lie off the beaten path, and reaching them can mean difficult driving on poorly maintained, rocky, rutted-out roads, so it's wise to use a vehicle with four-wheel drive. Be aware, however, that regulations require dispersed campsites to be set up near that road—it's illegal to go off-road four-wheeling across a pristine meadow just to reach that perfect campsite off in the distance.

At most developed campgrounds and occasionally some primitive campgrounds, you'll be able to find dumpsters where you can deposit garbage. In dispersed camping areas, though, you'll need to adhere to "leave no trace" rules, which means packing out your trash. Kids have a habit of dropping candy wrappers and other micro-trash on the ground, so hold them accountable for scouring the area for litter regularly during your stay and before you leave. If you dig your own fire pit and build a stone fire ring, you'll need to fill it back in and put the rocks back where you found them. This might seem excessive, but if you've ever seen a campsite strewn with trash or a fire pit lined with burnt-up beer cans and melted plastic, you'll know that it's worth teaching your children to put in a little extra work to preserve the integrity of the natural environment.

## BACKCOUNTRY CAMPING

Car camping is a great place to start with kids, and it's easy enough that you can do it on a regular basis. But if you're really looking to add some rawness and grit to your children's camping experience, backpacking is the way to go. And in order to reach areas that lack road access, or in federally designated wilderness areas where any form of motorized travel is illegal, backpacking in on foot will be your only option. Sure, a backcountry camping trip that requires hiking into a more remote setting involves a lot more preparation, effort, and gear, but it can be incredibly worthwhile. Your schedule won't be dictated by a campsite's checkout times, and you'll be able to pitch your tent wherever you want—in a grassy meadow, under a shady grove of trees, or next to a high alpine lake.

Be aware, however, that backpack camping also adds a level of difficulty and hassle that car camping lacks. Even on a single overnighter, at a minimum you'll need to pack a first-aid kit, a tent, sleeping bags and sleeping pads, rain gear, headlamps, and enough food to get everyone through a couple of days in the woods. You might need to pack water, too, if there isn't a reliable natural source that can be filtered or treated. Think about how you can distribute the weight across your family without overloading anyone.

Start simple and short. Merely hiking to wherever you'll pitch your tent for the night is a challenge, especially with very young kids. Even if you have some personal experience with long through-hikes and backpack camping, save the big multiday expeditions for later. Aim to pack in no more than a couple of miles on your first overnight backpack camping trip with kids.

## CAMPING GEAR

If you've ever been forced to suffer through a long, rainy night curled up in a damp sleeping bag inside a cheap, leaky tent, you'll know there's a direct correlation between the quality of your gear and the amount of fun you may or may not have on a camping trip. A lot of heartache, crying, and suffering can be avoided with quality camping gear.

If you're just getting started on your outdoor adventures, there's nothing wrong with borrowing gear from well-resourced friends. But pretty soon you're going to need your own. Start by investing in the foundational essentials that you absolutely can't get by without, like a good tent, sleeping bags, and outdoor clothing. Get the best gear you can afford and then move on to nice-to-haves that aren't strictly necessary but make your camp more efficient and comfortable. Choose camping gear made by companies with strong ties to mountaineering, backcountry hiking, hunting, and fishing lifestyles. The folks who enjoy those activities tend to be tough on gear and aren't afraid to be outside in nasty weather. Generally speaking, you'll be able to find everything you'll need at outdoor retail chains like REI and Sportsman's Warehouse. If you're looking to save a little money, keep an eye out for end-of-season sales and scour classified ads, thrift stores, and Craigslist for deals on lightly used high-quality gear.

Finally, make sure you are intimately familiar with how to use your gear before you hit the woods. As a family, practice staking out tents in your backyard, break in hiking boots before you wear them on the trail, try on last season's clothes to make sure your kids still fit into them, and teach your kids how to cram their own sleeping bags back into their stuff sacks. Make sure the adults know how to operate stoves and any other gear or tech. Check to see that your first-aid kit is fully stocked, download your maps, and test all batteries to make sure they're still functioning.

## CAMPING GEAR ESSENTIALS

Adjust the following list based on your needs, your preferences, and the type of camping you'll be doing. (For instance, a two-burner propane stove is ideal for car camping, but you'll need a lightweight, packable camping stove on backpacking trips.)

- First-aid and survival kits
- Sunscreen
- Insect repellent
- Tent
- Tent patch kit (Tenacious Tape)
- Tent pole repair kit
- Ground cloth
- Tarp for sun/rain shelter
- Sleeping bags
- Sleeping pads
- Headlamps and flashlights
- Lantern (battery-powered)

- Cooler(s)
- Nalgene water bottles
- 5-gallon water storage container with pour spout
- Portable cooking stove and/or grill, and fuel
- Fire grate
- Long-handled butane lighter
- Cookware, bowls, plates, cups, utensils, cutting board
- Dish soap, dishcloth, pot scrubber
- Collapsible camp table
- Folding camp chairs
- Pocketknife
- Multi-tool
- Shovel
- Hatchet (for chopping firewood and pounding tent stakes)
- Tool kit
- Lighters
- Garbage bags
- Personal hygiene kit
- Quick-dry camp towels
- Hand sanitizer and biodegradable camp soap
- Toilet paper
- Extra batteries for headlamps, etc.
- Portable battery chargers for electronic devices
- Small inflatable camp pillows for backpacking trips
- Deck of cards
- Books

### GEAR TIPS AND TRICKS

- Make sure you have a reliable source of communication on camping trips. Wireless providers wildly overstate reliable coverage in rural and remote areas. In the event of an emergency, a satellite messenger/emergency beacon like Garmin's inReach Mini provides a lifesaving line of communication to the outside world even where cellphones don't work.

- Upload a subscription GPS navigation app onto your smartphone. Apps like onX, Gaia, and AllTrails allow the user to navigate through the backcountry without wireless service.

- Don't rely completely on your smartphone for navigation—phones can break, get dropped in the water, or run out of power. It's smart to pack paper maps, too. DeLorme publishes an atlas and gazetteer for each individual state that shows roads and topography along with the location of everything from campgrounds to hiking trails to fishing access points. You can also buy more detailed trail guides and topo maps for specific areas. Carry a compass, too, and teach your kids to use these tools not only to navigate but also to gain a broader perspective of the landscape.

- Human food attracts bears, so it needs to be stored safely, and not just in grizzly bear country—black bears are found in forty-one out of fifty states. At night or whenever you're away from your campsite, lock all food inside vehicles. On backpacking trips, store all food in a stuff sack or dry bag and hang it in a tree at least ten feet off the ground, six feet away from the tree trunk, and a hundred yards from your tent.

- Cute cotton sleeping bags decorated with cartoon characters are designed for sleepover parties, not camping. They're cheaply built, useless when wet, and quick to fall apart. REI, The North Face, and Kelty all make kid-sized sleeping bags with high-quality synthetic insulation that retains heat even when wet. Choose one with a temperature comfort rating lower than the lowest nighttime temperatures you expect to run into while camping. Nighttime temperatures in the Rocky Mountains can dip below freezing in the summer. Unless you're going to do all your camping in warmer climates, go with a fifteen-degree sleeping bag for your kids and consider adding a sleeping bag liner for extra warmth on really cold nights.

- Double-walled, three-season dome-style tents made by companies like Nemo, Big Agnes, and Black Diamond handle wind, rain, and condensation well. Look for one that has a covered vestibule outside the main body of the tent where you can store boots and packs overnight. Tents are sized according to the number of people who can sleep in them, but these specifications rarely account for much breathing room. A family of four might want to size up to a six-person car camping tent. Make sure to pack a tent patch kit and pole repair kit.

- Store and transport your camping gear in plastic totes labeled and neatly organized by category. Stuff sacks are great for packing clothes, and roll-top dry bags are a must-have for storing important gear and clothing in wet environments or on river trips.

- Fine-tune your first-aid kit for children by carrying plenty of Band-Aids, children's Tylenol, cold and allergy medication, extra sunscreen, and calamine lotion.

- Waterproof boots made by Muck and Bogs are tops for all-purpose kids' footwear. Pack a pair of sneakers or Crocs for "camp shoes" for kids so they're not tracking mud from their boots into the tent or camper, or in case their boots need to dry out. Flip-flops invite splinters, cuts, blisters, and other headaches. Unless you're camping on the beach, avoid them altogether.

- Sleeping clothes or pajamas should be kept dry and be worn only for sleeping. Likewise, bring an extra set of clothes and socks for kids that is always kept dry and is only available for emergency use.

- You can use old household stuff for camping cookware or buy a complete set that's designed specifically for camping. If you choose to purchase cookware, get the good stuff and stay away from thin, super-cheap aluminum camping pots and pans, since food burns easily in them and they become impossible to clean properly. For plates, bowls, cups, and silverware you can go with either plastic or metal. Don't forget to include things like spatulas for flipping pancakes and burgers and a big serving spoon for ladling soup or stew. Travel mugs with lids are good for preventing spills at camp, too.
- Pack a pair of binoculars with you on your camping trips for observing birds and other wildlife.
- Hammocks are great for napping and also make a fine portable swing set.
- Puffy jackets crammed into a sleeping bag stuff sack make great pillows on backpack camping trips.

## KID-FRIENDLY CAMP FOODS

Hungry kids are ornery kids, and on camping trips they'll be burning even more calories than usual. A lot of temper tantrums and hysterical bouts of crying can be avoided by regularly doling out snacks. Carrot sticks, apple slices, and even some energy bars are some of the healthier options, but don't be afraid to bend your normal rules. It's amazing how fast a single piece of candy can turn around a situation that's heading in the wrong direction, and dosing kids with a little extra sugar now and then isn't going to kill them.

When it comes to breakfast, lunch, and dinner, it's best to keep things simple and hearty. You want food that your kids will eat without complaint and meals that can be prepared without a lot of fuss. Instant oatmeal makes for an easy hot breakfast, especially if you're backpacking. If you have concerns about the added sugar and corn syrup in most of the pre-flavored varieties, go with plain and bring along a little maple syrup or honey. Kids also appreciate a bagel toasted in a frying pan or small backpacking cookpot with some added butter. Of course, you can also go with a full-on cooked breakfast on car camping trips, though it's probably not something you'll want to do every morning. If you're getting out of your sleeping bags before the sun rises to go out for a morning of hunting or fishing, grab a couple of protein bars to tide you over until you get back to camp. Then you can cook up a big midmorning meal of pancakes and eggs.

Camp lunches can range from reheating the previous night's leftovers to packing sandwiches into the field. For kids, it's hard to beat a classic PB&J or cold cuts and cheese slices, but stay away from soft sliced bread on backpacking trips and opt for sturdier stuff like bagels, pita pockets, or hard rolls that won't get smashed and soggy inside your pack. For cold days, come prepared with the makings of a bowl of soup (canned or dry packets work well for camping) and a cup of hot cocoa. If you're combining your camping trip with fishing or hunting and have had a successful morning, celebrate the occasion by frying up some fresh fish for lunch.

Camp dinners always seem to take place when it's dark out, even on long summer days, so simplicity is even more important. When camping with another family or two, rotating between cooking group dinners and cleanup duties spreads out the workload. Cooking hot dogs over the campfire while potatoes wrapped in foil are baking on the coals is a time-honored move with zero cleanup, but a fire grate and cast-iron skillet or griddle come in handy for more involved campfire cooking. If you'd rather not build a campfire to cook every meal, a small propane grill works great for brats and burgers, and a portable two-burner propane stove is ideal for kid-friendly sides like egg noodles, rice, or mac and cheese. You can also try pre-cooking dinners and freezing them in vacuum sealer bags. That way, all you need to do is plop a bag of frozen chili or taco meat into a pot of heated water and leave it there until the meal is warm enough to eat. There's virtually no prep time, no worries of over- or undercooking, and fewer dishes to wash. Even if a frozen pre-cooked meal thaws in the cooler before it's reheated, it'll keep for a few days as long as it stays cold.

To make sure nutrition doesn't fall entirely by the wayside, bring along raw veggies and fruits to cut up as side dishes.

On backpacking trips, you'll be limited to using a portable camp stove and a small cookpot or two. You'll also need to limit the amount of weight you're carrying in the form of heavy, perishable food items. This doesn't completely rule out preparing well-balanced meals with fresh ingredients, but it does make pulling them off a pain in the ass. An easier option is stocking up on some freeze-dried meals from companies like Peak Refuel and Mountain House. They've got a wide variety of pretty tasty meals that even kids who are picky eaters will enjoy, and they're light and compact. All you have to do is boil some water on your camp stove, pour the water into the bag and reseal it, and let the food rehydrate and warm up for ten minutes or so. Then you get to eat the whole meal right out of the bag with a long-handled spork, which kids find kind of cool.

Whatever type of camping you're doing, mealtime will always be extra special when you incorporate fresh ingredients you've sourced yourself. You can prepare for those spontaneous menus by folding up a couple of square feet of aluminum foil and packing small plastic vials of olive oil and seasoned salt—even backpackers can make room for these items. That way a fresh-caught trout or some crayfish can be paired with foraged morel mushrooms, seasoned with salt and a drizzle of olive oil, then wrapped in foil and tossed directly on the campfire's coals. After ten or fifteen minutes, you've got yourself a fine meal that's about as simple and pure as it gets.

## THE OUTDOOR BATHROOM

If your kids are out of diapers, your days of worrying about trips to the bathroom are mercifully in the rearview mirror. Camping trips, however, can be a backward time warp. Unless you're staying at a developed campground, you're going to have to deal with the challenges that arise when kids need to poop or pee in the outdoors. This is particularly true with kids who are past the full-time diaper stage but not yet self-sufficient enough to get the job done on their own without a flush toilet and running water. At campgrounds with nothing but primitive vault toilets, you'll need to go in with toddlers, and grade-schoolers may need some outside assurance they're not going to fall into that creepy, smelly hole. You'll have to provide even more of a helping hand on camping trips where toilets in any form aren't an option. Children under age ten or so often find going to the bathroom outside to be an unpleasant and even frightening experience, at least initially.

Obviously, peeing is less complicated than pooping—cop a squat behind a bush or take aim at a tree stump and skip the smelly outhouse—but it's still not without challenges. That goes for both boys and girls. Keep an eye on little boys who aren't yet used to peeing standing up and fail to clear their pants or underwear. The same thing happens with girls who don't get their clothing out of the way. You may even need to hold their hands while they pee since they don't have a toilet to balance on. After a fair bit of practice, most young kids will be comfortable peeing on their own, although it's wise to make sure they're dry afterward. And remember to scout the area for poison oak and poison ivy before any trips to the outdoor privy.

Regardless of their outdoor peeing prowess, both boys and girls in this age group will need assistance with pooping. Backcountry rules, both informal and written, expect that everyone bury their solid waste far from high-use areas and water sources. Even if your kid just needs to pee, the best practice is to go well away from hiking trails and campsites; for poop, two hundred feet from trails, campsites, creeks, or lakes is the generally accepted distance to maintain a pristine environment and prevent disease transmission. First, you'll need to dig a cat hole at least eight inches deep. If you're car camping, bring a shovel—you'll definitely find it useful for more than just this job. On backpacking trips, you can use a sturdy stick or other naturally sourced tool to dig your hole, or you can flip over partially buried basketball-sized rocks to expose a hole. Once that task is complete, position your kid's behind over the hole and help them balance there if needed. Biodegradable toilet paper can be tossed into the cat hole, but you'll have to burn or pack out used wet wipes in a sealed plastic bag. Lastly, cover everything up by burying the works with the soil you dug up or by flipping the rock back into the original position.

Afterward, *always* make sure children's hands are washed thoroughly with biodegradable camp soap and water or hand sanitizer. Intestinal illnesses are one of the most common reasons camping trips are cut short, and the majority are attributed to fecal contamination passed around by dirty hands.

Needless to say, that same rigor need not apply to the rest of your personal hygiene routine when you're out in the woods. As long as hands and faces are getting washed regularly, permission to get dirty and stay that way is part of the fun. On longer camping trips, you can wipe down your kids with a damp, soapy washcloth and rinse them with some warm water heated up on the camp stove every couple of days.

## II.
### FORAGING

## FIRST STEPS

Foraging doesn't need to begin with a grand expedition to some remote outpost in search of a specific root. Instead, it can start small and
close to home.

Just about everyone has access to some type of edible plant, fruit,
fungus, root, or nut—from the dandelions that pop up in your backyard every spring to the wild asparagus growing in a roadside ditch. If
that sounds far-fetched given where you live, you might be surprised
by what you find once you start to do a little research. The scope of
what can be sourced in urban and suburban settings is probably wider
than you think. Your yard is a great place to start foraging, but if you
don't have a yard, there is almost certainly a neighborhood park or
open space within walking distance that is home to an edible specimen or two. Incorporating those foraged foods into family meals can
be as simple as throwing a salad together from those spring dandelion

greens, or as involved as making flour from all the acorns that pile up under that old oak tree every fall.

Before any wild food is ingested, of course, it must be positively identified. Toxic plants and mushrooms abound. Although a quick search online should turn up some edible plants that are commonly available near you, picking up a field guide is a great idea. Samuel Thayer's *Nature's Garden* is an excellent general field guide for commonly available North American edible wild plants, but you might also seek out a book focused on the specific region of the country where you live. You can use your laptop to access websites like foraging.com or the USDA plant database, and apps such as iNaturalist and PlantSnap are extremely useful for on-the-spot identification. And although these resources don't completely rule out misidentification, they will not only help keep you safe—they'll also turn an undifferentiated mass of weeds into a treasure trove of wild edibles that are free (with some exceptions, as noted below) for the taking.

Another good way for you and your kids to get familiar with local foraging opportunities is to enroll in a foraging workshop. There are scads offered virtually, but in-person training from a wild foods expert is a better choice. Workshops range from one-day sessions that teach folks to find edible plants in their own backyards to in-depth, weekslong courses that include regular forays into local woods and fields. Some are geared specifically for city dwellers. Some are fine-tuned for specific types of plants, while others cast a wide net for anything and everything edible. If you're particularly interested in finding edible mushrooms (more on that ahead), it's a good idea to join a local mycology club.

As your family gets hooked, the goal of finding more elusive wild edibles can become yet another reason to get outside and discover new places. A tangible goal helps ramp up kids' excitement about getting outdoors, and kids have a natural inclination to put a bunch of energy into scavenger hunts of all sorts.

Since you don't need much more than a pocketknife and a sack of some sort for most types of foraging, it can happen on the fly while you're out and about doing other activities, and it's a great fallback when an outing falls flat. An unsuccessful fishing trip can be saved by the discovery of a small patch of raspberries, and any camp meal will be enhanced by the addition of a handful of morels. As an added bonus, even kids who are squeamish about trying new foods will burst with excitement at the moment of discovery. That excitement can be an avenue toward a more adventurous palate. Children will be more inclined to eat a salad that they foraged themselves than one that gets dumped out of a sealed plastic bag onto their plate.

## FORAGING SAFELY AND LEGALLY

When foraging with little ones, it's imperative to impress upon your kids that they must check in with you before putting anything in their mouths. While eating easily recognized fruit from neighboring trees is a risk-free endeavor, there are strict safety protocols you'll need to follow before eating any wild edibles. Mistaking a toxic plant or mushroom for an edible one can have serious consequences. Though fatalities are rare, there are some poisonous plants and fungi that can kill you if they're ingested. Many more can cause symptoms ranging from vomiting and diarrhea to seizures and lasting kidney or liver damage. Some wild foods are mildly toxic if they're eaten raw but perfectly edible if they're cooked. And even eating too much of some of the more desirable plants or mushrooms that are widely considered to be tasty and safe to eat can cause some folks to experience mild nausea and an upset stomach. But assiduously following these foraging safety rules will almost always prevent such outcomes:

- Never eat a plant or mushroom you can't positively identify. Don't guess, ever.

- Never assume that plants, mushrooms, or berries that are eaten by birds or animals are safe for human consumption.
- Don't overeat any plant or mushroom the first time you try it. Start with a small amount—your digestive system may need time to adjust to new food sources.
- Cooking, and boiling in particular, makes mushrooms and plants more digestible and releases more nutrients.
- If you decide to look for wild edibles in public open spaces, be sure you're foraging in an area where toxic pesticides and herbicides aren't being used.
- While foragers are usually free to harvest whatever they want on public lands, there are occasional exceptions. Regulations that limit the amount of any given wild edible people may take are generally aimed at large-scale commercial harvest. But in some national parks and other protected areas, you may be required to secure a recreational foraging permit or follow harvest limits on foraged items; in some areas you may even be completely prohibited from harvesting any wild plants and fungi at all.
- Finally, it's easy to get greedy when the abundance of any given wild edible seems unlimited. A smarter and more sustainable approach is to take only what you can use within a reasonable amount of time. Rather than overharvesting, teach your children to play the long game by leaving some seed for the future.

## TUNING IN TO TIMING AND LOCATION

Foraging is all about being in the right place at the right time. In western Montana, wild mountain huckleberries grow in the acidic soil of sub-alpine pine and fir forests. Our huckleberry season usually begins in early August and ends with the first hard frosts in mid-September. It's a long enough stretch of harvesting time to allow local families to gather enough wild berries to last through the winter. But the timing, length, and crop yield of huckleberry season can vary wildly from year to year depending on factors like cold snaps, extreme droughts, disease, or wildfires. A single but severe early summer frost could wipe out a mountain's entire berry crop, although it won't prevent anyone from going mountain biking. Likewise, the annual flush of spring snowmelt into a river is a boon to whitewater rafters but could very well inundate your favorite mushroom-hunting spot. Assuming you're going to get what you want based simply on the location, time of year, previous experience, or word of mouth is a mistake; the only way to verify the availability of wild edibles in your area is to go look for them. But first you need to know where to start.

Certain regions and environments tend to be more productive for certain types of wild foods. For instance, in the cool, wet climate of the Pacific Northwest, a wide variety of edible mushrooms is available almost all year round. Meanwhile, only a few inches of precipitation fall annually in the arid desert Southwest, and the availability of mushrooms is highly dependent on whether the summer monsoon season brings enough rain. In dry years, mushrooms may never appear in numbers sufficient enough to make looking for them a worthwhile endeavor.

Though you can harvest pine needles for tea or cattail roots with which to make flour year-round, seasonal guidelines apply to most foraged foods. For instance, the season for picking ramps, a wild relative of onions and leeks, begins in early April and lasts through May in the Upper Midwest. Some degree of seasonal overlap is common in temperate regions of the country, but generally speaking, greens are a spring target, berries pop in the summer, and nuts are ready for harvesting in the fall; mushrooms appear in different varieties in spring, summer, and fall.

These are only loose guidelines, especially in warmer climates. With many wild foods, you'll also need to consider the specific micro-environments within a region where certain plants and fungi can be found. In Montana, foragers search for morel mushrooms in late spring, but their efforts are typically focused in river bottoms lined with cottonwood trees and in recently burned Ponderosa pine forests. When you're foraging for something that may only be available for a week or two in a very specific microenvironment during ideal weather, the perfect conditions may not line up in any given year. Take away some of the guesswork by taking advantage of the previously mentioned resources. The more you know, the better your chances of a successful foraging outing.

## TYPES OF FOODS TO FORAGE

It would be impossible to fully catalog the vast scope of wild edibles found throughout the country in the space we have available here. If you really want to take a deep dive into foraging, dozens of encyclopedic books like the ones mentioned earlier have been written on the subject. For simplicity's sake, we'll stick to the most popular categories of wild edibles with a focus on some of the most widely available examples. The following examples are only a small representation of the foraging opportunities you might be able to find in your neck of the woods, but they should be more than enough to get you and your kids on the path to sourcing a variety of sustainable, delicious wild foods.

### BERRIES

Wild berries are the most obvious and attractive starting point for foraging with kids, though if you want to gather enough for pies, cobbler, jams, and syrup you'll need to put in a little work. During late-summer hikes, whatever trailside berries that haven't been thoroughly cleaned out by other hikers can provide a tasty diversion, but usually you'll need to venture away from well-worn trails to find the thickest, most productive berry patches. Luckily, as far as kids are concerned, a patch of ripe, sweet wild berries is the candy aisle of the foraging grocery store. You probably won't have to coerce your kids into a targeted berry-picking excursion. In fact, the hardest part will be getting your kids to stop shoving berries into their faces long enough to make a meaningful contribution toward future desserts. Certainly let them enjoy the reward of their efforts in real time, but try to shift their focus away from eating every berry that passes through their hands and toward the value of stockpiling for leaner times by setting a goal of filling a bucket or two. A neat trick for gathering a large number of berries in short order is to lay a blanket or small tarp under a heavily laden berry bush and whack or shake the branches so the ripe berries that are ready to drop naturally fall on the blanket, where it's easy to collect them.

Other than in the most arid desert environments, throughout most of the country you can find a multitude of different wild berries. Bramble berries such as blackberries and raspberries are some of the most widely distributed. Though Himalayan blackberries are considered an invasive pest, various species of native American wild raspberries thrive in disturbed woodland environments and field edges around most of the United States. They're often found in huge numbers where selective logging has recently occurred. Just remember, they're called bramble berries for a reason—these plants grow sharp prickers that will leave the bare hands and arms of young foragers covered in scratches. It's a price most kids are willing to pay for a tasty treat.

Foragers can also find different varieties of wild strawberries in meadows and forests all over the continental United States. They can be harder to find than bramble berries, since their plants hug the ground and the berries are quite small, but the search is worth the effort. What wild strawberries lack in size compared to their store-bought counterparts, they make up for with an intense flavor that farm-raised berries can't compete with.

Depending on where you live or are traveling, there are many other types of wild berries you might find. Lowbush blueberries are found in the northeastern quadrant of the United States. Highbush blueberries have a wider though more scattered distribution. Huckleberries and serviceberries, or saskatoons, are similar to blueberries and grow throughout the Rocky Mountains and Northern Plains states. And from gooseberries to mulberries to cranberries, the list of other wild berries that can be foraged is a long one. Generally speaking, most wild berries ripen between early summer and early fall, though the berry-picking season may be longer in mild climates like the Pacific Northwest or the southeastern portion of the country.

## MUSHROOMS

Serious mushroom hunters occupy their own fanatic, dedicated space among the foraging community. That's because foraging mushrooms isn't something that you can afford to be casual about, especially with young children. The consequences of eating the wrong mushroom can be grave, and there are plenty of opportunities for cases of mistaken identity to send someone to the emergency room. For example, the little brown mushrooms, or LBMs, that pop up in your lawn after a spring or summer rainfall might appear similar to the ones found in grocery stores, but for the layperson it's nearly impossible to positively identify what species of LBM you might be looking at, and many are at least mildly toxic. The first rule of thumb when foraging mushrooms with kids is to teach them to keep on walking when they come across clusters of LBMs.

Fortunately, there are many species of edible mushrooms that are more easily identified by their unique appearance, including some of the most delicious varieties. Rookie mushroom hunters should concentrate their efforts on the following species. As you get further along in your mushroom hunting exploits, check out *Mushrooms Demystified* by David Arora.

**Morels.** Found throughout most of the United States, with the exception of the desert Southwest, they can appear as early as March in the Southeast and as late as June in the northern Rockies. Morels tend to grow in wooded areas and are particularly fond of dead or dying elm, ash, and apple trees, recently burned areas, and river corridors lined with cottonwood trees. Their bumpy, honeycombed, egg-shaped cap is often described as looking a bit like a brain.

**Chanterelles.** Found throughout the summer and into early fall in moist, wooded areas, they are often associated with conifer trees in western mountains and near deciduous hardwood trees elsewhere. They range in color from whitish yellow to a light peach to a deep orange and are distinguished by the forked ridges, or gills, that run under their thin, undulating caps; unlike with many other mushrooms, these ridges continue down the stem below the cap. They emerge as individual mushrooms and are always found growing directly on the forest floor.

**Giant puffballs.** Appearing in spring through fall in meadows, fields, and deciduous forests in the central and eastern United States, these smooth, gill-less golfball- to volleyball-sized globes are easy to spot and fun to cook with. You'll know you've got a good one if the inner flesh is white and firm. For kids, try slicing the big ones into a pizza crust of sorts and pile on their favorite sauce and toppings, then throw the whole thing onto the grill for a few minutes.

**Chicken of the woods.** Growing on tree trunks or at the base of trees, these wavy-edged, orange-hued mushrooms can be found

throughout summer and fall. Look for them on fallen trees, as they are a saprotrophic fungi (one that feeds on dead trees) that can occasionally become parasitic, causing trees to rot.

No matter the species of mushroom being targeted, new mushroom hunters will discover that they are always in a race against time. Most species of fungus only emerge under very specific weather conditions at certain times of the year, and they have a rather fleeting existence. Individual mushrooms usually last only a few days before they either dry up and wither away or begin to get slimy and rotten. You'll also find that you and your kids aren't the only ones utilizing mushrooms as a food source, and you don't want to be second in line to the various bugs and worms who like to eat 'shrooms and most other foraged edibles. Inspect each one as you and your kids are picking—it's an unfortunate inevitability that you'll have to toss some specimens that are infested with creepy-crawlies.

Even if they're bug-free, wild mushrooms grow in the dirt and muck, so they'll need to be cleaned before eating. You can use a baby toothbrush to remove dirt and debris before gently washing them. After washing, run them through a salad spinner to remove excess moisture, and allow them to dry on a sheet pan in the fridge before storing in a paper bag. Mushrooms stored this way will keep for several days. You can also use a food dehydrator to dry mushrooms for later use. Dehydrated mushrooms will keep indefinitely stored in a mason jar; soak them in water for an hour to reconstitute before cooking as you normally would, or just add them to soups or stews and they'll rehydrate in the cooking liquid. And remember that some mushrooms may cause digestive distress when eaten raw, so it's generally safest to err on the side of caution by cooking all foraged mushrooms.

## GREENS

Wild greens are probably the least appealing of the foraging categories for many children, but kids who fight tooth and nail against eating salads tend to be open to trying something they've found in the woods and pulled from the ground with their own two hands. A dose of ranch or sweetened salad dressing can work wonders, too, especially with bitter greens like dandelion leaves.

Most greens are a spring foraging target, though some are available through the summer as well. Found throughout the eastern half of the country in moist hardwood forests, ramps belong to the onion family and are one of the first wild greens to appear in early spring. Their popularity among foragers is unparalleled, and in recent years they've also become a favorite among chefs. Though most folks consider the taste mild, some find ramps overpowering; but if you enjoy the taste of onion and garlic, the green leaves of ramps are what you're after. To do a test run for picky eaters, slip a few chopped-up ramp leaves into your pasta sauce as it heats up—chances are they won't even notice they're ingesting some extra greens. Be aware that the toxic lily-of-the-valley is similar in appearance to ramps; you can tell the two species apart by smell. Ramps smell distinctly like onions when the leaves are torn. Also, the root of ramps features a white bulb, whereas the lily-of-the-valley has a thinner root with no bulb. Check the leaves as your primary method of detection, and only use the root test on a single stalk in order to verify you're getting what you're after. Because wild ramp patches are prone to being overharvested for commercial markets, you can ensure their future sustainability by taking only the leaves. If you cut the leaves cleanly at the base instead of yanking the entire plant root out of the ground, you'll be able to return the following year for more.

There are a host of other wild greens that can be used in fresh salads or for cooking. If you live in an area where ramps aren't available, chances are good you'll be able to find some wild onions or leeks. Asparagus has been growing in the wild and spreading throughout North America since the continent was colonized by Europeans who brought it here for cultivation. Even though you might find it growing in a ditch alongside a country road, it's the same stuff you find in the grocery store. Wild mint is also found all over the United States and can be used in tea or to flavor a bowl of ice cream. Wild grape leaves, watercress, wild mustard and fennel, and various types of seaweed and kelp are just a few more examples of wild greens that you and your children might be able to utilize.

Many of these wild greens can be eaten raw, but some greens need cooking in order to become more digestible—or in some cases to purge toxins that can make you ill. Fiddleheads are a prime example. The term is actually the name for a growth stage that manifests in all ferns, when the young green shoots of the fern plants mimic the appearance of the tuning end of a fiddle as they emerge in the spring from moist soil in forests, often near rivers and streams. The exact timing of the spring fiddlehead emergence varies depending on latitude, but regardless of the location, edible fern varieties are only forageable for those couple of weeks each year when the young leaves and stem are coiled into a tight ball. East of the Mississippi, foragers target the ostrich fern, and out west it's lady ferns. Positive identification is important, as many other species of ferns aren't edible. Even the edible varieties need to be blanched in boiling water for several minutes before consumption; eating them raw can cause nausea, vomiting, and diarrhea. But after they're cooked, fiddleheads are great in soups and salads, and they're fantastic when pickled. At farmer's markets, they can sell for $20 per pound.

## WILD FRUIT TREES

During the summer and into early fall, wild fruit trees offer young foragers a potentially more appealing (and sweeter) payoff than wild greens. Crabapples, the only apples that are native to North America, appear in several varieties that are scattered across the continent. They may be more bitter and sour than the apples your kids are used to eating, but they can be used to make great jams and ciders.

When eaten straight off the tree, black cherries and chokecherries are also bitter compared to the domesticated variety, but cooking them intensifies their sweetness—they're excellent in pies. Wild plum trees produce a sweet fruit that can be eaten fresh or used to make preserves. Pawpaws abound in the eastern United States, and kids love them blended into slushies and smoothies. If you find wild persimmons, some folks claim the fruit tastes like caramel—let your kids be the judge.

Native wild species aren't your only option for foraging fruits. In many warmer southern and West Coast communities, citrus trees are so common that oranges and lemons can be gathered off the sidewalk on neighborhood strolls. In the Midwest, it's not uncommon to stumble on an old apple orchard that was left to go feral in a forgotten corner of a suburban field or woodlot. You also might find pear, cherry, or peach trees growing on abandoned farmsteads. The fruit gathered from these trees might be abundant, and it often tastes much better than the store-bought stuff.

## NUTS

After the spoils of summer, autumn signals the arrival of wild nuts. The most common edible nuts are easily identifiable, and the types of poisonous look-alikes that can trip up foragers looking for mushrooms or greens aren't a big concern. The time frame for collecting them also tends to be much longer than that of more ephemeral wild foods like berries, mushrooms, and greens. Nuts are built to last; their hard outer shell protects them from the elements, preventing them from drying out or rotting while also creating a barrier against critters like worms and insects. When nuts drop in the fall, you'll have a few weeks, or longer, as opposed to a few days, to gather them. Of course, that doesn't mean you're always guaranteed to come home with a couple of five-gallon buckets full of walnuts or pecans. From year to year, nut-bearing trees and their "mast crop" are prone to fluctuations of productivity. During what are known as mast years, trees produce a bumper crop of nuts that fall to the ground in seemingly limitless numbers, and collecting a year's worth of nuts from a single tree might only take a couple of hours. However, the following year, the mast crop might be so sparse that you'll have to spend a few days searching under an entire grove of trees to collect enough to suit your needs. But the great thing about nuts is that, unlike fruits, greens, or mushrooms, which need to be eaten right away or frozen or dehydrated for later use, for the most part nuts remain shelf stable long after they've been harvested. And with several varieties of wild nuts to forage, in years when one particular mast crop is sparse, chances are that others will be available in good numbers.

The black walnuts that so many people view as more of a nuisance than a food source are found throughout most of the eastern United States along with hickory nuts, hazelnuts, and beechnuts. Though the vast majority of pecans eaten in America are commercially harvested, wild pecan trees are found across the south-central and southeastern portions of the country. Farther west, it's a tradition for many families to forage for one of the most expensive nuts in the world; every fall, locals gather along roadsides in northern New Mexico and other parts of the Southwest to collect the cones that house pine nuts. It's a lot of work to actually get to the nuts, but considering the price for a pound of wild pinyon pine nuts, the effort can be worth the reward. Then there's the ubiquitous acorn to consider. With some regional exceptions, most folks in the United States live within close proximity to some type of oak tree and the acorns they bear. Although acorns were once a staple food among some groups of Native Americans, today it seems only the most hard-core foragers bother with them even though they're available in great abundance. That's because, before they can be eaten, acorns require a special preparation technique. Critters like squirrels, black bears, whitetail deer, wild turkeys, and many others take advantage of this nutritious, energy-rich nut and have no trouble digesting raw acorns, but the human digestive system can't handle their harsh tannins, which can cause liver damage when consumed in large quantities. However, with proper treatment acorns are completely safe to eat; before they can be roasted and eaten or ground into flour, acorns must be blanched in water multiple times in order to leach out the tannins.

Sadly, we can no longer count American chestnuts among this trove of wild nuts. As many as 4 billion American chestnut trees (not to be confused with the non-native and toxic horse chestnut) once dominated the landscape of the Appalachian corridor and Ohio River Valley, but during the first half of the twentieth century the species was largely extirpated by a widespread fungal disease commonly known as chestnut blight. Which means that roasting wild American chestnuts over an open fire is no longer a possibility—the chestnuts you might see in a grocery store were likely hybrids cultivated in California or overseas.

### BEYOND THE BASICS

While you and your kids should have your hands full foraging for berries, mushrooms, greens, and nuts, there is a myriad of other wild edibles out there on the landscape just waiting to be found, no matter where you live or play. Scads of edible roots and tubers can be harvested from cattails and other wild plants. Many wildflowers are edible. Teas can be made from the needles of several species of coniferous trees. The inner flesh of prickly pear cactus fruits can be cooked on the grill or made into syrup. If you live in the Upper Midwest or in the Great Lakes region and you're willing to invest some time and elbow grease, it's possible to harvest enough wild rice to feed a family of four throughout the year. Tapping maple trees and turning their sap into syrup is a lengthy and involved process that requires some special equipment and know-how, but what kid doesn't like pancakes drenched in maple syrup? They'll appreciate them even more if they made the syrup themselves. The world of foraging can be as contained or vast as you and your children are willing to make it, but chances are good that once you get them started, they'll soon be willing, perhaps craving, to branch out into areas you never expected.

III.

GARDENING

## GROWING A PLANT FROM SEED

At some point during their elementary school years, just about every kid comes home with a couple of seeds in a styrofoam cup or small plastic starter planter full of potting soil. Often, however, these young plants are forgotten and abandoned by their young caretakers soon after they've sprouted a few leaves. Don't let that opportunity go to waste. If your child brings home a seedling, especially one that produces an edible product, encourage them to see the process through all the way to the end. Involving your kids in caring for houseplants and flowers is certainly worthwhile, but their interest tends to skyrocket when a plant does more than serve as a decorative addition to your home. You'll usually be looking at pumpkin, corn, or sunflower seeds, but the actual type of plant doesn't really matter. The important thing, from a learning perspective, is that with a little care on their part and a little time for Mother Nature to work her magic, kids are able to witness the magical transformation of a lowly, boring seed into a living, growing plant.

Of course, you don't need to wait for a germination project to happen at school—start your own plant by having your child pick out a small packet of seeds of their choice at any home and garden store and do the entire project at home. After the seeds have been planted, watered, and sprouted, have the child carefully transfer the seedlings to a larger pot that can be cared for indoors or on the porch if the weather is suitable. Even better, after several days of growth, the seedling can be transplanted into your garden. From here on out, the care and work necessary for the plant's long-term survival should be the child's responsibility, though this will un-doubtedly require frequent supervision and encouragement on your part. In due time, you'll be able to celebrate their success by roasting some sunflower seeds, buttering an ear of corn, or carving a pump-kin for Halloween. And don't forget to save some of the seeds their plant produced for next year.

Graduating from that germination project to getting your kids in-volved in gardening is a logical next step. If you don't have a yard, you can use a porch or a windowsill. If you're new to gardening yourself, resources abound in the form of books such as *Plants You Can't Kill,* *The Vegetable Gardener's Bible,* and the four regionally specific volumes of the Month-by-Month Gardening series. Experienced mentors should be easy to come by—there's probably one or more in your family or neighborhood.

Unlike a special outing to camp, forage, fish, or hunt, a garden, even a small one, will be a day-in, day-out labor of love for at least a few months each year. Including children in the process of gardening will provide a very real education about the kind of long-term com-mitment that's necessary to get from seed to harvest. Though you'll probably find that kids are eager to jump in when it's time to do the planting and harvesting, prepare for some resistance when they're called upon for mundane chores like pulling weeds. Luckily, there's a tangible reward that comes from all those weeks of garden chores. That reward may be a long time in coming ("Are these strawberries *ever* going to turn red?"), but to have something—whether it is one plant in a pot or a big patch of dirt full of all kinds of plants—that is designated as *theirs* and which will succeed, or fail, based on their effort alone is a wonderful life lesson.

## PLANNING AND PREPPING YOUR GARDEN

Full-fledged food-producing gardens take a lot of work and some planning to maintain. Don't fear the planning stage, as it will make your initial forays into gardening much easier. Here's a checklist to take into account.

### KNOW YOUR ZONE

Before you decide what you want to plant, you'll need at least a basic understanding of what will actually grow in the area where you live. That starts by knowing what gardening zone you occupy; the United States, including Alaska and Hawaii, is divided into different plant hardiness zones by the United States Department of Agriculture. For reference, interior Alaska, which can have freezing temperatures during the summer and where the growing season is short, lies in Zone 1. Much of Hawaii, where ambient air temperatures remain warm throughout the year, is designated Zone 10. The majority of the lower 48 falls between Zone 4 in the north and Zone 9 in the south. Individual zones are further divided into sub-zones, but that's getting nitpicky. Each zone has a list of corresponding crops that tend to do well in that climate. Gardening manuals like the ones mentioned earlier will provide a more detailed explanation of the different zones and the length of their growing seasons and what types of plants grow best at certain latitudes, and information is abundant online. These zones are guidelines, and you can certainly experiment a bit, but don't be surprised if you have trouble growing a warm-weather species like bell peppers in a northern hardiness zone. When in doubt, it's a good idea to focus on plants that can be grown successfully in a wide range of hardiness zones, and particularly the zone you live in.

## SELECT YOUR GARDENING STYLE

What type of gardening you're going to do is partly a matter of space, among other considerations. Potted plants work well for many people who don't have a lot of outdoor space or want to expand their capacity beyond an actual garden. Raised beds are popular with gardeners these days, and they're convenient for a number of reasons. You can strategically place them wherever you want on your property, even on a concrete patio or a patch of gravel where digging a garden isn't an option. Essentially just large containers filled with dirt, they allow gardeners to cultivate a variety of plants in a deep layer of rock-free store-bought gardening soil. It's a great fix if the soil in your yard is too shallow, too rocky, or lacking the right composition for gardening. Raised beds also provide some measure of protection against ground-dwelling garden raiders like rabbits and mice, and they can be quickly covered to protect plants from insects and birds, hot sun, and killing frosts. Lastly, they're much easier to keep weed-free than in-ground gardens. You'll find raised-bed kits sized to suit your needs, or you and your kids can build your own. Most are constructed out of water-resistant treated lumber that will last many years, but they can also be made with concrete or metal sheeting. You can even use repurposed old bookshelves, bathtubs, livestock water and feed troughs, or tractor tires. The one drawback to raised beds is that they put a finite limit on the amount of space you'll be working with. Planting directly in your soil allows you more flexibility, but it means you'll have to contend with that soil.

## GARDENING INDOORS AND OUT

Novice gardeners may be surprised to learn that indoor gardening is often the easiest way to tiptoe into growing food. For some families, it might be the only option. But even for those with plentiful outdoor space, growing food inside offers simplicity and convenience. It's easier to keep an eye on plants when they're within arm's reach, and a controlled indoor environment eliminates many of the challenges that outdoor gardeners must contend with on a daily basis, such as pests and weather events. The outdoor gardening season also ends for many folks when the first hard frosts of autumn hit, while indoor gardening can be done year-round, regardless of the temperature outside.

The more space you have for plants, the more options you'll have, but even a corner of your kitchen counter or a couple of windowsills can provide room enough to get started. Obviously, there will be limitations to what you and your children can accomplish indoors with limited space. You certainly won't be producing enough fruits and vegetables to eliminate the need for trips to the grocery store, but it is possible to supplement your diet with some that are homegrown. Commercially produced countertop hydroponic herb gardens that don't require any soil are popular in many households. For a modest investment, it's possible to maintain a steady supply of mint, basil, thyme, rosemary, or whatever other herbs your family might get the most use out of. Similar hydroponic systems allow people to grow tomatoes, peppers, strawberries, and many other fruits and vegetables inside. But growing these plants potted in soil indoors is easily accomplished as well, provided you have the space in your home. You can buy the soil, pots, and seeds separately from any home and garden store, or you can purchase kits that come with everything you'll need. Mushroom-growing kits are becoming more popular with indoor gardeners, too—they're equal parts fun science experiment and food source.

Lastly, there are practical reasons for dedicated outdoor gardeners to engage in at least some indoor gardening. If you live in an area with significant seasonal temperature swings, you can get a jump on spring planting by starting your outdoor plants inside. Your garden will be more productive if you start your seedlings indoors for a few weeks in late winter and early spring and wait until the danger of killing frosts has passed before transplanting them outside as hardy, well-developed plants. Many outdoor gardeners extend their growing season by utilizing greenhouses for this purpose; these also allow plants to keep producing well into the fall, when outdoor temperatures begin to drop below the freezing point at night.

## KNOW YOUR SOIL

If you plan on gardening directly in the native soil of your yard or property, you must pay attention to the type of soil you're planting in. Soil quality varies widely, even within the same zones and localities. One area on the side of a mountain might have dry, rocky, low-nutrient soil, while just a mile away down in the river valley, the soil is moist, loamy, and nutrient-rich. Dirt is mostly made up of a mixture of organic matter and minerals, and for many fruits and vegetables the quality of that mixture largely determines the quality of their output. The pH of your soil (a measure of how acidic or alkaline it is) is also important. For example, some plants can tolerate and even thrive in acidic soil, while others cannot. This kind of information can be found in any decent gardening handbook, but you'll still need to test your soil to find out its makeup. Soil test kits are available at any gardening retailer, and they'll tell you not only what pH you're working with but also what nutrients your soil might be lacking. These tests provide crucial information you need to have before you start planting, and they're another one of those fun science experiments to engage children in. After testing, you'll know whether you need to add soil amendments such as natural organic matter (manure and compost) or prepared fertilizers that contribute nutrients and help achieve ideal pH levels in your garden.

## CHOOSE YOUR SEEDS OR STARTER PLANTS

If you're growing food, focus on foods your kids will actually eat. Plant your garden accordingly, and maintain interest by allowing them to choose a few things they'd like to grow. If they like green beans and cucumbers, dedicate a large portion  of your garden space to those vegetables while still setting aside some space for expanding their palate with veggies they're reluctant to eat but that you enjoy.

Whether you choose seeds or starter seedlings depends partly on the plant. Some plants (such as radishes and carrots), can only be grown from seeds. Others (like beans) are widely available as starter plants but are also very easy to grow from seeds, and they don't need to be started indoors. At several dollars apiece for a starter, growing beans from seeds will save you some money. Beyond their modest expense, it's fair to say that some dedicated gardeners view buying starters as lazy or a form of cheating. And it is true that using starter plants skips some steps in the seed-to-harvest process, but there's no shame in using them. Tomatoes, cucumbers, and many other staples can be started from seed indoors and transplanted into the garden, but it's much less time-consuming to buy starter plants and transfer those into the garden. In other words, there is no one best way for all plants.

## DESIGN YOUR GARDEN

When you've finalized your plan for what plants you're going to grow and how you're going to get them started, you'll also need to decide where in your garden they'll end up. Some species of plants don't do well when they are planted next to other species; tomatoes, for example, struggle if they're planted close to members of the brassica family like broccoli and cabbage. There are also plants that you *should* grow next to one another. This is known as companion planting, and it can help gardeners by repelling pests, attracting beneficial pollinators and pest-eating insects, providing shade or support, and improving soil fertility. For instance, when basil is planted next to tomatoes, it wards off aphids; pole beans provide shade that prevents lettuce and the leaves of cucumber plants from wilting on hot, sunny days. A good way to go about deciding what to plant where is to draw a grid-style map of your garden with your kids and label each section appropriately. Then it's time to plant, work, and wait for a few weeks for the payoff to begin.

## KEEP A GARDEN JOURNAL

Encourage your children to document their experience for future reference. Keeping a gardening journal is a way to celebrate successes, and it will help you make each successive gardening season more fruitful. Together, you can record how much food was put up as well as the recipes that your family enjoys. From year to year, it can be hard to remember the details of what was planted where, what seed varietals were used, and why something flourished or didn't. In time, you might find that journal becomes a cherished heirloom that gets passed on from one generation to the next.

## SHARE AND PRESERVE YOUR BOUNTY

People who plant large in-ground gardens and fruit-bearing trees do so with the intention of enjoying their bounty months after the growing season has ended. In good years, even a couple of raised garden beds or a fruit tree can produce more food than a small family is able to eat fresh throughout the summer. With that in mind, it's a good plan to learn how to preserve fruits and vegetables. Freezing is one option, and in many cases a good one. But you can save some freezer space and make some simple, quick meals, desserts, and snacks by dehydrating and canning some of your harvest (look up and follow the USDA safety recommendations on canning if you're going that route). Both processes are easy to do with kids and leave your family with a store of shelf-stable food that doesn't require refrigeration or freezing. Don't forget to share with friends and neighbors—giving away the fruits of your labor is one of the great pleasures of caring for a food-producing garden, and it teaches kids a great lesson about generosity and community.

## START A COMPOST PILE

If you're already doing some outdoor gardening or considering making the leap, it's a good idea to start composting. Your family probably has some food in the fridge right now that's going to end up in the trash and eventually the landfill. Consider reducing your waste stream and turning leftover fruit and vegetables that have gone bad back into fruits and vegetables by making your own compost pile. It might seem like a mundane chore at first, but it's another one of those simple long-term projects that teach kids the value of taking part in a natural and beneficial process. You only need a small corner of your yard to make one, and the resulting decomposed organic matter is a high-energy boost for the plants in your garden. You can maintain a compost pile directly on the ground, where you'll attain the added benefit of attracting a whole bunch of earthworms for fishing bait, or you can buy commercially produced composting containers; you can also find simple plans online to build your own.

## BASIC GARDENING GEAR LIST

Gardening is more time-consuming than it is expensive, but there are some things that you can't get by without. What you'll need will vary depending on the size and scope of your garden. Chances are that you already have some of these items or have something that can be repurposed for gardening. Eventually you might find you end up with a shed or garage full of gardening equipment, but here are some of the basics for getting started:

- Seeds and starter plants
- Seed starter trays and containers
- Soil mixes, compost, and fertilizer
- Trellises, stakes, posts, and garden cord or wire
- Pots and barrel planters
- Raised bed materials
- Work gloves
- Shovel, garden rake, garden hoe, hand trowel, and pitchfork
- Pruning shears, garden scissors, and small pruning saw (for fruit trees)
- Wheelbarrow
- Watering hose and water wand, watering bucket, or a drip irrigation system
- Material for sun or frost protection—shade cloth, blankets, tarps, etc.

# THE INEVITABILITY OF FAILURE

Anyone who's gardening, kids and adults alike, should be prepared for the fact that even with all the information at your disposal in the form of books and websites and mentors, you *will* experience at least some level of failure in your garden. From pests and disease to drought and hailstorms, plants, both wild and garden varieties, die for many reasons. Sometimes they die because of mistakes their caretakers made, such as under- or overwatering. Overcrowding plants by planting too many of them too close together is also a common reason for failure. And then there are the times when you do everything right and the growing conditions are perfect and garden plants still fail.

Given all this inevitable failure, persistence is an attribute that aspiring gardeners must adopt—one of many lessons a garden can teach. Walk away from a garden failure without starting over, and there won't be any fruits of your labor to enjoy at the dinner table. And even in failure, gardening teaches its participants about natural phenomena that many folks never stop to think about, from the appetites of hungry pests to the interrelationships of plant species. Although some frustration is as inevitable as the failure that spawns it, the ability of a garden to renew itself under the watchful eye of a loving caretaker may be the greatest lesson of all.

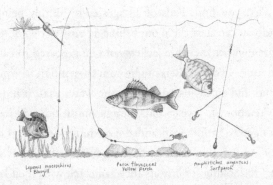

Lepomis macrochirus
Bluegill

Perca flavescens
Yellow Perch

Amphistichus argenteus
Surfperch

## I V .

## F I S H I N G

## THE LURE OF LOCAL WATERS

You will certainly find wilder places, more seclusion, and the possibility of better fishing if you're willing to travel, but for kids, a small farm pond down the road that's full of sunfish can be just as productive and magical as a remote Alaskan river during the salmon run. Some easily accessible small bodies of water are designated as "kids-only" fishing spots that are stocked regularly with rainbow trout or channel catfish. If you live near the ocean, there should be good fishing opportunities at or near the same beach where you take your kids swimming. There are also dozens of public fishing piers and private piers that charge a small access fee scattered all along both coasts. Head boats that run a couple of fishing trips per day for as many as twenty or thirty people are another saltwater option. For a modest fee, you'll be provided with fishing gear and bait as well as assistance from the captain and mates.

But to start your family fishing career in the simplest way possible, just find the closest local body of water with stuff living in it. Then head over there with an aquarium net and a bucket to muck around and see what you find. Kids of all ages enjoy simply being around water, and you can start them out fishing as early as two or three years old. Just remember their life jackets, and be prepared to call it a day after an hour or two. Toddlers might want to spend more time playing in the mud and throwing rocks into the water than fishing. By the time they're about five years old, though, most kids will have developed a longer attention span and the dexterity needed to catch fish with a rod and reel on their own, though if the fishing is slow they may revert to looking for critters they can catch with their hands or a small aquarium net.

If this happens, consider jumping right in and joining them. After all, they're still having a blast and learning about aquatic environments and the creatures that live there. Kids can put snails and crabs in buckets as temporary pets or bring aquatic bugs, salamanders, and tadpoles home to observe for a day or two before releasing them back into their natural habitat. Sometimes they even catch other things that can be eaten—a batch of deep-fried frog legs or boiled crayfish is a nice consolation prize if you don't bring home any fish. Regardless of the size or shape of your early fishing ventures, if you orient yourselves toward getting as close to the wild world as possible, take turns leading and letting the kids lead, and keep an eye out for ways to extend the experience beyond the outing itself, you're on the right track.

If you and your kids have never wet a line, it pays to seek out a fishing mentor. Don't be afraid to ask a friend, neighbor, or family member who has some fishing experience for help. You can also visit the nearest state fish and game agency office to talk to a game warden or fisheries biologist. These folks are usually very forthcoming with advice about taking kids fishing.

You can find a wealth of information on state fish and game agency websites, including maps of public fishing access sites, what fish species are present in certain bodies of water, regularly updated fishing reports, and even a calendar of free fishing days when adults don't need a license as well as "learn to fish" programs that are open to the public. It's a good idea to check the fishing reports at your local tackle shop and get friendly with the employees there. If you make a habit of stopping in with your kids to buy some gear or bait now and then and ask for advice politely, you'll more than likely score some insider tips and tricks for catching fish in local waters.

If you really want to speed up your learning curve, consider hiring a professional fishing guide; it's a worthwhile investment. Whether you're trying to figure out your local fisheries or you're on vacation in an unfamiliar area, you'll save a lot of time and misery by taking advantage of a guide's knowledge and skill. Just be sure to let your guide know you'll be bringing kids, and be honest about their experience level. Not all guides like taking kids, but the really good ones enjoy teaching young anglers new skills, and some specialize in teaching kids.

## FISHING GEAR

Like many other outdoor activities kids enjoy—skiing, mountain biking, or even playing on a baseball or football team—fishing is a gear-intensive pastime. Sure, you can pare it down and try your luck catching a few fish out of a farm pond with just a long cane pole, a short length of line, and a baited hook, like kids did in the old days. Practically speaking, however, both you and your children will have a much better experience if you invest in a basic set of quality gear that will allow you to fish multiple water types for multiple species. You don't need to spend a fortune (although it's certainly possible), but if you're planning on making fishing a regular activity, you don't want to make the mistake of starting out with cheap stuff that is going to fail or break after a couple of trips. If you're unsure of whether your kids will catch the fishing bug, try borrowing equipment the first few times you go out.

## RODS AND REELS

Resist the urge to buy your kids cheapo Marvel superhero or Disney character miniature fishing combos—they're designed to catch gullible parents, not fish. However, millions of kids have caught millions of fish with the classic Zebco spincast combo. The push-button reel is very easy for kids to operate and the fiberglass rod is very durable, casts pretty well, and can handle everything from small sunfish to big bass. At about thirty bucks, it's a good option until you and your kids have built up a year or two of experience and want to upgrade your equipment.

Later, you may want to look into getting some higher-quality open-faced spinning reels and fishing rods made out of graphite composites. A versatile general-use setup would be a six-foot medium-action rod and a midsized spinning reel. If you mostly fish for small sunfish or trout, though, a light or ultralight package might be better. Conversely, if you fish mostly for bigger fish like salmon or redfish, a heavy-action setup may be needed. Companies like Cabela's and Bass Pro Shops sell quality, affordable combo packages. You also can't go wrong with Ugly Stik or St. Croix rods, and reels made by Shimano or Okuma.

## FISHING LINE

Many of the fishing combo packages purchased at places like Walmart will come with a reel pre-spooled with fishing line, but you're much better off buying good line and spooling your own reels. It's simple enough to do, and there's nothing more heartbreaking than watching a kid lose a nice fish because the cheap fishing line that was on their reel when you bought it snapped just as you were about to net their trophy.

For castability, you will need to match your fishing line to the type of rod you're using.

All fishing lines are rated according to their breaking strength. For instance, if you were using 4-lb. test and tried to lift a five-pound catfish out of the water up onto a fishing dock by grabbing the line, it would more than likely snap. These ratings are deceiving, though: A five-pound catfish in the water actually "weighs" much less than five pounds since the mass of submerged objects is supported by the water around them. It's therefore possible to land fish much heavier than the strength rating of the line being used. Fish like halibut and tuna weighing hundreds of pounds are commonly landed on fishing lines rated as 80-lb. test. Most general-use medium-action rods used for freshwater fishing are rated for lines between 8 and 15 lb., depending on the species being targeted.

The most common and affordable fishing lines are made out of monofilament, which is a single strand of nylon. Monofilament line is versatile and has worked well for decades. Some anglers prefer fluoro-carbon lines because they're less visible to fish, a little stronger than mono lines, and a little more resistant to abrasion, but they're also more expensive.

The strongest option of all is braided line made with tiny, woven strands of polyethylene called microfilaments. Braided lines used to be made out of strands of woven horsehair and plant fibers; today's versions are much stronger than mono or fluorocarbon lines of the same diameter, and they don't break down and weaken over time. They're much pricier, but many anglers find the extra strength and smaller diameter worth the money. Braid does have some drawbacks, how-ever. Thin braided line can slice open a finger like a sharp knife if it isn't handled properly, so never yank on it when it's under a lot of tension. Since it's not as stiff as monofilament, it's also more prone to getting knotted and tangled.

Speaking of tangles, no matter what kind of line you're using or how carefully you keep an eye on your kids, children will always manage to turn their fishing line into a confusing bird's nest of overlapping loops and knots. With really bad tangles, cutting the line and starting over is a faster fix than trying to untangle the knots.

## HOOKS

Hooks are sized by number, but it's a confusing system for beginners. For most hooks used by recreational anglers, the larger the number, the smaller the hook. A tiny #12 hook is used for catching small panfish, while a #1 hook might be used for big catfish. But for hooks bigger than #1, the system reverses and adds a zero. So a #4/0 is much bigger than a #4. Generally speaking, the bigger the bait and fish, the bigger the hook you use. Carry a range of hook types and sizes for different baits and different fish; you'll be covered for most freshwater game fish with a selection of #1/0–#10 bait hooks.

There are also a vast array of hook shapes designed for different purposes. It's not important to know them all, but the most basic is a J-hook. They're shaped just like—wait for it—the letter *J,* with varying shank (the straight part of the hook) lengths as well as hook gapes or gaps (the space between the shank and the point). Circle hooks have a similarly self-explanatory shape, but there are important differences in how they work. With J-hooks, when a fish bites, you need to "set" the hook by pulling back hard on the rod. When you get a bite on a circle hook, though, you just reel until the line tightens up and the fish hooks itself in the corner of the mouth.

Regardless of what specific type of hook you're using, most have a sharp barb that faces the opposite direction of the point of the hook. Barbed hooks help to prevent fish from getting away, but they're very difficult to remove from human flesh; barbless hooks are a safer bet when fishing with kids. You can use pliers to mash down the barb until the point is flush and unexposed. And should a barbed hook get lodged in a child's hand or eye (or anywhere else), don't try to force it out; tape it down so it doesn't move and head to the emergency room.

## BAIT

There's no question that using live bait is typically the best way to catch fish. Worms will catch panfish, trout, suckers, and a host of other fish. Minnows work extremely well for some of these fish, too, and for piscivorous (fish-eating) predators like bass, walleye, and northern pike, live minnows are deadly. Other worthwhile live baits include maggots, mealworms, waxworms, grasshoppers, crickets, and leeches. In saltwater, you can't get by without baitfish like pilchards or menhaden, as well as shrimp and small crabs.

Dead baits are also very effective in some situations. Dead shrimp work well for catfish in freshwater and for many saltwater species. "Cutbait" is nothing more than strips of fish flesh. Cutbait is simply cast out and pinned to the bottom with a lead weight, where it will attract fish by scent alone. Strips of squid meat are also a popular bait with saltwater anglers because the meat is tough and stays on the hook well. Prepared baits (concoctions of dyed and scented dough-like material) are used for catfish and stocked trout. There are also liquid scents that you can add to baits and lures to make them more noticeable and attractive to fish. And, finally, odd as it might seem, everything from canned corn to pieces of bread to chunks of hot dog catches its fair share of fish, too.

You can buy bait of all types at local tackle shops, sporting goods stores, and even some gas stations, but there's another option for securing live bait that will be way more fun for kids and lets them get their hands dirty while helping them develop a better understanding of the natural food chain. Rather than spending a few bucks for a dozen nightcrawlers, collect enough for an entire fishing season in your own backyard. The compost pile you maintain for your garden is a great place to find smaller garden worms, and during the spring and summer, the large earthworms known as nightcrawlers leave the safety of underground burrows to mate in grassy areas on rainy nights. You'll need a flashlight with the lens covered in transparent red plastic, or headlamps that have a red light setting. Nightcrawlers don't have eyes, but sensors on their skin are alarmed by bright yellow or white light that resembles natural sunlight. Sneak up to them quietly so that they don't retract back into their holes when they feel the ground vibrating from heavy footsteps. Grasp their bodies firmly between thumb and forefinger, as close to their burrows as possible, and pull them up slowly, being careful not to tug so hard that you break them in half.

You can store worms in a refrigerator, inside a styrofoam bait container full of moist soil and newspaper shreds; they'll keep for a few weeks. Toss in a small amount of used coffee grounds, grass clippings, or bits of raw vegetables now and then to feed them. Other live baits that kids will have fun catching include grasshoppers and crickets. Aquatic baits like crayfish and minnows can be trapped and kept in the garage in a tub of cool water that's oxygenated with an aquarium aerator. Throw some goldfish food flakes into the tub periodically.

## LURES

Fishing with bait is how most of us got started, but you'll also want a basic assortment of artificial lures. For beginner anglers, lure selection can be daunting. The tackle-shop wall displaying dozens of different lures in hundreds of sizes, shapes, and colors can overwhelm, and no matter which ones you buy, you need to know how to fish them the right way. Some are cast out and reeled back in fast, others slow; some are designed to be fished erratically or jerked up and down off the bottom. Some float, and others sink. Don't be afraid to tell the sales clerk you're a beginner and ask what lures are working well locally for different game fish and how to use them.

The best lures for beginners are in-line metal spinners like Panther Martins and Rooster Tails, metal spoons like Kastmasters, hard-bodied baitfish plugs made by Rapala, and leadhead jig hooks with bucktail bodies, soft plastic twister tails, and Gulp minnows. Spinners, spoons, and plugs are easy for kids to master; they're simply cast out and reeled in. Vary the depth you let them sink to and the speed of the retrieve until you find what the fish want. These lures can also be trolled slowly behind a boat to cover a lot of water effectively. Jigs are usually fished near the bottom with an up-and-down "jigging" motion, but they can also be cast out and reeled in like other lures. Most predatory game fish respond well to lures with bright, flashy colors, but sometimes dull, natural patterns work best. Buy a selection of lures in various sizes and colors, giving you the option to change things up and experiment if the fish aren't interested in what you're using.

## BOBBERS AND SINKERS

Depending on the species, its feeding habits, and a host of other variables, fish can be found just under the surface of the water, suspended in the middle of the water column, or down near the bottom. A worm pinned down on the bottom isn't going to get noticed by bluegills that are eating ants blown onto the water's surface. Likewise, it's difficult to coax a yellow perch that's down in twenty feet of water up to the surface to eat a minnow. Thus you need a collection of items that will help you adjust the depth of your bait or lure.

To keep your bases covered, add a handful of different sizes and shapes of lead weights and a couple of different styles and sizes of bobbers or floats to your tackle box. Get some pinch-on weights (called split shots), some sliding bullet sinkers, and some stationary sinkers with a brass eyelet. The ubiquitous, inexpensive red-and-white plastic spheres most people picture when they think of a bobber work well for detecting strikes and for hanging baits just below the surface. You'll also want some more sensitive "stick" bobbers, also known as "floats" by some anglers. They have a narrower, elongated shape that detects light strikes very well, and they slide easily up and down your line so you can quickly adjust your depth as needed.

## TACKLE BOXES AND BAGS

These days, old-school canvas fishing vests have been replaced by lightweight, technically advanced packs, and you don't see very many beat-up metal tackle boxes sitting around in the bottom of boats. But whether you're in a boat or fishing from shore, you need a way to organize, store, and transport your gear. A waterproof, rigid, TPU-coated vinyl tackle bag is a great place to store fishing gear when you're boating. To keep things tidy, try storing your tackle inside transparent plastic utility boxes with dividers. There's a box for hooks, one for sinkers, and several for different types of lures. Depending on where you're headed and what you're fishing, you can move different boxes in and out of the bag.

When fishing from shore or wade fishing, a waterproof sling pack comes in handy. You can fill it with a pared-down version of your utility box fishing kit.

## ADDITIONAL GEAR TO CONSIDER

The basic kit outlined in the preceeding sections will allow you and your kids to catch fish just about anywhere. You'll add more items as your fishing knowledge, experience, and methodology grow, but there are a few more things you'll probably want to have on hand sooner rather than later.

- **Multi-tool.** A multi-tool is practically a must-have item when you're fishing. You can use them to repair or modify gear, cut line, sharpen hooks, unhook fish, gut fish, and more. Get a stainless steel model that's impervious to rust. You can also use long needle-nose pliers to remove hooks from fish. Medical hemostats are cheap and work well, too, though they're not as durable or as useful for other tasks. Just make sure you have some kind of tool that can be used to safely remove hooks and avoid sharp teeth.

- **Stringer.** Stringers are used to secure your catch and keep them alive while you keep fishing. Some stringers are just lengths of thin nylon cord. Look for sturdier models with a series of large metal clips that can each hold multiple small fish or one big one.

- **Landing net.** Landing nets greatly increase the likelihood of putting some fish in the freezer. Many fish escape at the last moment as they thrash around next to shore or the boat. Get one with a long handle that makes scooping fish easier, and a rubber bag—hooks get stuck in net bags made out of nylon cord.

- **Polarized sunglasses.** Anglers favor sunglasses with polarized lenses that reduce the glare of light reflecting off the water. This allows them to more easily spot fish. Kids are tough on sunglasses—they break and lose them at an astonishing rate—but beyond the benefit of being able to see fish, wrap-around sunglasses with shatterproof lenses are one of the most important pieces of safety gear you can bring on a fishing trip, and not just for kids. Think of them like the safety goggles worn when using power tools and chainsaws, only they protect your eyes from the fishing hooks that are flying around in the air all day long.

- **Waders.** Hip boots and chest waders allow you to access deeper water and cross shallow streams, and they're also a godsend when it comes to keeping your kids relatively dry and warm. You may even find yourself putting them on your kids when you're fishing on shore as added insurance in case some unexpected wading occurs. When you are planning on wading with kids, don't get over-confident about taking them into cold water, fast current, or water over their knees. Make sure the belt on their chest waders is cinched down tight, and if they can't swim, put a life jacket on them even if you're wading in shallow water.

- **Boats.** Boats aren't a necessity for a successful day on the water, but they sure do open up a lot more opportunities to catch fish. This is especially true if you want to escape crowded fishing access sites where shorebound anglers congregate or if you're trying to catch game fish that prefer deeper waters away from the shoreline. Boats also give anglers the ability to cover much more water than you could ever hope to fish on foot. Even small human-powered watercraft like rowboats, canoes, and kayaks will allow you to reach water inaccessible by roads or trails. Many untouched, remote fishing, hunting, and camping spots in wilderness settings like the Boundary Waters Canoe Area and other locations can only be reached by boat.

- **Sonar flasher.** A sonar flasher is a fish-finder made for ice fishing; they aren't strictly necessary, but they sure do improve your odds of success.

- **Crayfish traps.** Catching crayfish the hands-on way may be more engaging for children, but if you're looking to catch a bucket's worth, the more efficient method is to trap them just like crabs or lobsters. You can buy crayfish traps that look like smaller versions of commercially produced crab traps, or you and your children can find instructions on YouTube for building your own crayfish traps out of anything from a five-gallon bucket to pieces of plastic or wire mesh. For bait, use the guts and carcasses of fish you've caught, or punch some holes into a can of cat food to coax crayfish into the trap. Crayfish are most active at night, so it's best to place your traps in the afternoon and come back early the next morning to check them.

# CLEANING YOUR CATCH

There's a lot of important work that needs to happen in the hours after a fish is caught, the most immediate being short-term storage. If you put your catch on a stringer in the water to keep them alive while you con-

Ictalurus punctatus - Channel Catfish

tinue to fish, you can clean them later. But keep an eye out for fish that die on the stringer. Fish flesh begins to deteriorate quickly, especially if it's warm outside. A good alternative to keeping fish on a stringer is to dispatch them immediately after they're caught and place them in an ice bath inside a cooler. You can use a stout wooden club to administer a quick blow to the head of larger fish or use the point of a fillet knife to pierce the brain of smaller fish. Bleeding large fish and dark-fleshed fish like salmon and bluefish by cutting their gills also helps to minimize off-flavors. To ensure the best eating experience, even fish that are bled and kept on ice are best cooked within a few hours of being caught. If you can't get to them within a day, they should be frozen.

Before you freeze or cook your fish, however, you'll need to clean them.

## GUTTING FISH

There are a couple of ways to go about cleaning fish, depending on their size and how you're going to cook them. The first is gutting fish that will either be cooked whole or cut crosswise into steaks. Gutting fish is a simple process that kids with a little experience handling knives can manage pretty easily; affordable fillet knives made by companies like Rapala and Kershaw are much better suited to the task than standard kitchen or butcher knives, though they need regular sharpening to maintain the serious edge required for cleaning fish. Insert the tip of the knife into the fish's vent, a small hole in their belly where waste is expelled. Make an incision through the belly running from the vent all the way to their gills. Then remove the guts and gills and rinse the cavity clean. You'll need to scrape the line of dark, congealed blood on the underside of the spine away with a spoon or your thumbnail. The head can be removed, though it's not necessary. Don't forget to have your kids check the stomach contents for some valuable insight into what the fish were eating.

## FILLETING FISH

Filleting fish is a necessary first step if you want a boneless piece of meat, but keep in mind that many fish, notably salmon, also have pinbones that will need to be removed with tweezers, and some fish that are great to eat, like whitefish, have so many bones that it's almost impossible to remove them all. You'll also want to cut away any layers of fat or dark, bloody meat clinging to the fillets, which is what gives fish the powerful fishy flavors that turn some people off. Removing it will ensure you're eating the highest-quality, best-tasting product.

## SKINNING AND SCALING FISH

A pair of pliers with toothed jaws can be useful for gripping fish fillets while you skin them or for peeling the skin off whole fish. For preparations that include the skin, you'll still need a tool to remove the scales. You can use a knife, but a scaling tool with a rough, serrated edge works better—you can purchase one or use a bottle cap on a wooden handle. Scaling is a great job for kids, but it can get messy, so it's best done outside or in the garage.

## STORING FISH

Any fish that won't be eaten right away needs to be properly packaged and frozen in order to preserve its texture and flavor. Don't just throw fish in a plastic bag and toss it in the freezer—exposure to air will quickly turn your catch freezer-burned and practically inedible. Ideally, you should store your fish in vacuum-sealed, heavy-duty plastic packaging. Fish can also be frozen in water inside freezer-grade zipper-lock bags or plastic Tupperware containers; the ice acts as a barrier that protects the fish from freezer burn, though this method takes up a lot more space in your freezer. Keep in mind, even fish that's properly packaged has a limited shelf life. Frozen fish will keep for six months or so before you begin to see a serious decline in quality, and it's best when it's eaten within a month or two.

A word to the wise: Many fish are outfitted with parts that poke to protect them from predators and to capture food. Along with panfish, many freshwater and saltwater species have dorsal fins with defensive, needle-like spines that make it harder for bigger fish and avian predators to swallow them. You can't completely avoid getting poked now and then, but when you're handling these fish, make a habit of folding their fins down so the spines lie back against their body. Most catfish have a single, sturdy spine in their dorsal and pectoral fins. Some of these are mildly venomous and may cause irritation or minor swelling, and the puncture wounds can become infected if they're not washed and treated with antibiotic ointment. The gill cover is the bony plate that protects the sensitive red gill filaments underneath that fish use to extract oxygen from water. Many fish, from crappies to snook, have sharply pointed gill covers. There's also teeth to consider. Game fish like northern pike and bluefish and many others have razor-sharp teeth they use to hold or slice prey. Never stick fingers inside the mouth of a toothy fish to unhook it.

## COOKING AND EATING YOUR CATCH

If your child manages to catch even a single, small fish, you should celebrate the occasion by cooking and eating that catch together. Make sure to choose a simple preparation so that everyone can get involved. Cooking techniques for fish vary widely, but if you already cook and eat store-bought fish, the same recipes will work for fish you catch in the wild. Depending on the species, fish can be excellent poached, baked, grilled, fried, or even pickled.

Frying works well with any fish that has firm, flaky white flesh. Everything from whole bluegills to a big chunk of a giant halibut fillet cut into small pieces can be dipped in batter or coated in breading and dropped in hot oil, then served with a dash of lemon juice and a side of ketchup or tartar sauce for dipping. Although it can get a little messy, using an assembly-line process to prepare deep-fried fish makes it easy to employ the help of children—kids can dip the fish in an egg or milk wash and then coat it in breading before adults handle the frying.

Fish with oily, fatty flesh like trout, salmon, and mackerel are well suited for grilling or broiling, and they're also great for smoking. This last technique requires more prep and cooking time, but it's easy to execute, and the payoff is worth the wait. First, make a simple dry brine of equal parts salt and brown sugar. Make enough to cover the fish on both sides and place in a glass, plastic, or nonreactive metal container overnight. You can spice things up by adding Cajun seasoning, teriyaki sauce, or whatever else your kids might like to the salt-and-sugar mix. You can also dissolve the brine ingredients in a gallon of water and soak the fish in the liquid solution. Once the fish has cured overnight in the brine, rinse and allow to dry in the fridge for a couple of hours. Complete the process by smoking the fish at 160–180 degrees Farenheit over apple or cherry wood chips on a pellet grill or an electric or propane smoker. Depending on how moist or dry you and your kids like your smoked fish, it may take anywhere from two to four hours.

## KID-FRIENDLY FISH

"Panfish" like bluegills, pumpkinseeds, and shellcrackers are perfect targets for youngsters because they're generally pretty easily caught using simple equipment, and they're present in abundant numbers in a wide variety of waterways. You'll find them in tiny farm ponds, giant lakes, and slow-moving rivers throughout the country. In the North, you'll hear folks generally refer to this group of fish as sunfish or "sunnies"; in the South, they're known as bream. Other species that are also lumped into the panfish category include yellow perch, white bass, and white and black crappie. Although none of these species grow very big, they are called panfish for a reason: They're very good to eat. That these smallish fish are almost always colorfully decorated with spots, stripes, and vividly bright colors seems to indicate some divine plan for making them all the more appealing to kids.

Of course, you needn't limit yourselves to panfish, especially once your kids get more experienced. You might even find them leading the way. If your kids get interested in catching a particular kind of fish, spend a little time with them on your state's fish and game website researching places they can be caught. Many kinds of fish can be caught using the same basic tackle and techniques used for panfish, though you'll have to make some adjustments.

That'll also present an opportunity to expand your vocabulary. Fish are known by all kinds of different names, depending on where you find them, and learning their names and origins can make for an entertaining game. For instance, freshwater drum are called sheepshead around the Great Lakes area, but down south they're commonly referred to as gaspergou, a French Cajun term that goes back hundreds of years. To make things more confusing, there's also a completely different fish called sheepshead that lives in saltwater. Then there's striped bass, which are known locally as rockfish in the Chesapeake Bay area. All along the rest of the East Coast, they're called linesiders or stripers. And on the West Coast, around the San Francisco Bay Area, where striped bass aren't native but have been introduced, "rockfish" is a general term that encompasses a large family of fish that aren't even closely related to striped bass.

A note on timing: Some of the best fishing happens late at night, which isn't always practical when you're fishing with young children. But you can take advantage of the low light conditions of dawn and dusk, when fish feed more aggressively than during the middle of the day. Cloudy days can keep fish feeding throughout the day, which provides great incentive to fish in the rain. It's no fun to fish in heavy downpours, but some fantastic fishing can be had during light drizzles—rain often flushes terrestrial insects, earthworms, and other food sources into the water. Too much rain, or even snowmelt, can make the water muddy, though, making it harder for the fish to see your bait. To offset that issue, use bait that puts off scent to attract fish, or lures like spinners or minnow plugs with noisy rattles that make vibrations in the water that fish feel with the sensitive lateral line that runs the length of their body.

## PANFISH

Throughout their range, panfish can be readily caught year-round, but the best fishing, especially for sunfish like bluegills, is in the spring when they're spawning in shallow water. This breeding activity is dictated by the photoperiod (the amount of daylight in a twenty-four-hour period) and water temperature. It might begin as early as March in Florida or as late as June in Minnesota. In northern latitudes, spawning may start and stop and start up again if a long period of cold weather sets in and is followed by more seasonal conditions. In warmer climates, sunfish may spawn multiple times over the course of several weeks.

When sunfish spawn, they dig a shallow depression in the sand, mud, or gravel that ranges from the size of a dinner plate to as wide as a hula hoop. The female stays in the nest until she's laid her eggs, while males circle the area around her, waiting until it's time to fertilize the eggs. Afterward, male sunfish move onto the nest to guard the eggs and the newly hatched fry against predators. Just before, during, and directly after the spawn, sunfish are exceptionally aggressive and will attack any small bait or lure that invades their space. This can lead to some hot fishing. You'll often be able to see the nests, which stand out as light circles on a darker bottom. In turn, the fish are easily spotted hovering over the nest.

Sight-fishing opportunities like this are the pinnacle of excitement; kids will also learn a lot just by watching how the fish react to a bait or lure. Sunfish are most easily caught using live bait like earthworms, maggots, and crickets. Small artificial lures and flies work well, too.

When they are done spawning, sunfish move to the closest drop-off that gives them access to deeper water. You won't be able to see them as well, or at all, but they can be caught using the same tactics by adjusting the depth of your presentation.

Other panfish species like yellow perch and crappie don't exhibit the same shallow-water, nest-building spawning behavior as sunfish, but they do gather in large schools in the spring to breed and feed on small baitfish near bridge pilings, boat docks, weedlines, woody debris, and submerged rock piles. Once you locate them, it's often possible to quickly catch the limit by dropping small live minnows or soft plastic jigs into the school. Unlike sunfish, schools of perch and crappie can move around a lot, so you may only catch a few before they disappear. Moving to another area with the same depth and underwater features might be necessary, or you might get another chance if you're patient enough to wait for them to return or for another school to move into the area.

Panfish of all species tend to gather in schools made up of individuals of roughly the same size. If you're catching mostly tiny specimens, you might want to switch spots. Kids who are new to fishing will have fun catching panfish that only measure a few inches long, but the individual meat yield on a catch of this size is very low; you'll need a significant haul to make a family meal. If you're lucky enough to find a cluster of giant bluegills the size of an adult's hand on their spawning beds, or a school of jumbo yellow perch that span the length of a ruler, you've hit the jackpot. Panfish are a vastly underutilized resource in many areas, and they tend to be prolific reproducers; without angler harvest to keep their numbers in check, they can become overpopulated and stunted. Because of that, bag limits are very liberal in most places, with anglers often being allowed to keep twenty fish each.

## BASS

Wherever you find sunfish like bluegills and pumpkinseeds, you'll almost certainly find their piscivorous cousins—the larger, more aggressive bass—lurking nearby, looking for lunch. Largemouth bass are America's most popular game fish species, due to their abundance, size, and willingness to attack lures and baits, and smallmouth bass aren't far behind in the popularity category. Millions of hard-core bass anglers invest millions of dollars on souped-up "bass boats," high-tech sonar fish-finders, fancy lifelike lures, and the latest and greatest rods and reels for the sole purpose of catch-and-release bass fishing. That's great if that's the kind of fishing that gets you excited, but most bass only weigh a pound or two, and you don't need a garage full of expensive tackle to catch them. In fact, it often happens by accident while you're just trying to catch sunfish.

One of the most effective ways to catch bass with kids is to cast a live minnow, like a golden shiner or a creek chub, suspending it under a bobber near weedlines, docks, and underwater rocks, where bass like to hide in ambush. In fact, all sorts of game fish can be caught this way, including walleye, northern pike, and chain pickerel.

## TROUT

In areas where the water is too cold to support populations of bluegills and bass, you'll find various species of trout. Though they're native to only a handful of states on the West Coast, rainbow trout reign supreme throughout the United States, due to widespread stocking efforts over the last couple of hundred years. Native to Europe and parts of Asia, brown trout have also been stocked throughout North America for well over a century. In many waters, stocked trout are incapable of successful reproduction for reasons ranging from warm water temperature to a lack of appropriate spawning habitat, so they are managed as a "put-and-take" fishery that exists solely to provide a recreational angling opportunity. However, many stocking efforts have led to self-sustaining wild populations of rainbow and brown trout.

Though rainbow and brown trout are widely loved both for sport and table fare, their popularity has come at a cost to native salmonid populations in the United States. There are all kinds of examples you can use to teach kids about the deleterious effects of non-native species on native plants and wildlife, whether they've been introduced intentionally or not. But if you're looking for a prime example of what happens when mankind tries to outdo Mother Nature, look no further than the trout family. Brook trout (actually a species of char) were once found in mountain creeks, coastal rivers, and many inland lakes throughout the eastern seaboard and the Upper Midwest. Today, they've been largely extirpated from most of their native range and replaced by non-native rainbow and brown trout. And in the Rocky Mountains and coastal Northwest, native cutthroat trout have suffered due to widespread introductions of rainbows and browns. To make things even more complicated, the eastern brook trout that were eliminated from most of their native eastern waters were stocked in western states, where their populations have exploded to the point that they now outcompete native cutthroat trout. This scenario isn't limited to trout, either. Wherever non-native game fish have been stocked to create more fishing opportunities, native game fish numbers tend to decline.

Still, introduced trout now exist as a fairly natural, healthy part of many aquatic ecosystems where angler demand ensures they'll continue to be managed as a wild, sustainable resource. In these places, and where they're managed as a put-and-take fishery, it would be foolish not to take advantage of the angling opportunities they provide. And there are still plenty of places left where native trout populations are doing well enough to sustain some recreational harvest.

All species of trout, both wild and stocked, can be caught in lakes and ponds as well as moving water, from giant rivers to tiny creeks. Your kids can use the same rods and reels they use for panfish, and many of the same baits and lures, to catch trout, though they'll need to learn the nuances of fishing in current to catch them out of streams. In lakes, trout swim around looking for food just like other fish, but in streams they tend to hold in one spot, waiting to intercept worms, aquatic insects, and small baitfish carried to them by the current. Trout in rivers in coastal Alaska and Washington and some Great Lakes tributaries gorge on salmon eggs when their larger cousins are spawning. Salmon eggs, or roe, can be used as bait by curing them in salt so they'll harden enough to stay on a hook. Innumerable stocked rainbow trout have also been caught using canned corn, which the fish may mistake for a fish egg. Whatever bait you're using, a natural presentation is achieved by casting upstream and letting your offering drift downstream to the fish. Trout will also aggressively attack small in-line spinners and spoons cast and reeled across the current. And trout are the most popular target for anglers using fly fishing equipment. Fly fishing is often perceived to be a difficult skill to master, but I have a lot of friends who have made a living as fly fishing guides and most of them say kids pick up fly fishing pretty fast, provided they're old enough to have developed a certain level of dexterity.

## CATFISH

Catfish are fun because you can get them with a passive fishing technique known as trot-lining or limb-lining. Both variations use the same basic system and equipment, with minor differences in how they're set up. First, a number of evenly spaced hooks are attached to a length of heavy cord and baited with chicken gizzards, live bait, or cutbait. Trot lines are weighted on both ends, with one end of the cord placed on or near shore and the other stretched out and placed in the water. With limb lining, one end of the line is unweighted and tied to a tree branch or a long, springy limb that's driven into a muddy bank to anchor the line. Once the lines are placed, the hooked baits are left to soak anywhere from a few hours to overnight.

While fishing this way is most popular in the southeastern portion of the country, three species of catfish that are commonly targeted using trot lines and limb lines—channel catfish, blue catfish, and flathead catfish—can be found throughout the United States. All are good eating, and blue cats and flatheads can occasionally reach weights over one hundred pounds.

Sometimes while trot-lining you might be surprised by a fish like gar, and catching a snapping turtle is a real possibility. Snapping turtles have a powerful bite, and gar have dozens of needle-like teeth. If you and your kids are feeling adventurous, these species can be eaten. Otherwise release them, but take care when handling, and keep small fingers well away from their jaws. The safest way to release bycatches of unwanted species is to just cut the line near the hook. Don't worry about hurting the fish or turtle—the hook will rust and fall out in a few days.

## RULES, REGULATIONS, AND RESPONSIBILITIES

Keep in mind that there are special regulations surrounding passive fishing methods and trapping crustaceans. In some states or individual bodies of water, trot-lining is illegal. Where it's legal, there may be a limit to the number of traps that can be placed and/or the number of hooks that can be used, and all lines or traps will need to include a tag with the owner's name, phone number, and fishing license number and must be checked regularly, usually on a daily basis. Both trot-lining and limb-lining are best accomplished with a boat since you need to haul a lot of gear around if you're placing multiple lines.

Overall, as mentioned throughout the book, as accessible and fun as fishing can be, it is important to understand that it isn't a free-for-all activity, nor a risk-free one. Whether you're casting for perch or harvesting shellfish, you can't necessarily fish for whatever you want, wherever and whenever you want—and you won't always be able to keep what you catch. You'll need to follow state and, in some cases, federal regulations aimed at maintaining sustainable populations of game fish while at the same time providing recreational fishing opportunities. You can pick up free copies of regulations booklets at state fish and game agency offices or download digital copies onto your smartphone. And you can always call an agency office and ask to speak to a game warden if you have any questions that you can't find the answer to in the regulations.

All anglers (even children) are expected to follow the rules surrounding season dates, fishing license requirements, legal fishing methods, size and possession limits, and more. These regulations are extensive and subject to change, and to be honest, they are sometimes quite confusing. For instance, it might be legal to keep a certain kind of fish in one body of water but not in another just a few miles away. In other cases, the number of fish you're allowed to legally keep might change depending on the time of year. As an adult, you'll be required to have a state-issued fishing license, though children under a certain age will not need a license. All this is to say that it's a good idea to carry a copy of the fishing regulations with you when you're out on the water.

Some species of fish have been so depleted by dams that block access to spawning areas, excessive commercial harvest, competition with invasive species, or habitat and water quality degradation that only recreational catch-and-release fishing is allowed for those species in order to preserve existing stocks. A prime example is the steelhead that spawn in coastal rivers throughout the Pacific Northwest; this ocean-going strain of large rainbow trout is popular with anglers, but its numbers have fallen drastically in recent years. All wild steelhead must be released. You can keep hatchery-raised steelhead, but you had better make sure you know how to tell the difference: hatchery-raised fish have the adipose fin—the small one on their back near the tail—clipped before they're released into the wild.

Other fish species can only sustain a very limited amount of harvest and are strictly managed under a quota system that implements closures to open seasons once a certain number of fish have been caught by recreational anglers. In some cases, regulations designed to ensure future sustainability prohibit keeping fish that fall above or below a certain size, in order to protect small, young fish or older breeding-sized fish; these "slot limits" are implemented with popular game fish species ranging from walleye to redfish. Depending on the location, even game fish that are generally very abundant, like largemouth bass, might be off-limits during their spawning season, when they are particularly vulnerable to being caught in large numbers.

V.

HUNTING

## WHERE TO BEGIN

Historically, children were introduced to hunting by parents, guardians, or relatives who hunted. There are lots of other ways to source information about hunting these days (books, podcasts, videos, and so on), making it more available to anyone who's interested. But despite all of the opportunities for self-guided learning, for adults who are new to hunting and looking to give their children some exposure, finding an experienced mentor is key. While there are opportunities for newbies to go on mentored hunts through fish and game agencies, these can be limited. Forging long-term relationships with experienced hunters is your best bet for continued education.

Ideally, long before children are handling hunting weapons in the field, both you and they should be familiar with firearm safety protocols. Kids should begin by practicing safe and accurate shooting by plinking soda cans or paper targets with BB guns. From there, move on to target practice at the shooting range with real firearms. Only after children have proven they can handle firearms responsibly and safely is it time to start thinking seriously about hunting. Many children and novice adults begin by accompanying an experienced mentor on a hunt for ducks, wild turkeys, or whitetail deer. By all means, you should jump at chances like that if they're offered, but if you and your child are going out your first time together without the aid of a mentor, one of the best choices for an introductory hunt is small game. Squirrels and rabbits are an ideal place to begin; they're abundant and easily accessible in most of the country. As you gain small game hunting experience together, moving on to bigger or more challenging animals like turkeys and deer won't seem so daunting. You'll find plenty of information on hunting all of these species in this section, but remember that this information is only designed to give new and prospective hunters a basic understanding of hunting. There is no substitute for the knowledge and experience gained from hands-on learning.

## HUNTER SAFETY COURSES

New hunters are required to complete a state-certified education and safety course in order to become eligible to purchase a hunting license. There are some exceptions designed to make initial forays into hunting easier: In some states, adults born before a certain date aren't required to take the class, and more and more states are allowing new hunters to hunt with a qualified, licensed mentor for a year or two before taking the course. But don't underestimate the value of hunter safety classes even if you're a parent, guardian, or caregiver who's old enough to forgo taking the course. Sure, completing one of these day- or two-day-long courses is a prerequisite to meeting certain legal requirements, but the courses are also full of information that will make you a better hunter. And since all children will need to complete hunter education as soon as their mentoring exception expires, it's a great chance to do something worthwhile together.

Conducted by state fish and game agencies and taught by trained instructors, the courses are primarily focused on general and hunting-specific firearm operation and safety protocols; they also cover an overview of hunting regulations, ethical hunting practices, basic marksmanship skills, basic hunting skills, game animal identification, and other relevant topics. The courses are designed to be passed by all students (youngsters included) who study the material; practice tests are given for each section, and even if you happen to fail the official test, you can take it again.

In the past, hunter safety courses were held periodically throughout the year, with part of the course held in a classroom and some out in the field, in several different locations across any given state. Later, some states began giving students the option to complete a portion of the course online but still required classroom attendance for certain lessons. More recently, social distancing measures during the Covid-19 pandemic took the courses completely online, but ideally, vaccinations will allow the system to revert back to some in-person learning.

All state fish and game agencies (sometimes called departments of natural resources) conduct regular "learn to hunt" seminars for various game animals and birds that are free and open to members of the public of all ages. These agencies also organize and oversee mentored youth hunts with game wardens and other agency staff members, though these opportunities are more limited in scope. Keep an eye on your state's fish and game website for chances to apply for these hunts. Some hunter-based wildlife conservation organizations like Ducks Unlimited, the Rocky Mountain Elk Foundation, and the National

Wild Turkey Federation also offer special mentored youth hunts. These groups are worth joining and supporting regardless of those opportunities. For a small membership fee you'll get access to a website full of hunting tips and wildlife behavior information. Most of them also publish magazines just for their members. And if you make a habit of helping out with habitat restoration projects and wildlife conservation fund-raisers, you'll almost certainly find some friendly folks willing to play the role of guide and mentor. The same can be said by joining a local sportsmen's club if there's one in your area; these clubs often have shooting ranges where you can practice. And just as with fishing, hiring a hunting guide can be a worthwhile investment, though the best outfitters come at a significant cost.

Eventually, you and your kids will want to go it alone, and the role of mentor will fall squarely on your shoulders. Hunting is uniquely suited to providing children a deep, hands-on understanding of the natural world that can't be found on a suburban hiking trail or at a KOA campground, but in order to get there, everyone involved will need to become a studied observer of the landscape and its inhabitants while also developing some basic woodsmanship skills. For instance, if you understand that most wild animals are crepuscular in nature, meaning they're most active in the hour or two just after dawn and just before dusk, then you'll stand a better chance of finding them. But you'll do even better if you know how they tend to move across the landscape where they live and for what reasons. You'll also need to pay attention to the wind direction, know what food sources are available for the animals you're hunting, and even be aware of when those animals breed. Just walking quietly through the woods isn't a skill that comes naturally to most people. Being able to identify what bird made a call or what animal left droppings or tracks will only further increase your odds of success. And a truly devoted hunter will be able to follow those tracks to learn even more about the animal and maybe even get a shot. Then, in order to find the animal after the shot is made, a hunter might need to follow a blood trail left on a forest floor carpeted in dark brown and red leaves. The point of all this is that even if you're lucky enough to find a dedicated hunting mentor, there are still a lot of things you'll need to learn on your own. You'll make some mistakes, but that's all part of the process.

## THE TEN GOLDEN RULES
## OF GUN SAFETY

The first and most important rule of hunting is that only a safe hunt is a good hunt. When hunting with children, this rule obviously needs to be reinforced again and again. Storing guns safely is vital. Handling them safely is arguably even more important. Make it clear to children that firearms are a tool—one that is safe to use when handled properly, but also one capable of killing someone if it is handled carelessly. When hunting with a young, inexperienced child, an adult should carry the firearm until it's time to shoot. And don't even consider allowing a child to handle a gun or take a child hunting until they've learned the ten commandments of firearm safety:

1. Treat every gun as if it were loaded.
2. Always keep the muzzle of the gun pointed in a safe direction.
3. Never point the gun at anything you don't intend to destroy.
4. Be sure of your target and what is beyond it.
5. Keep the gun on safety until you are ready to shoot.
6. Never assume the safety will prevent the gun from firing.
7. Keep your finger off the trigger until you are ready to shoot.
8. Keep the gun unloaded until you are ready to use it.
9. Learn how to operate the gun you are using.
10. Make sure you are using the proper ammunition and that the barrel is free of obstructions.

# FIREARMS BASICS

The vast majority of hunting is done with three types of guns: rimfire rifles, shotguns, and centerfire high-powered rifles. What type of gun you and your kids use will largely depend on what species or group of species you'll be hunting, and in some cases how you'll be hunting them. But first you'll need to know what caliber and cartridge to choose.

Rimfire and centerfire rifles are classified by their caliber and cartridge sizes. Caliber is the diameter of a firearm's bore, measured using the decimal value for fractions of an inch or by millimeters using the metric system. Cartridges are ammunition—a brass case containing the bullet, gunpowder, and a primer. The primer is located either on the rim (rimfire) or at the center (centerfire) of the base of the cartridge. When the trigger is pulled, the firing pin hits the primer, which contains a chemical compound that ignites the gunpowder, creating a contained explosion that propels the bullet through the bore and out of the barrel of the gun.

All guns are designed to fire a specific type of ammunition. This is important because different cartridges aren't interchangeable between firearms, even if they share the same caliber. For instance, the .30/30, .30-06, and .308 are all very popular choices for deer hunting, but each uses completely different ammunition even though they all have the same exact caliber, or bore measurement, of .308 inches. Firing, or attempting to fire, the wrong ammunition out of a gun can be extremely dangerous. Always make sure you're using ammunition that matches the cartridge that's stamped onto a gun's barrel.

The same goes for shotguns, but unlike rifles, shotguns and their ammunition are categorized by the gauge of the bore. Gauge is a weight measurement of how many lead balls with a diameter equal to a shotgun barrel's bore it would take to get a pound of lead. The smaller the gauge, the bigger the ammunition. The most common and versatile sizes used in hunting are the 12 gauge and the 20 gauge. (There are 10, 16, and 28 gauges, but only a tiny percentage of hunters use them; and for reasons we won't get into here, the .410 shotgun's name breaks with the gauge system and falls back on the caliber bore measurement used for rifles.) Shotgun ammunition is constructed with a brass base attached to a plastic shell containing a load of pellets, or sometimes a single projectile.

## CHOOSING THE RIGHT FIREARM

Among hunters and target shooters, the .22 long rifle is by far the most popular rimfire rifle cartridge. There are other, faster, more powerful options, but rifles chambered for .22LR make ideal starter guns for new hunters; the gun manufacturer Savage makes extremely affordable, accurate models. These rifles shoot small, light, single projectiles at modest velocities, so they're perfect for hunting small game animals like rabbits and squirrels. They're light and easily handled, have virtually no recoil (the force of the gun pushing back against the shooter), and aren't very loud, all of which makes them pleasant to shoot for kids as young as five or six years old. The best .22 rifles for hunting have a bolt action that loads and unloads cartridges into and out of the chamber by cycling the bolt handle. Rifles with these actions provide the best blend of safety and accuracy. Ammunition for .22s is cheap; you can shoot a box of fifty shells at the shooting range for a few bucks. And practicing is something you and your kids will want to do as much as possible. You can outfit .22 rifles with a magnified scope sight, which makes accurate shooting much easier, but even with a scope it requires a lot of skill to consistently hit a quarter-sized target out to fifty yards. That's the kind of accuracy you'll need to kill a squirrel.

Shotguns are a little more versatile and forgiving than .22 rifles. Because they shoot a load of dozens of small pellets in a wide pattern, hitting your target, especially a stationary one, doesn't require pinpoint accuracy. So a shotgun enables you to hunt small game animals, and it's a must-have for hunting birds. Another helpful feature is that shotguns have different chokes—tubes that screw into the end of the barrel—allowing hunters to adjust the width and density of the load of pellets they're shooting. An improved cylinder choke throws a wide pattern that's ideal for shooting small, fast-moving targets at close range, while a full choke throws a small, dense pattern, which is better when you're taking longer shots, especially at big birds like turkeys. Shotgun ammunition, too, is available in a wide range of pellet sizes used for different hunting applications. Pellets are sized according to an arcane system of numbers and letters, but, essentially, shotgun shells loaded with pellets on the small, light end of the spectrum are used for animals like mourning doves, while larger, heavier pellets are needed to take down something like a Canada goose. (Those are very general rules with all kinds of exceptions that you can dive into as you gain hunting experience.)

A single-shot break-action .410 shotgun is a great choice for children, especially young kids with small frames. They hold only one shell and can be carried around with the action broken open, so that even if the gun is loaded, it can't fire. That means adults accompanying children can easily verify that the gun is being carried safely. Additionally, this type of shotgun has redundant safety features; there is a safety that prevents the firing pin from engaging with the primer, and the gun has a hammer that needs to be cocked before the gun can be fired. Since .410 shells carry a relatively small payload of pellets, shots on small game and birds should be limited to distances no longer than twenty-five yards. Even with these limitations, my son has used his .410 to kill pigeons, grouse, rabbits, and squirrels, and there are .410 loads specifically designed for killing wild turkeys effectively. It's important to note that children will probably grow out of a single-shot .410 within a couple of years. Eventually, you'll want to upgrade them to a 20-gauge pump-action shotgun; older children can start with one. A 20-gauge shotgun has the power and increased pellet load needed to make longer shots, and a pump action allows shooters to take multiple shots quickly. These factors become important when you're hunting large birds like wild turkey and Canada geese and fast-flying birds like mourning doves and ringneck pheasants. Several gun manufacturers make compact youth versions that are just scaled-down versions of their regular models.

In addition to small game and birds, deer can be hunted with shotguns loaded with shells containing a single heavy projectile called a slug. Depending on where you live, these may be your only option during deer season; in many eastern and midwestern rural areas with relatively high densities of people and dwellings, regulations dictate the use of a shotgun as opposed to a rifle. These regulations greatly diminish the chance of accidentally injuring someone or damaging property, since shotgun slugs don't fly nearly as fast or far as bullets fired out of high-powered rifles. Some shotguns can be set up with one barrel for small game and one for deer hunting, an affordable way to double their usefulness.

Outside of these aforementioned zones, deer and other big game animals are most commonly hunted and killed with high-powered centerfire rifles. These guns fire an aerodynamic lead or copper bullet at extremely high velocities, and they're used to hunt everything from wild pigs and whitetail deer to black bears and moose. A shooter with sufficient target practice and hunting experience is capable of cleanly killing big game animals at ranges exceeding three hundred yards with centerfire rifles, especially with the modern telescopic sights, more commonly known as "scopes." Up until a few decades ago, many deer hunters got by without telescopic sights and just used the simple iron sights that all rifles came equipped with. But these days most hunting rifles aren't even made with iron sights, and scopes made by companies like Vortex are considered standard equipment for shooters who need to make precise shots at long distances. (At a minimum, novice big game hunters need to be able to routinely put a group of three consecutive shots inside a three-inch circle on a target that is one hundred yards away, though three-shot groups inside a six-inch circle at two hundred yards is an even better goal.)

There are a few centerfire hunting rifle cartridges with ideal characteristics for novices and youngsters (accuracy, mild recoil, and bullets heavy enough to kill large animals). The .243 Winchester has been a favorite cartridge of young deer hunters for decades, though it lacks the power needed for big animals like elk. If you're looking for an all-purpose big game cartridge with mild recoil that's capable of handling animals up to and including elk, it's hard to beat the 6.5mm Creedmoor or the 7mm-08 Remington. Both of these cartridges are available in the accurate, economically priced bolt action Weatherby Vanguard compact model that is designed specifically for young hunters.

## ARCHERY HUNTING

Although the stories and recommendations in this book have thus far focused primarily on hunting with firearms, many folks, kids included, hunt big game animals with archery gear. That certainly isn't the most efficient option, as an arrow flying out of a compound bow at three hundred feet per second doesn't come close to the power of a bullet flying ten times as fast. Nor is it the easiest for beginners—it takes a lot of time and practice to become a good archery shot. Since the accurate range for arrows is only about fifty yards at maximum, archery hunters also need to be extra stealthy and quiet in order to avoid getting detected by an animal. (In places where the use of crossbows—as opposed to standard bows—is legal during archery seasons, accurate shooting will be more attainable, but the big-picture challenges still remain.)

All of this isn't to say you and your kids shouldn't try archery hunting if it's something you're interested in; many archery hunters say that challenge is what they enjoy the most, and shooting at targets in the backyard is great fun for all. When it is time to hunt and the opportunity arises, keep your shots short, and only let an arrow fly if you're confident the result will be a dead animal.

## TAKING YOUR SHOT

No matter what kind of weaponry you're working with, shots should never be taken at movement alone, or through thick brush that obscures an animal. Just seeing a deer or turkey isn't enough, especially if you're carrying a license that only allows the take of one sex or the other. In cases like these, you'll need to know whether the deer has antlers or if the turkey has a beard *before* you pull the trigger. And once the target has been identified as legal, the shooter will need to wait until the animal's vitals are exposed, making a clean kill possible.

When hunting squirrels or rabbits with a .22 rifle, the ideal shot placement is to the head, though chest shots will also kill them instantly. But if you're hunting big game with a rifle or a bow, head shots are considered unethical by most hunters. A deer's brain is about half the size of a man's fist. If your aim is just a little off, there's a good chance you'll give the animal an injury that isn't immediately fatal but will lead to a long, painful death. The preferred shot placement on big game animals is to the heart/lung area through the rib cage. A whitetail deer's vital heart/lung area is a little bigger than a volleyball; aiming here gives a hunter some room for error to make a clean kill, and animals shot in this area will die very quickly from blood loss and massive trauma. New hunters should be encouraged to only take broadside shots on stationary big game animals, as this shot angle provides the clearest view and exposes the largest profile of the vital area. Running shots should always be avoided unless a hunter is trying to finish off an animal that's already been wounded.

Take the time to study the anatomy of big game animals and the location of their vitals with young hunters. You can even buy rifle and bow targets of different game animals designed for practicing shots to the vital areas at different angles.

When you're hunting rabbits, quail, or other game birds with a shotgun that shoots a wide pattern of small pellets, shooting at a fast-moving target is perfectly acceptable if the hunter has practiced making those types of shots. Wild turkeys are also hunted with shotguns, but they're much harder to kill than smaller critters, so you're likely to only wound them by shooting at them when they're flying. Turkey hunters must wait until the bird is at close range and standing still to make a well-placed shot to the head and neck area.

## A FEW MORE GUN SAFETY RULES FOR HUNTERS

- Always wear hearing and eye protection when operating a firearm. Shooting glasses and earplugs are inexpensive insurance against eye injuries and hearing damage.
- Always identify your target before shooting. When there is any doubt, don't shoot.
- When hunting in a group, always be aware of everyone's location and only fire in a safe direction.
- Never climb over fences or other obstructions with a loaded gun in your hand or on your person.
- Never use the scope on a gun like a pair of binoculars.
- If you fall or trip, point the muzzle in a safe direction. Check the gun for damage and the barrel for obstructions.

## RULES AND REGULATIONS

If you've read the hunting chapter in my book, or if you're a lifelong hunter yourself, you'll have some familiarity with the intricacies of the regulations that surround the sport. Given how variable these factors are—depending on your location, what you're hunting, when you're hunting, and the state of a critter's stock in any given year—there's little we could do in a document of this scope to provide any meaningful overview on the particulars. But I will say that I've been hunting for my entire life, and I still encounter situations where I feel compelled to call a game warden in order to clarify my understanding of the rules.

That said, these regulations exist for very good reasons—to maintain the sustainability of our resources for present and future generations alike. When and where populations of game animals and birds are stable and abundant, hunting opportunities for those species are easy to come by. But if the population of a certain animal is less abundant or limited to just a small area, hunting opportunities will be strictly managed to ensure the future viability of the species. Know that with only a few extremely rare exceptions, no game animal can be hunted without a license.

The caribou hunting grounds I described in the hunting chapter are an example of one such way that game managers can limit harvest of a resource. For caribou, the particular herd we were hunting is managed under a strict quota system that caps how many of the animals can be killed by hunters every year. If the quota is reached before the regular hunting season ends, the state will close the season early. But more abundant small game animals like squirrels and rabbits have more liberal bag limits, with licenses purchasable online or at your local sporting goods store. Getting your hands on a big game license may be just as easy. In many midwestern and southern states, whitetail deer populations are far above the management objectives set by state wildlife biologists. In these places, open seasons are long and hunters can often secure permits to kill multiple deer per year.

To find out what regulations govern the type of hunting you have in mind, check the state fish and game agency website for the state where you'd like to hunt, or give them a call. Every state has a detailed regulations book that you can pick up at the local outpost of your state's fish and game office or download digitally online; once you get a license from any particular state, they'll mail you updated copies of the regulations every year. In the event of confusion, give your local fish and game agency a call and they'll be happy to help with any questions you might have.

## FIGURING OUT WHERE TO HUNT

Fifty years ago, rural landscapes dominated a much greater percentage of our total landmass. Small farms, ranches, and unoccupied woodlots abounded in places that are now dominated by subdivisions and strip malls. We were also a more neighborly and less litigious society. Back then, private landowners were more receptive to allowing hunters onto their property. In most cases, if a farm or woodlot wasn't posted with No Trespassing signs, it was generally considered okay to go and hunt there. That's simply no longer the case. Finding access to a place to hunt can be difficult, and the challenge is magnified for novices who don't benefit from a lifetime's worth of exploration and social connections with other hunters. There are fewer acres available to hunters, and the landowners who manage the existing private lands are generally more likely to post those signs on their property or to charge lease fees in exchange for access.

It's not all bad news, though. If you're willing to put in the necessary time and effort, access is a solvable problem. Plenty of landowners still welcome hunters with open arms, as long as they're willing to ask for permission and abide by the rules. Start the process of meeting landowners by exploring personal connections through work, church, or social organizations. Follow any and all leads that you can turn up. More often than not, you'll find that getting permission for a child to hunt is easier than getting permission for an adult. It seems that people's desire to help kids often overrides any impulse of theirs to keep folks off their land. The best way to ask for hunting permission is to ask in person, though it's perfectly acceptable to make a phone call or write a letter as an initial way of establishing contact with a landowner. However, you'll still want to meet with them in person to talk about what animals you'd like to hunt, when you're welcome, and where you can and can't go on their property.

A great many hunters avoid the need for permissions by avoiding private land altogether and focusing their hunting efforts entirely on public land. Though some hunters complain about the dearth of accessible hunting areas, with just a little effort you'll find an abundance of public lands that are open to hunting, especially in western states, where nearly half of the land is public property, most of which is federally managed; some areas are even actively managed for the specific purpose of providing good habitat for various species of game animals and birds. State fish and game agencies provide hunting and/or fishing opportunities for the public on properties they own or lease, such as state game lands, state wildlife areas, and wildlife management areas; some state forests and state parks are also open to hunting. At the federal level, hunting is permitted in many of the dozens of national wildlife refuges throughout the country as well as on hundreds of millions of acres of federally managed national forests, wilderness areas, and Bureau of Land Management parcels. Additionally, some private landowners allow public access to their properties through various specially regulated cooperative programs; you'll find information about these programs on state fish and game agency websites.

One of the handiest pieces of technology available to hunters interested in contacting private landowners about hunting permission or locating public land on which to hunt is a smartphone GPS mapping app called onX. The app outlines property boundaries and even identifies the names and addresses of landowners so that you can begin the process of securing access to private property. Alternately, you can check out some Trails Illustrated paper maps, which feature a color-coded key letting you know what type of land you're looking at.

## HUNTING GEAR 101

Hunting is just like any other gear-intensive pastime: the more you're willing to invest, the better the quality of the gear. On the plus side, if you and your kids already fish, camp, or hike, or you plan to start, a lot of the gear used for those activities will cross over to hunting. Beginners should focus on getting set up with the foundational hunting gear they don't yet have. You can't get by without a gun, ammunition, and a hunting knife, but you don't need a highly specialized hunting backpack to hunt deer or a pair of waders to go duck hunting when the stuff you already have for hiking and fishing will do.

### BASIC HUNTING GEAR LIST

- Hunting regulations booklet. Keep a hard copy of your state's hunting regulations in your backpack or a digital copy on your phone.
- Hunting license and permits.
- Firearm and ammunition or bow and arrows.
- Gun case or sleeve for transporting firearms in a vehicle.
- Hunting knife. Get your kid their own hunting knife as a gift—they'll appreciate being treated like an adult. Choose a knife with a three- to four-inch fixed or lockable folding blade with a clip point or drop point. Carry a small knife sharpener, and pack a multi-tool as a backup knife that also allows you to make quick gear fixes.

- Binoculars. You don't need them for kicking rabbits out of brush piles, but they're invaluable for many other hunting applications.
- Backpack. You'll need something to carry around food, water, rain jacket, survival and first-aid kits, and all kinds of other gear.
- Communication and navigation aids. Carry a cellphone and portable battery, maps, compass, GPS unit, etc.
- Clothing. For most types of hunting, camouflage clothing isn't necessary, although concealment is a top priority in waterfowl and turkey hunting. Otherwise, you'll be fine as long as you and your kids are wearing clothes, hats, and gloves that will keep you warm and dry. If you plan on using outdoor clothing for multiple activities including hunting, consider getting earth tones that will blend in with natural surroundings. Regulations in most states do require hunters to wear a minimum amount of fluorescent safety orange for certain types of hunting. At a minimum, you'll want an orange hat and vest for you and your kids.
- Footwear. Think of hunting footwear the same way you think of clothing. Wear boots that are suited to match the environment and weather where and when you'll be hunting.
- Surveyor's tape. Bring some surveyor's tape for flagging the path to your stand so that you can find your way back and forth in the dark. It's also used to mark the blood trail of animals.
- Rubber gloves. Keep a couple of pairs of these in your pack to wear while you're gutting and skinning animals.
- Laser rangefinder. These devices allow hunters to accurately judge the distance of an animal in order to make the most accurate shot possible and rule out shots on animals that are too far away.
- Game bags and drag ropes. Drag ropes are used to pull deer from the field to your vehicle. When steep terrain or long distances rule out dragging, big game animals are broken down into four quarters and placed in game bags so that the meat can be carried out in

a backpack. (You may also want to carry a small, foldable bone saw if you'll be hunting where animals will need to be quartered and packed out on your back.)

- Calls and decoys. See pages 255–257.
- Pop-up blind. If you're going to hunt turkeys or deer with kids, the concealment and protection from the elements provided by a portable pop-up blind will save you a lot of heartache.
- Shooting sticks. Lightweight, packable bipod shooting sticks like the Bog Pod provide a steady shooting rest. They're a must-have for young hunters.
- Headlamp.
- Toilet paper.
- Handwarmers.
- Snacks.
- Zip ties. Multiple uses, including attaching tags to deer and turkeys.
- First-aid and survival kits.

## GAME ANIMALS FOR BEGINNERS

Generally speaking, hunting is broken down by the size of the game being pursued. Animals like deer, elk, black bears, and wild pigs are considered big game, while small mammals such as rab-

Sciurus carolinensis - Eastern Gray Squirrel

bits and squirrels and birds like quail, grouse, pheasants, and ducks are classified as small game. The best way for beginners to approach hunting is to follow a progression, from the easiest and most accessible animals to the ones that are harder to find and hunt.

There's nothing wrong with starting out by hunting deer, but getting your feet wet with small game has a lot of built-in appeal for beginners looking to gain experience, skill, and knowledge that will prove useful later. Remember, kids are usually pretty easily pleased. Try to think about hunting with kids the same way you do fishing: When they're first starting out, kids will be happy to catch a bunch of small panfish. Likewise, their first game animal needn't be a trophy-sized buck when they'll get fired up over a couple of doves or squirrels. And although taking any animal's life is a significant act and should be treated as such, emotions seem to run higher with the death of big game animals. Children may find it easier to begin with small game or even wild turkeys. And, practically speaking, hunting rabbits and squirrels is an excellent way to work on the shooting and stalking skills that are needed for pursuing big game like deer and elk.

Some small game species are easier for newbies to hunt than others. For instance, ducks and geese can be hunted on the cheap by "jump-shooting" them off small ponds or creeks, but you'll open up a whole new world of opportunities by investing in decoys, calls, waterproof camouflage rain gear, neoprene chest waders, and maybe even a dog and a boat if you want to get really serious. For most folks, it will be a lot easier to start out with doves, which can be hunted effectively without a pile of special gear.

If you do want to start with big game, consider the context. Going after whitetail deer on a friend's or relative's farm isn't nearly as time-consuming or physically demanding as chasing elk high in the Rocky Mountains.

## HUNTING METHODS

Though more days end in failure than in success even for experienced hunters, beginners need to know that there is more to hunting than just walking around in the woods with a gun hoping you'll get lucky and bump into whatever critter you're after. Some hunting methods and techniques are focused on a narrow range of species, while others are more universal. Being able to employ different tactics will give novices more opportunities for success.

## AMBUSH HUNTING

Ambush hunting is about as straightforward as it gets. A hunter picks out a spot where the target species will likely be feeding or traveling and simply hunkers down and waits for them to show up. Seasonal food sources are a good place to start. In the fall, sitting quietly in a grove of red or white oaks that are dropping their acorns is a good plan of attack for the squirrels, turkeys, and whitetail deer that feed on these mast crops. Alfalfa fields draw deer like flies, and all sorts of game animals and birds feed on waste grain that's left on the ground where corn, soybean, and wheat crops have been harvested. Hunters can also do well posting up where game trails made by wild pigs, deer, and elk show signs of heavy use in the form of lots of fresh tracks and droppings. Specific spots to look for along game trails are spots where several game trails converge, stretches of game trail that cross a creek, or strips of dry land surrounded by swamps.

Edge habitat, the place where two different types of habitat meet, is also very attractive to most game animals. The junction where a meadow butts up against thick woods is a go-to ambush location for deer and turkey hunters. Pinch points that funnel wildlife into small areas are also good ambush zones—creek beds, draws, the spine of ridges, low-lying saddles between two hills or mountains, flat benches on otherwise steep hillsides, and narrow strips of woods between two fields are all examples of pinch points where game animals prefer to travel, feed, and bed.

Sitting against a tree or a rock works just fine for ambush hunting, but hunters often place stands or blinds in places where animals tend to congregate. Blinds can be fashioned on the spot out of naturally available materials like dead sticks and logs, leafy branches, reeds, and clumps of grass that will make it harder for animals to see the hunter—kids love this job, as you're basically building a small, makeshift fort. You can also make a quick blind out of a length of camouflage screen or cloth attached to two stakes. Other types of stands are more substantial, from portable pop-up tent blinds and folding camp chairs to ladder treestands with one or two swivel seats and a shooting rest, and even permanent blind structures with shooting windows and roofs and walls that protect hunters from the elements. In addition to keeping kids shielded from rain, snow, and cold winds, portable pop-up blinds and permanent blind structures are also ideally suited for hunting with young children who have a hard time staying still. Game animals like turkeys and deer are always on the lookout for predators, and their eyesight is highly adapted for detecting movement. Learning to be comfortable and attentive while sitting still for long periods of time is something that takes years to master; in the meantime, blinds hide kids who are constantly fidgeting around. The goal for kids should be to patiently watch for animals as long as it takes, but the reality is that sitting in a blind can get monotonous for anyone when the animals aren't moving. After a good stretch of staring at the same trees and bushes, it's perfectly fine for kids to open a book, eat some snacks, or take a short nap inside the blind.

Elevated treestands leave hunters more exposed to the elements, but they do a great job of keeping hunters out of sight while providing a much larger and longer field of view than ground blinds. However, treestand hunting demands taking extra safety precautions that aren't necessary in a ground blind. If you and your kids are going to hunt out of a treestand, it is vitally important that you use safety harnesses and lines when you're climbing up and down and sitting in the stand. Several thousand hunters are injured each year because they failed to adhere to simple treestand safety instructions.

## STILL HUNTING

The term "still hunting" can be confusing to rookies who aren't fully familiar with hunting lingo. It suggests the hunter is sitting or standing in one spot in an ambush position, but in reality, still hunters stalk slowly through the woods, trying to spot animals before they become aware of the hunter's presence. The hunters who find the most success using this method are the ones who move so slowly that they're almost standing still. In order to be an effective still hunter, you'll need to creep along quietly at a snail's pace through the same areas where you'd expect to see animals on an ambush hunt. A good still hunter takes a step or two, then pauses to scan the surrounding area for a few minutes before moving a few more steps and pausing again. Sometimes you'll get lucky and spot a whole animal, but more often it will just be the flicker of a deer's ear or squirrel's tail. You'll want to use your ears, too. A buck's grunt, the soft cluck of a turkey, or the sound of twigs cracking and leaves rustling may tip you off before you see anything. Then you'll need to wait until the animal reveals itself. In open country with long sight lines, you can still hunt faster than in thick woods, where it could take an hour or more to cover just a couple hundred yards.

Hunters who have a really hard time sitting in one spot for hours at a time often prefer still hunting, but it's probably the most difficult way to consistently kill big game animals like deer and elk, which have eyesight that's at least equal to our own, much better hearing, and a nose that can pick up human scent from hundreds of yards away. Generally speaking, you're wasting your time still hunting for big game in wide-open meadows and fields, on forest floors carpeted in dry, crunchy leaves and sticks, or anytime the wind is blowing in the direction you're walking. The ideal place to still hunt is in open woods with just enough trees and vegetation to give you some cover and enough visibility to see animals at a distance. The best conditions for still hunting happen when there is a light breeze blowing in your face and a drizzle of rain or light snow that makes the ground soft enough for quiet walking. These days can be very productive—although if you pull off a successful still hunt with a child in even the most favorable conditions, you've really accomplished something. In order to minimize movement, noise, and scent, still hunting is best accomplished solo. It can be done with a kid or two in tow, but that scenario can quickly turn into an exercise in frustration if the kids have a hard time moving slow and keeping quiet. Try still hunting for squirrels first. You don't need to worry about the wind direction and you'll often spot squirrels that are inside shooting range scurrying around in trees or foraging for acorns on the ground. When a squirrel is too far away to take a shot, it's a perfect time to practice stalking skills.

## SPOT-AND-STALK HUNTING

Spot-and-stalk hunting is sort of a mishmash of stand hunting and still hunting that's most typically done in the mountains and prairies of the West, where hunters hike to a high vantage point that provides a good view of the surrounding country. From that vantage point, they use binoculars and spotting scopes to locate far-off mule deer, elk, pronghorn antelope, or black bears before selecting a route for the stalking portion; good routes keep the wind in the hunter's face to disperse their scent away from the animal while allowing the hunter to remain out of sight until they can reach a predetermined concealed location to make a shot. Sometimes stalks may cover a mile or more, and during this time the animal may move. Efforts to re-locate the animal in order to repeat the process are sometimes unsuccessful. However, it's not uncommon for another animal to suddenly appear nearby, out of nowhere, while a hunter is busy concentrating on finding one much farther away. Don't forget to periodically look over the terrain close to you.

Since optics are crucial to finding animals during spot-and-stalk hunts, you'll want to get your kids their own pair of binoculars. Otherwise they'll feel left out or get bored and frustrated because they're not seeing any animals. On western spot-and-stalk hunts, kids should be prepared for a fair bit of hiking through steep and uneven terrain, and shots in open country may be long. But don't assume spot-and-stalk hunting is only applicable to western big game hunting. Whether it's a cottontail resting under a bush or a whitetail feeding at the edge of a soybean field, you can try pulling it off with kids anytime you see a game animal from a distance.

## CALLING

Calling an animal in—coaxing an animal into shooting range by speaking its language—is an exciting and interactive experience for kids. Turkeys and elk are most effectively called during their breeding season, spring for turkeys and early fall for elk. During this time males of both species are very vocal and will react well to calls. Male turkeys, also known as toms and gobblers, respond best to yelps, clucks, and purrs that mimic a hen turkey. Sometimes they'll also "shock gobble" at loud, piercing sounds like car horns and barking dogs, but hunters use "locator calls" that sound like owls, crows, and coyotes to make tom turkeys gobble. During the elk rut in September, a bull will move toward mews and whines that sound like a cow that's left his harem, and he'll also come in looking for a fight when he hears a hunter challenge him with a loud bugle call that sounds like another bull elk trying to steal his cows. Similarly, whitetail deer can be called in using buck grunts and doe bleats during their late fall breeding season. Rattling antlers together loudly to imitate two bucks fighting over breeding territory will also get the attention of nearby deer. All manner of waterfowl species are also hunted using calls during the fall and winter migration period. Waterfowlers use calls to boost the confidence of geese and ducks that might be hesitant to come flying into decoy spreads.

There are several types of calls used to make the sounds of different animals, and each works a little differently. Diaphragm or mouth calls are small pieces of thin latex material that are placed between the tongue and the roof of the mouth and used to make turkey or elk sounds. Diaphragms are the most difficult kind of call to master but can be very realistic when the air is passed through them just right. Reed calls are easier-to-use tube-shaped devices that you press against your lips to make calls for turkey, elk, deer, and waterfowl. Turkey callers also use hand-operated wooden box calls and round pot calls; these are fairly easy to get the hang of, and some kid-friendly versions are controlled by a small spring-loaded plunger. But don't shy away from encouraging kids to practice with any type of call, and let them do some calling out in the woods even if they don't sound perfect. It'll be a magical experience for them if they rattle in a buck or call some ducks into range. Even just getting a response out of a distant gobbler or bull elk will make them eager for more.

## DECOYS

Decoys that look like the real thing are used to pull waterfowl, mourning doves, wild turkeys, elk, pronghorn antelope, and whitetail deer toward hunters. They are often used in conjunction with calls but can work well on their own—sometimes the sight of a decoy is enough to pique the curiosity or territorial aggression of animals, who'll move in for a closer look. The nice thing about decoys is they can be placed to give young hunters shorter shots, and they'll often cause animals to stop and linger in the area for longer periods, giving young hunters more time to wait for the perfect shot opportunity. Remember to always use a little extra caution when carrying and using decoys—though very rare, shooting accidents involving decoys do happen. The overwhelming majority of them can be avoided just by hanging highly visible wraps of fluorescent orange surveyor's tape on deer or turkey decoys when you're carrying them around in the woods. You should also mark your shooting location with the same material when you're hunkered down waiting for an animal to approach your decoy setup. For safety's sake, decoys should not be used at all on public land during rifle big game seasons.

## DRIVING AND PUSHING

The technique of driving, or pushing animals out of cover so they can be shot, is most typically associated with whitetail deer hunting, though it can be used for a number of other game animals. With deer, one or more hunters called "drivers" walk with the wind at their backs through an area that's likely to hold deer and toward one or more "posters" waiting in an area that the deer are likely to move toward when they smell, hear, or see the drivers. This can be a very effective means of moving deer out of cover, but shots on stationary deer can be hard to come by since the animals are often running. Additionally, with one group of hunters moving toward another, great care needs to be taken when shooting. Driving deer isn't dangerous when the plan is well organized and communicated, but young hunters should be accompanied by an experienced adult to ensure things stay safe.

Driving animals is also a common technique for cottontail rabbits and upland birds. Cottontails like to hole up under tall grass, brush piles, briar patches, and even old farm equipment and junk piles. Upland birds such as grouse, quail, and pheasants take cover in similar places, and you'll also find them in berry patches and crop fields. One hunter can try kicking them out of these spots while the other waits for them to pop out, but sometimes when game birds are approached, they will stay hidden out of sight under thick cover or run away before the hunter ever sees them. That's when having a trained bird dog really pays off.

## HUNTING WITH DOGS

Dog breeds like pointers and spaniels are used to help hunters locate upland game birds by scent before pointing or flushing them into the air, while Labs and some other breeds retrieve downed waterfowl by sight. Some bird dog breeds are capable of doing both. There are beagles that run cottontail rabbits and snowshoe hares and cur dogs that chase squirrels into trees. In some states, dogs like bluetick and black-and-tan coonhounds are used to scent-track and chase raccoons, mountain lions, and black bears into trees.

No matter the breed, when it comes to hunting dogs, it's generally true that you'll have to pay a pretty penny for one with good hunting genetics, and training any dog to become a good hunter requires a significant investment in terms of time. It's enough work that some folks are willing to ship their puppy off to a professional trainer for a few months, another significant cost. If you and your kids are thinking about getting your own hunting dog, be aware you're committing to a project that will take a year or more to complete.

## BAITING ANIMALS

Baiting animals with regular doses of attractive food sources is a tried-and-true hunting method for many deer and bear hunters. Baiting greatly increases the odds of actually seeing animals, which helps keep young hunters focused and interested. Additionally, feeding animals tend to stay put for a while, allowing young hunters to select the animal they want to shoot and take the time to aim carefully; in places like Texas, Kansas, and Maryland, it's fair to say that most young hunters shoot their first deer with the aid of feeders that dispense dried corn. If the bait is placed a short distance from a hunter concealed in a blind or up in a treestand, the shot will be that much easier for them to make. Baiting also gives hunters more time to look over an animal to be sure it's the one they want to kill. This comes into play if regulations called antler restrictions dictate that a buck must have a certain number of points on its antlers to be legally harvested. Similarly, it is universally illegal to shoot female black bears, or sows, with cubs in tow, and most bear hunters prefer shooting males, or boars, over females without cubs. The use of bait affords hunters the extra time needed to verify they aren't shooting the wrong bear.

Still, baiting isn't without controversy in some hunting circles. A fair knock against the practice is that you'll learn a lot less sitting over bait than you would by carefully observing the natural behavior and daily patterns of a species. There are also some hunters who believe baiting wild game is unethical and violates the rules of "fair chase" because the animals become so habituated to free handouts that you can expect them to show up like clockwork at bait sites. Some state fish and game agencies agree; baiting is illegal in about half of the states in the country. Where baiting is legal, it's a widely used practice with a long, traditional use pattern among hunters. It's not unreasonable to give youngsters a chance to take an animal at a bait site if your state allows it, but it's also worthwhile to have a chat about the pros and cons of baiting and the idea of hunting ethics with them beforehand.

## FAIR CHASE VERSUS CANNED HUNTS

Hunting ethics are in part concerned with keeping the relationship between hunter and hunted on a level playing field. Hunter and author Jim Posewitz described what is generally known as "fair chase" hunting as "a balance that allows hunters to occasionally succeed while animals generally avoid being taken." In other words, the killing part of hunting shouldn't be a foregone conclusion. The philosophy of fair chase mandates that hunting is fair and ethical only when game animals are able to use all of their natural abilities—sight, smell, hearing, and an instinctive sense of self-preservation—to escape.

Your kids should understand that stacking the deck too heavily in your favor only cheapens the hunting experience. Baiting, for example, is a technique open to debate on ethical grounds. What's not debatable, however, are the high-fence canned hunting operations that guarantee success. Even though selling canned hunts is a completely legitimate business in the eyes of the law in many states, the practice is a clear violation of the concept of fair chase.

These outfits often call themselves "hunting preserves," which makes them sound more appealing to hunters and the general public. In reality, these facilities are run just like commercial livestock operations, where all manner of big game animals are fed and bred behind fifteen-foot high-tension wire fences. In fact, canned hunting operations are overseen by the U.S. Department of Agriculture, not state fish and game agencies, which ought to tell you something. But a high fence alone isn't necessarily indicative of canned hunting operations. In Texas, many large ranches offer guided high-fence hunts, but the game animals behind those fences are wild and a hunting license is required to go after them.

However, you should be extremely suspicious of advertisements that offer "100 percent guaranteed success" without any need for a hunting license. The game animals at these places are more akin to cattle or sheep than their wild counterparts. Still, there are those who are willing to skip all the work, uncertainty, and potential disappointment that's baked into fair chase hunting. Just hop online, pick out the animal you want to put on your wall, plop down a deposit, and choose a date and time to go take care of the messy part. Then after the deed is done, you snap a few pictures, pay the rest of the money owed, and you're home by dinnertime. There are other versions of this where pen-raised game birds like pheasants, chukar, and quail with no more natural survival skills than barnyard chickens are placed out in a field an hour or two before the shooters arrive. You won't be doing kids any favors by teaching them that such transactional shortcuts are not only acceptable but preferable to the realities and principles of fair chase hunting.

## CLEANING AND BUTCHERING YOUR MEAT

Outside of children who grow up on farms where animals are raised and slaughtered for food, most kids have virtually no understanding of how the meat they eat ends up on their plate. The same goes for adults— many have gone through their lives without stopping to con-

Columbia livia - Street Pigeon

sider all the steps that occur before a farm-raised cow gets turned into the packaged steaks they buy at the grocery store.

Any such ignorance is lost the moment you're forced to reckon with a dead animal. New hunters will either need to learn to do the work of making meat or pay someone else to do it. For a fee, big game animals can be dropped off at a wild game processor who will take care of skinning and butchering as well as processing, packaging, and labeling the meat. But there's no outsourcing the task of gutting big game animals in the field—a task that needs to be completed immediately after the kill. If an animal is killed far from a vehicle, new hunters will also need to learn how to break it down into pieces small enough to haul out in a backpack. This is especially pertinent with elk, which weigh several hundred pounds on the hoof, but it can apply to any big game animal that's killed in rough, broken terrain where dragging them out whole is impractical or even impossible. Lastly, when it comes to small game and birds, taking them to a commercial meat processor isn't an option, so neophytes will need to know how to do everything themselves, from skinning and plucking to gutting to butchering.

Perhaps unsurprisingly, the fieldwork that needs to take place after the trigger gets pulled is often even more intimidating to beginners than the finding and killing parts. It's understandable that someone who has never butchered anything with their own hands would be squeamish, or would fret about where to even begin and the consequences of making a mistake, but converting a whole animal into usable pieces of edible meat isn't actually all that difficult. And as convenient as it is for someone else to do everything but the cooking for you, when you're grilling venison steaks that you cut and packaged with your kids, they'll know exactly where the meat came from and all the adventure, time, and toil that went into putting it there. That's powerful stuff.

Still, some children may recoil when faced with the realities of field dressing, but shielding them from blood and guts prevents them from engaging in the entire process from start to finish. If skinning, gutting, and cleaning are presented to them as natural and necessary steps, they'll likely be more curious than grossed out—in fact, children are usually less freaked out than most adult newbies. Cleaning and butchering your own meat also yields a plethora of valuable teaching moments for young biophiles in training. After a successful grouse-hunting trip, the pouch under the skin at the base of the bird's throat called the crop might hold the same wild blueberries your kids were just picking and eating themselves. Or they might be curious about all the tiny round pebbles that are found when the bird's gizzard is cut open; the birds ingest small pebbles to help their gizzard muscles grind up the food so it's more digestible in their intestines. During that process, the rough edges of the pebbles are smoothed over.

There are, of course, very practical reasons for knowing how to clean game animals. The quality, texture, and taste of any raw meat begin to deteriorate quickly if it is allowed to sit too long in warm conditions. You wouldn't leave a raw chicken sitting out on your counter all day, and the same rule applies to meat you've hunted. Folks who believe game meat is dry, tough, and chewy or has strong "gamey" or off-putting flavors have usually eaten game meat that wasn't cooked the right way (more on that later) or wasn't cared for properly in the minutes and hours directly following the animal's death. Game birds and animals should be gutted immediately after death; removing the innards prevents spoiling by allowing the surrounding meat to begin cooling. Skinning animals right away isn't strictly necessary in cooler temperatures, but it does help to quickly dissipate heat away from muscles when it's warm out.

Of course, field dressing involves handling sharp knives, which may worry some parents. Caution is warranted, but with some instruction and supervision, children as young as six or seven are fully capable of handling knives safely. It may seem intimidating at first, but the cleaning process is not a complicated one and the same basic steps apply to all birds and all mammals. If you can skin and gut a rabbit, you'll be able to handle a deer. Likewise, you'll know what to do with a turkey if you've already cleaned some ducks.

Beyond cleaning animals, the first step of meat processing, there is a lot to learn about butchering birds and animals into different cuts. Online video tutorials are good starting points, and wild game cookbooks often include detailed instructions for breaking down small game and birds and turning a deer into steaks and roasts. After an animal is butchered, you'll need to preserve any meat that won't get eaten within a day or two. Meat packaged in vacuum-sealed plastic bags or wrapped tightly in thick freezer paper will keep in the freezer for a year.

## COOKING WILD GAME

Hunting with kids means cooking wild game with kids—another valuable source of education and enjoyment, not to mention nutrition. If you're concerned about the implications processed food and factory-farmed meat might have for the health of your children, there's plenty of evidence out there showing that wild game meat is more nutritious and healthier than meat sourced from the commercial food supply chain.

There's a widely held misperception that cooking wild game requires a lot of complicated techniques and special recipes, but you'll have the best results if your early efforts are geared toward simple preparations. The most important factor to consider when you're cooking any kind of game, be it deer, ducks, or rabbits, is that wild animals have much leaner meat and less fat than domestic animals. You'll do fine if you follow the rule that wild game is best cooked either hot and fast or low and slow. Overcooking red meat like venison steaks or waterfowl breasts is a sure path to a bad meal; these cuts shouldn't be cooked past medium rare or they'll get tough and rubbery and develop a strong, livery flavor. Tougher cuts with lots of connective tissue like venison shoulder roasts and wild turkey legs should be slow-cooked until they're fork tender; after several hours of braising in a Dutch oven or a crockpot, the tough tendons and ligaments in the muscles will break down into a silky liquid that bastes the meat from within, acting almost like the fat that game animals lack. White meat from upland game birds, squirrels, and rabbits is leaner and more flavorful than domestic chicken, but keep in mind that it will dry out if it's overcooked; if undercooked, the meat will be tough. Cooking techniques are interchangeable within similar groups of game birds and animals, so don't worry too much about finding species-specific recipes. In other words, you can use the same recipe for whitetail deer and elk or for wild turkeys and pheasants. Similarly, if you adjust cooking times and sometimes temperatures for the leaner nature of game, you can use recipes from standard cookbooks, too.

Let children have a say in how they'd like their meal prepared, and involve them in cooking it. Young kids might not be able to connect their venison sloppy joes to the wonders of the natural world, but at least they'll be able to share in the pride, satisfaction, and joy that come with being able to complete each step of the field-to-table process on your own. When it comes to making meals for kids who haven't had much exposure to wild game, keep things approachable and familiar. Burgers and tacos are fast and easy to make, and kids will eat them without any cajoling. Turkey or pheasant breasts can be cut into nugget-sized pieces, breaded, and deep-fried for a kid-friendly preparation that'll blow away the chicken fingers on the kids' menu at most restaurants.

# INDEX

PHOTO: © GARRET SMITH
FOR MEATEATER

STEVEN RINELLA is the host of the television show *MeatEater* and The MeatEater Podcast. He is the author of *The MeatEater Guide to Wilderness Skills and Survival; The MeatEater Fish and Game Cookbook;* two volumes of *The Complete Guide to Hunting, Butchering, and Cooking Wild Game; Meat Eater: Adventures from the Life of an American Hunter; American Buffalo: In Search of a Lost Icon;* and *The Scavenger's Guide to Haute Cuisine.* He is the recipient of the Conservation Achievement Award from the Theodore Roosevelt Conservation Partnership.

themeateater.com
Facebook.com/StevenRinellaMeatEater
Instagram: @stevenrinella and @meateater

## ABOUT THE TYPE

This book was set in Garamond, a typeface originally designed by the Parisian type cutter Claude Garamond (c. 1500–61). This version of Garamond was modeled on a 1592 specimen sheet from the Egenolff-Berner foundry, which was produced from types assumed to have been brought to Frankfurt by the punch cutter Jacques Sabon (c. 1520–80).

Claude Garamond's distinguished romans and italics first appeared in *Opera Ciceronis* in 1543–44. The Garamond types are clear, open, and elegant.